"Historically, Biblical Christianity is a credal or confessional faith. By examining in detail the evidence of the New Testament about this area of church life in the first century AD, this new study by Tony Costa convincingly demonstrates this to be a vital aspect of the Christian Faith. The idea that Christianity is simply about love is thus shown to be a patent misreading of Apostolic Christianity. Our Faith is grounded on both love and truth. A very helpful book: ideal for personal or group study."

MICHAEL A.G. HAYKIN, Th.D, FRHistS
Chair and Professor of Church History & Director of The Andrew Fuller Center for Baptist Studies, The Southern Baptist Theological Seminary

"If someone says 'I believe the Bible,' is that sufficient to really tell you what he or she believes? Throughout Church History, Christians have rightly felt the need to clarify their belief in God's Word by summarizing its core teachings in creeds and confessions. And, because 'the hymnbook is the theology text of the church,' we can also learn much about what Christians actually believed and valued by studying the hymns of the church. In this fascinating and well-written book, Dr. Tony Costa, points us back to the earliest confessions and hymns found within the Scriptures themselves."

ROBERT L. PLUMMER, Ph.D.
Collin and Eveyln Aikman Professor of Biblical Studies
The Southern Baptist Theological Seminary

"In this clearly argued, well-researched, groundbreaking work, Dr. Tony Costa demonstrates that all the core beliefs associated with 'Christian orthodoxy' were already laid out in the New Testament documents themselves, in particular in their creedal and hymnic statements about Jesus. This will be a great resource for apologists, theologians, and New Testament scholars. Highly recommended!"

MICHAEL L. BROWN, Ph.D.
Author of *Answering Jewish Objections to Jesus* (5 vols); Adjunct Professor, Southern Evangelical Seminary, Gordon Conwell Theological Seminary (Charlotte), Trinity Evangelical Divinity School

"After an historical overview of the content and importance of creeds in early Christianity, Costa rightly demonstrates that Christian hymns and creeds have their roots in the Jewish Scriptures. Old Testament believers had their own creeds, such as the *Shema* and the 'Song of the Sea,' and a number of songs collected in the book of Psalms confessing and reviewing God's salvific dealings with the nation of Israel. Most intriguing, then, is the fact that the high Christology expressed by the New Testament creeds and hymns was birthed among Jesus' disciples, who were faithful monotheistic Jews. An edifying piece of work!"

PIERRE CONSTANT, Ph.D.
Chair of New Testament Studies, Toronto Baptist Seminary

"Tony Costa gives us a book solidly grounded in important biblical and theological facts: Singing to and about Jesus Christ was important to the earliest Christians, and their original hymnody was heavily theological, with an emphasis upon Christology. Costa suggests several linguistic criteria for picking out plausible candidates for hymnic material in the New Testament, and he carefully analyzes its theological content. Admitting openly that the musical settings for these segments of Scripture are lost to history, Costa nonetheless points to practical ramifications for our own worship. For example, he emphasizes the fact that the songs we sing in church should not be mantras; rather, they should contain a robust theological element. His analysis of these passages also contributes helpfully to the discussion of high Christology in earliest Christianity."

LYDIA MCGREW, Ph.D.
Author of *The Mirror or the Mask: Liberating the Gospels from Literary Devices*

"It's difficult to overstate how important Dr Costa's look at the earliest creeds and hymns of the New Testament is. It demonstrates a fully-developed understanding of the person and work of Christ centuries before their re-articulation in the ecumenical councils of the church. Thereby he tacitly undercuts those who would drive a wedge between the Bible and traditional church teaching."

SCOTT MASSON, Ph.D.
Associate Professor of English, Tyndale University

"In response to attacks on the divine glory of Jesus, the Church should never be caught on the defensive. Instead, like this book, the Church should always be calmly and consistently affirming the high Christology of the New Testament. Tony Costa highlights and carefully explains the creeds and hymns of scripture in order to portray the very earliest Christian beliefs about Jesus. In so doing he preempts the efforts of religions and ideologies to belittle the identity of Jesus and to caricature the deity and redemptive death of Jesus as inventions of later times. For the Apostolate to Islam, this book will prove a much-needed source of encouragement and practical knowledge for its confident witness to the Son of God."

GORDON NICKEL, Ph.D.
Director of the Centre for Islamic Studies at South Asia Institute of Advanced Christian Studies in Bangalore, India; Author, *A Gentle Answer to the Muslim Accusation of Biblical Falsification* and *The Quran with Christian Commentary: A Guide to Understanding the Scripture of Islam*.

"Dr Costa is probably one of the best people I know to not only understand the creeds and hymns themselves, and their impact on the church, but their importance as a defense against the attacks by those from outside the church, particularly those coming from Islam. He has tirelessly put himself forward in public debates, live-streams and recordings to not only defend the foundations of Christianity but confront the foundations of those challenging our faith, using the doctrines found in the creeds and hymns as one of his most potent weapons."

JAY SMITH, Ph.D.
Christian apologist and polemicist to Islam

"I am not aware of any other book that is devoted to offering a comprehensive summary of the creeds and hymns found in the Bible and how they encapsulate early Christian beliefs concerning Christ and the gospel. Tony Costa has done a fine job of distilling the current scholarship on early Christian creeds and hymns, while retaining accessibility to the general reader. Whether you are a lay-Christian, seminary student, pastor or academic, this book serves as an excellent introduction to this fascinating subject, and I warmly commend it to your reading."

JONATHAN MCLATCHIE, Ph.D.
Writer, Speaker, Scholar; Professor, Sattler College

Early Christian Creeds & Hymns

|*Studies in the Ancient Church*|

Early Christian Creeds & Hymns

What the Earliest Christians Believed in Word and Song:

An Exegetical-Theological Study

Tony Costa

H&E
Academic

Early Christian Creeds and Hymns—What the Earliest Christians Believed in Word and Song: An Exegetical and Theological Study

Series: Studies in the Ancient Church

Copyright © 2021 Tony Costa

All rights reserved. This book may not be reproduced, in whole or in part, without written permission from the publishers.

Unless otherwise indicated, all Scripture quotations are from The ESV® Bible (The Holy Bible, English Standard Version®), copyright © 2001 by Crossway, a publishing ministry of Good News Publishers. Used by permission. All rights reserved.

H&E Academic, Peterborough, Ontario
www.hesedandemet.com

Cover design by Corey M.K. Hughes
Interior font: Equity Text A

Paperback ISBN: 978-1-77484-013-9
Hardcover ISBN: 978-1-77484-015-3
eBook ISBN: 978-1-77484-014-6

To Vida, meu amor.

Contents

Series Preface xv

Foreword xviiii
   James White

Part 1: The creeds

  1. What are creeds? 1

  2. The Old Testament as the forerunner of Christian creeds 11

  3. Creeds in the New Testament 25

  4. The earliest Christian creed: 1 Corinthians 15:3-4 29

  5. The shortest creed: "Jesus is Lord" 45

  6. Jesus is the Christ 63

  7. Jesus is the Son of God 71

  8. The Christian Shema: 1 Corinthians 8:6 87

Part 2: Hymns

  9. What are hymns? 97

  10. Hymns edify the Church: 1 Corinthians 14:26 103

  11. Hymns sung to the Lord Jesus and God the Father 105

  12. The *Carmen Christi*: Philippians 2:6-11 113

  13. The great confession in a hymn: 1 Timothy 3:16 125

  14. The wake-up hymn: Ephesians 5:14 135

  15. The hymn of the suffering Messiah: 1 Peter 2:22-24 141

  16. A Jewish hymn: Hebrews 1:2b-4 149

  17. The longest Christian hymn found in a gospel: John 1:1-18 163

  18. The grand finale hymn: Colossians 1:15-20 173

  Conclusion 197

Appendix 1
    The term Son of God in the Apocrypha, Pseudepigrapha,
    the Targums, and Rabbinic Literature 211

Appendix 2
    Jesus is the Son of Man 215

Subject Index 219

Scripture Index.. 223

ABBREVIATIONS

AD	Anno Domini
AJBT	The American Journal of Biblical Theology
AMP	Amplified Bible
ASV	American Standard Bible
AV	Authorized Version (King James Version)
BC	Before Christ
BDAG	Bauer, W., F. W. Danker, W. F. Arndt, and F.W. Gingrich. *Greek-English Lexicon of the New Testament and Other Early Christian Literature*. 3rd ed. Chicago, 2000.
BT	Bible Translator
ca.	circa
CBQ	Catholic Biblical Quarterly
cf.	*confer*, compare
d.	died
ed.	editor, edited by, edition
eds.	editors
eg.	*exempli gratia*, for example
ESV	English Standard Bible
et al.	and others
etc.	*et cetera*, and others, and so on
HCSB	Holman Christian Study Bible
i.e.	*id est*, that is
JSOT	Journal for Studies in the Old Testament
LXX	Septuagint
MT	Masoretic Text
NASB	New American Standard Bible
NEB	New English Bible
NET	New English Translation
NICNT	New International Commentary on the New Testament
NIGTC	New International Greek Testament Commentary
NIV	New International Version (1984, 1996)
NJB	New Jerusalem Bible

NKJV	New King James Version
NLT	New Living Translation
NRSV	New Revised Standard Version
NT	New Testament
OT	Old Testament
Ps	Psalm
rev.	revised (by)
RSV	Revised Standard Version
SBJT	Southern Baptist Journal of Theology
s.v.	*sub verbo*, under the word
TDNT	*Theological Dictionary of the New Testament*. Edited by G. Kittel and G. Friedrich. Translated by G. W. Bromiley. 1 10 vols. Grand Rapids, 1964–1976
TJT	Toronto Journal of Theology
TNTC	Tyndale New Testament Commentary
TOTC	Tyndale Old Testament Commentary
trans.	translator, translated (by)
v.	verse
vol.	volume
vols.	volumes
vs.	versus
YLT	Young's Literal Translation

Series Preface

Study of the Ancient Church was a common feature of Protestant theological reflection from the Reformation to the close of the long eighteenth century. Many of the Reformers, like John Calvin and Thomas Cranmer, were avid readers of extra-biblical, early Christian literature, as were most of the Puritans. They did not believe that this literature was canonical or on the same level as Holy Scripture, but they rightly recognized that the roots of the Reformed churches of Europe needed to be grounded in elements of Christian orthodoxy from the first five or six centuries of church history. Doctrinal convictions on the Trinity and the Incarnation that had been hammered out in those first centuries, for instance, still very much informed true Christian thinking. Moreover, Protestant claims to catholicity demanded recognition and evidence of continuity with the Ancient Church.

It is in the spirit of those Protestant and Evangelical forbears that these "Studies in the Ancient Church" are being published. Along with Calvin and Cranmer, Ussher and Owen, we recognize that early Christian thought has much to teach us. And in the various studies being published in this series, we listen afresh to those voices from the past, weighing what we hear against Scripture, discerning and cleaving to what is good and profitable for us in this day. These studies cover the entire range of the Ancient Church from the era of the so-called Apostolic Fathers down to the rise of Islam in the seventh century. We also include the occasional monograph on the New Testament texts, not because we consider the literature of that holy text to be on the same level as the literature that followed in the patristic era, but because the world of Roman Hellenism was a shared cultural context for both the New Testament period and the world of the Ancient Church.

It is the prayer of the publisher that this small academic series may, in its own small way, serve the cause of the Gospel and help advance the glory of God!

Foreword

The New Testament was not written to us as a theological textbook. It comes to us from the collective experience of the early church as they took the gospel out into the world and proclaimed this new and scandalous message, "Jesus, the Jewish Messiah, who was crucified by the Roman authorities, rose from the dead, ascended to the right hand of the Father, and is Lord of all." Theirs was a shared experience, one they communicated in preaching and teaching, singing and creed.

The reality of the truth that the one true God of Israel had revealed himself in three distinct, identifiable divine Persons, Father, Son, and Holy Spirit, set the Christian experience apart. Peter, for example, was an experiential Trinitarian. He had heard the Father speak on the mount, he had walked with the Son, he was now filled by the Spirit. The early believers truly believed those ancient words, "Immanuel," that is, God with us, not just for us, not just on our side, but truly, with us, amongst us, in the flesh, as Jesus of Nazareth.

It is hardly surprising then that we do not find the authors of the New Testament stopping each time they make an allusion to the shared faith of the church in their writings and explaining themselves as if this was some new teaching that needed to be explained. Their writings are filled with easy references to Father, Son, and Spirit, or to expressions of exchange, such as "the Spirit of Christ" and then, a few words later, "the Spirit of God." They are not confused, they are just speaking the language of an already lived faith.

Tony Costa takes us on a journey through the fragments of confessions, creeds, and hymns buried in the text of the New Testament documents that give us a tantalizing glimpse into the life of the early believers as they lived out the faith that was once delivered to the saints. We have the privilege of hearing a chorus here, a verse there, from the early Christian hymnal, and we find that this amazing revelation of God in Christ was its central theme. We are amazed as Paul draws from the ancient confession of his people, the Jews, and expands it to attempt to contain the glory of the incarnation in Christ. We discover that the early Christians were concerned about divine revelation, about a consistent, revealed faith, and most especially about knowing, accurately and truthfully, this God who has condescended in the person of the Son to give himself for his people.

James White, Th.D.
Director of Alpha and Omega Ministries
Pastor, Apologia Church in Tempe, Arizona

Part 1
The creeds

1
WHAT ARE CREEDS?

This book will be divided into two parts. In the first part we will deal with creeds and then in the second part we will look at the subject of hymns. While we will primarily be focused on the creeds and hymns found in the New Testament, we will also refer to several in the Old Testament which we will refer to as a reference point.

What exactly are creeds? Most Christians have probably heard this word tossed around during theological discussions, seminary classes, and church settings; we may even have heard some churches recite the Apostles' or the Nicene Creed during their worship service. Such creeds are usually recited by Christians as they publicly come together to assert what exactly it is that they believe. The word "creed" comes from the Latin word *credo* which means, "I believe,"[1] and several other of our English words, such as "credible" and "credibility," are also sourced from this same Latin word. In short, the creeds of the historic church are primarily theological in nature and deal with the fundamental doctrines that constitute the Christian faith.

But while creeds seek to affirm what Christians have always believed, they are also, by their very nature, confessional. This makes sense in light of the Scriptural injunction to *confess* what you believe. As we go on to consider the importance of creeds, it is important to remember the maxim that you are what you think. The Bible agrees with this position when it states, "For as [a man] thinks within himself, so he is" (Prov. 23:7 NASB). The Greek philosopher Socrates also once remarked that "the unexamined life is not worth living."[2] I believe this principle should extend into the area of theology as well; after all, an unexamined faith is not really one worth believing in.

Creeds were one of the many ways in which Christians articulated what they believed about the Scriptures; and not only what they merely believed, but what they were willing to stake their life on. Confessions were not merely

---
[1] Philip Schaff, *The Creeds of Christendom* (1877; repr., Grand Rapids: Baker Book House, 1998), 3:3 n.1. Also see G.S.R. Cox, "Creed" in J. D. Douglas, ed., *The New International Dictionary of the Christian Church* (Grand Rapids: Zondervan, 1974), 270.
[2] Plato, *Apology* 38a.

EARLY CHRISTIAN CREEDS AND HYMNS

an exercise in lip service towards the Christian faith, they were statements of heartfelt conviction and fact. That many early Christians were willing to die for their faith demonstrates the sheer depth of their convictions. The earliest Christians really believed it was their faith that would overcome the world, "For everyone who has been born of God overcomes the world. And this is the victory that has overcome the world—our faith. Who is it that overcomes the world except the one who believes that Jesus is the Son of God?" (1 John 5:4–5).[3] It should not be lost on the reader that in this text, three things are needed in order overcome the world. First, the one who overcomes must be "born of God," that is, they must be regenerate; second, they must hold to the "victory" of the Christian faith; thirdly, they must believe that Jesus is the Son of God. It is also important to note that all of these statements *together* constitute true faith. Only the regenerate believer who has faith in Jesus as the Son of God will overcome the world.

As we shall see, this same faith was communicated from the earliest periods of Christianity in the form of creeds; first orally, and then written down. Thus, in early Christianity, believers were to first *believe* the words or traditions (relayed teaching) *spoken* from the mouths of the apostles, and then apply themselves to what they had *written down*. We see this for instance in the exhortation of the apostle Paul, "So then, brothers, stand firm and hold to the traditions that you were taught by us, either by our *spoken word* or by our *letter*" (2 Thess. 2:15; italics mine).[4]

Christians believed what these creeds said about Jesus Christ and the gospel. In fact, they were so committed to their veracity that they were ready and willing to lay down their lives for them. Indeed, as the testimony of the early Church Fathers repeatedly attests, many did so. People do not generally die for that which they believe to be a lie. People only die for that which they believe to be true. Even those who have been deceived by a cult leader, if they are convinced that what they have been taught is the absolute truth, will not hesitate to sacrifice their own lives for it. This demonstrates once again that people do not knowingly lay down their lives for an error, but only for what they are convinced is true.

---

[3] Unless otherwise indicated, all biblical citations in this book are taken from *The Holy Bible: English Standard Version* (Wheaton: Crossway, 2001) and abbreviated as ESV.

[4] Earlier in 2 Thessalonians 2:2, Paul had issued a warning against false and fraudulent teachers who were trying to pass themselves off as having "a *spoken word*, or a *letter* seeming to be from us" (italics mine).

WHAT ARE CREEDS?

The words "to confess" comes from the Greek word ὁμολογέω (*homologeo*), which appears frequently in the New Testament and literally means "to say the same words." In other words, to "confess" is to verbally repeat in words what you already believe in your heart. The reader will immediately notice by now that there is an overlap between the terms "creed" and "confession;" this is because creeds are also confessions. Today many Christian denominations and groups will refer to their respective creeds as "Statements of Faith." Though the Protestant tradition has historically enunciated its various theological positions by means of the term "creeds," over the course of time, many have now come to be known as "confessions." Some notable Protestant confessions demonstrative of this trend include the *Augsburg Confession* (1530), the *Belgic Confession* (1561), the *Westminster Confession* (1647), and the *Second London Baptist Confession* (1689), to name a few. But while they may now be called confessions, they are also what have historically been known as creeds.

Creeds are the means by which Christians confess what it is that they, as a body of believers, believe. It is important to note that while creeds are positive in one respect, they are also negative; that is, while they clearly state what it is that Christians believe, they also clarify what it is that Christians do not believe. In this way, creeds do double duty in that they simultaneously affirm and negate certain beliefs. In logic this principle is known as the law of excluded middle, which states that a statement must either be true or false—middle alternatives are excluded. "A" can either be "A" or not "A," but it cannot be both.

Creeds tell us who is "in" and who is "out" of the confessional body of believers. When a Christian confesses with a creed that they believe in "one God," they are also asserting that the opposite of that statement—that there are many gods—is false. According to our logical principle, one cannot be a monotheist and polytheist at the same time. Similarly, when someone confesses Jesus Christ as the Son of God who has died and has risen from the dead, they are also confessing that the opposite of that statement is false. Jesus is not merely a prophet or man, as in Islam, who lived and died like all other religious leaders did. Rather, he is God's unique Son, the crucified and risen Saviour and sole Redeemer of sinners. So when Christians confessed that Jesus was the Messiah (Matt. 16:16; John 20:31), they were also affirming that its opposite claim, that Jesus is not the Messiah, was false. We see in the gospel accounts that this very question was a constant source of tension between Jesus and the Jewish religious leaders of his day.

We see a similar controversy at work between the early Jewish Christians and their unbelieving counterparts in the book of Acts. The fact is that everyone, whether they admit it or not, has their own creed or confession. Everyone, down to the most austere atheist, believes *something* about reality, the world, humanity and so on. There is no such thing as neutrality here. What a creed does is attempt to address and make public fundamental areas of belief.

Another aspect of creeds is that they are often polemical in nature—they set out to refute the opinions or positions of another party. In a sense, creeds are an attempt to hold out the brilliance of truth against the darkness of error. In this way, heresies actually highlight the truth of God in that their error also serves to magnify the light of God's truth.[5] As truth is known by it being the opposite of error, so light is known by its contrast to what is dark. You cannot understand one without the other.

Many of the historic ecumenical councils of the church gathered precisely to combat heresy, and produced creeds such as the Nicene Creed (AD 325), which was published to refute Arianism.[6] This heresy claimed that Jesus Christ was not truly God but rather the first of God's, and hence a creature. This is why the Nicene Creed has such a strong Christological emphasis. The Apostles' Creed also seems to be a polemic against Gnosticism, a philosophy which denied that God created the material world, that Jesus ever became a real human being, and that there will ever be a future resurrection of the body. Hence, the Apostles' Creed's emphasis on the physicality of creation, the incarnation, and the resurrection. Creeds that follow earlier creeds also tend to act as a snowball in that new content is often supplemented with previous material. Thus, the section of the Apostles' Creed which affirms God as Creator of heaven and earth has been added to the Nicene Creed with further elaboration.

Christian creeds invariably affirm the following central areas:

1. Theology (the doctrine of God)

---

[5] Augustine captured this idea when he wrote, "For the rejection of heretics makes the tenets of Thy Church and sound doctrine to stand out more clearly. For there must also be heresies, that the approved may be made manifest among the weak." Augustine, *Confessions* 7.25.

[6] As the Ecumenical Creeds will not be the focus of this book the reader is referred to Schaff, *The Creeds of Christendom*, 3:12–45.

2. Christology (the doctrine of Christ)
3. Soteriology (the doctrine of salvation)
4. Pneumatology (the doctrine of the Holy Spirit)
5. Ecclesiology (the doctrine of the church)
6. Eschatology (the doctrine of last things)

As an example, let us now consider two creeds: the Apostles' Creed and the Nicene Creed. We will begin with the Apostles' Creed:

> I believe in God, the Father almighty,
> creator of heaven and earth.
> I believe in Jesus Christ, his only Son, our Lord.
> He was conceived by the power of the Holy Spirit
> and born of the Virgin Mary.
> He suffered under Pontius Pilate,
> was crucified, died, and was buried.
> He descended to the dead.[7]
> On the third day he rose again.
> He ascended into heaven,
> and is seated at the right hand of the Father.
> He will come again
> to judge the living and the dead.
> I believe in the Holy Spirit,
> the holy catholic Church,
> the communion of saints,
> the forgiveness of sins,
> the resurrection of the body,
> and the life everlasting. Amen.

---

[7] The phrase "He descended to the dead," also traditionally translated, "he descended into hell" after the Latin text of the Creed *descendit ad inferos,* was a later addition believed to have been inserted after the fifth century AD. It was at this point that questions arose as to what happened to Jesus between his death and resurrection: did his soul or spirit linger in some kind of interim level between heaven and hell? Some Christians believed he went to Hades, the place of departed spirits, and freed the Old Testament saints and others who awaited his coming. They based this idea on certain New Testament texts such as Ephesians 4:8-10 and 1 Peter 3:18-20; 4:4-6. On this subject see Millard J. Erickson, *Christian Theology*, 3rd ed. (Grand Rapids: Baker Academic, 2013), 706-709.

EARLY CHRISTIAN CREEDS AND HYMNS

While this Creed is referred to as the Apostles' Creed, it was not actually authored by the apostles and in fact dates from before ca. AD 250.[8] The apostolic church father Irenaeus (AD 130–AD 202), bishop of Lyons, wrote a creed around the middle of the second century which bears an uncanny resemblance with what we know today as the Apostles' Creed.[9] Even earlier than this, Ignatius bishop of Antioch (AD 70–AD 110), in writing against the heretical Docetic Gnostics of his day, cited a creed that also shares an affinity with the Apostles' Creed, the only difference being that Ignatius emphasizes the veracity of Jesus' true humanity, suffering, death, and resurrection.[10] This should serve as a warning to gnostic-like thinkers today who lean towards viewing the death and resurrection of Jesus as some deeper, spiritual metaphors.

The Latin father Tertullian (ca. AD 155–AD 220) also recorded a creed which bears a remarkable similarity to the Apostles' Creed.[11] Tertullian emphasizes the apologetic importance of defending the articles of the creed, and

---

[8] John Tiller, "Apostles' Creed," in *New International Dictionary*, 58.

[9] Irenaeus, *Adversus Haereses* 1.10.1 wrote: "For the Church, although scattered throughout the whole world as far as the limits of the earth, has received from the Apostles and their disciples, handed down, its faith in one God the Father almighty, Who made the heavens and the earth and the seas and all the things in them; and in one Christ Jesus the Son of God, Who was made flesh for our salvation; and in the Holy Spirit, Who through the prophets proclaimed the saving dispensations, and the coming and birth from the Virgin, and the suffering, and the rising again from the dead, and the incarnate taking-up into the heavens of the beloved Christ Jesus our Lord, and His second coming from the heavens in the glory of the Father to sum up all things and to raise all flesh of all humanity."

[10] Ignatius, *Letter to the Trallians* 9:4 (italics mine): "Be deaf when anyone speaks to you apart from Jesus Christ, Who was of the stock of David, Who was born of Mary, Who was *truly* born, ate and drank, was *truly* persecuted under Pontius Pilate, was *truly* crucified and died in the sight of beings heavenly, earthly and under the earth, Who was *truly* raised from the dead, His Father raising Him."

[11] One of the more lamentable points in church history is Tertullian's adoption of the heretical movement known as the Montanists. The influence of Montanism on Tertullian was so effective that "the fiery African apologist Tertullian, fed up with the laxity of his orthodox brethren, ended his life a Montanist." Michael Collins and Matthew A. Price, *The Story of Christianity* (London: Oxford University Press, 1999), 43. Also see William Henn, *One Faith: Biblical and Patristic Contributions Towards Understanding Unity in Faith* (New York: Paulist Press, 1995), 102.

warns that their denial constitutes heresy.[12] Some early Christians, such as Rufinus in the early fifth century AD, believed that each of the apostles had contributed an article to the Apostles' Creed, but this view is rejected by virtually all church historians.[13]

The Apostles' Creed follows the order previously mentioned. It begins with God as Creator (theology), and then moves on to address Jesus Christ, the Son of God (Christology). What should be noted in this creed is that the section on Christ is more substantially worded than the other areas of belief. Note also how the Creed affirms first and foremost the person of the Son: who he is, his incarnation and virgin birth, his suffering and crucifixion, and his resurrection and ascension. The exaltation of Christ is affirmed in referencing his session at the right hand of the Father, from whence he will come again as the judge of all humanity. The Christocentricity of the church's creeds should not be missed and we shall see how the earliest creeds in the New Testament gravitate towards the person of Jesus Christ.

The creed also mentions belief in the Holy Spirit (Pneumatology), which reminds us that the trinitarian emphasis in this creed should not be overlooked. The usual pattern of the creeds is to begin with the person of the Father and then move to the person of the Son, whose treatment is typically substantially longer than the treatment of the other Persons of the Trinity. There is also mention of the church (Ecclesiology), and its nature—a fellowship of believers—and ends with a reference to the Second Coming of Christ and the resurrection of the dead (Eschatology). As the reader will notice, though the Apostles' Creed was not written by the apostles themselves, it does take the

---

[12] Tertullian, *Prescriptions* 13 also states, "Now, with regard to this rule of faith [*regula fidei*]—that we may from this point acknowledge *what it is which we defend*—it is, you must know, that which prescribes the belief that there is one only God, and that He is none other than the Creator of the world, who produced all things out of nothing through His Word, ... that this Word is called His Son ... at last brought down by the Spirit and Power of the Father into the Virgin Mary, was made flesh in her womb, and, being born of her, went forth as Jesus Christ ... having been crucified, He rose again the third day, (then) having ascended into the heavens, He sat at the right hand of the Father, sent instead of Himself the Power of the Holy Ghost to lead such as believe; will come with glory to take the saints to the enjoyment of everlasting life and of the heavenly promises, and to condemn the wicked to everlasting fire, after the resurrection of both of those classes shall have happened, together with the restoration of their flesh. This rule, as it will be proved, was taught by Christ, and raises amongst ourselves no other questions than those which heresies introduce, and which make men heretics."

As an apologist, it is no surprise to find concerning Tertullian as Henn notes that "[a]ll his writings are polemic" (Henn, *One Faith*, 102).

[13] Tiller, s.v. "Apostles' Creed" in *New International Dictionary*, 58.

doctrines and principles of Scripture as its basis. The wholesale acceptance and recitation of the Apostles' Creed throughout Christian history suggests that it is based on an old source; one which orthodox Christians of every stripe have universally confessed.[14]

Let us now turn our attention to the Nicene Creed, which states:

> We believe in one God, the Father almighty,
> Maker of heaven and earth,
> of all things visible and invisible.
>
> And in one Lord, Jesus Christ, the only-begotten Son of God,
> begotten of the Father before all ages;
> God of God, Light of Light, true God of true God;
> begotten, not made,
> of one substance with the Father;
> through whom all things were made.
> Who, for us men and our salvation, came down from heaven
> and became incarnate by the Holy Spirit of the virgin Mary
> and was made man.
> He was crucified for us under Pontius Pilate;
> he suffered and was buried;
> and the third day he arose, according to the Scriptures,
> and ascended into heaven, and sits at the right hand of the Father,
> and he will come again with glory to judge the living and the dead;
> whose kingdom shall have no end.
> And we believe in the Holy Spirit [the Lord and Giver of life,
> who proceeds from the Father and the Son;[15]
> who with the Father and the Son is worshipped and glorified;
> who spoke through the prophets.
> And we believe one holy catholic and apostolic church.
> We acknowledge one baptism for the forgiveness of sins;
> and we look forward to the resurrection of the dead,
> and the life of the world to come. Amen.]

---

[14] Even in the early third century AD, Tertullian could speak about a universal rule of faith that the churches shared and which could be traced back to the apostles' teachings, "We hold communion with the apostolic churches *because our doctrine is in no respect different from theirs*" (Tertullian, *The Prescription Against the Heretics*, 21). (Italics mine).

[15] The original Nicea-Constantinople Creed (AD 381) did not contain the words "and the Son." These words, also known in Latin as the *Filioque,* were added later by the Western Church in AD 589 at the regional Council of Toledo in Spain. See Wayne Grudem, *Systematic Theology: An Introduction to Biblical Doctrine* (Grand Rapids: Zondervan, 1994), 246.

WHAT ARE CREEDS?

The original form of the AD 325 Nicene Creed ends its final paragraph with the words, "And we believe in the Holy Spirit." The reader will notice that I added square brackets to the content that follows this statement. This is because though the Council of Constantinople (AD 381) originally adopted the Nicene Creed, it also added a fuller section on the Holy Spirit, the nature of the church, the ordinance of baptism, and the coming of the last day in AD 381. As was previously mentioned, later creeds tend to keep material from earlier creeds while at the same time expanding on certain material with a fuller explanation. One of the reasons why we have a fuller description on the Holy Spirit in the later version of the creed may have been in response to the so-called Pneumatachoi (literally "fighters against the Spirit"), a heretical group who denied the person and deity of the Holy Spirit.[16] It is interesting to note that the modern day Nicene Creed also includes the later section added at Constantinople.

The reader will notice that the creed begins with the Father as Creator of all things "visible and invisible" (a refutation of Gnosticism), followed by a substantial section dealing with the person of the Son. It first deals with titles associated with his status as our "one Lord"—Son of God who is begotten of the Father—and then, to emphasize his true deity, also asserts that the Son is "God of God, Light of Light, true God of true God." The key phrase that appears next is that the Son is "begotten, not made, of one substance with the Father." Much confusion has arisen concerning the language of the Son being begotten of the Father. It does *not* mean that the Son is created, as the doctrine of the Trinity maintains that there are three, eternal Persons in the Godhead, and their relationship with one another is also eternal. Rather, the relationship of the Son to the Father is that he is *eternally begotten.*[17] This is why the creed goes on to say that the Son is "of one substance with the Father."

The word "one substance" comes from the Greek word *homoousios*, which means of the same substance, nature, or being. This word was the centre of much debate in Nicaea. Did it mean that the Son was of similar substance (*homoiousios*) to the Father? A different substance (*heterousios*) with him? The same substance (*homoousios*)? Nicaea argued along biblical lines that it was the

---

[16] The Pneumatachoi were also known as Macedonians, after their supposed leader Macedonius. See Michael A.G. Haykin, *The Spirit of God: The Exegesis of 1 and 2 Corinthians in the Pneumatomachian Controversy of the Fourth Century* (Leiden: Brill, 1994).

[17] On this and other Christological questions relating to the eternal begetting of the Son, the reader is encouraged to consult Stephen J. Wellum, *God the Son Incarnate: The Doctrine of Christ* (ed. John S. Feinberg; Wheaton: Crossway, 2016).

latter—that the Son is of the *same* substance as the Father. In much the same way as the Apostles' Creed, the Nicene Creed then proceeds to address Christ's incarnation, his passion and resurrection, his ascension into heaven, and the hope of his Second Coming, which will usher in the final judgement. A trinitarian emphasis, as was seen in the Apostles' Creed, is highlighted in the references to the Holy Spirit and his inclusion with the Father and Son in Christian worship. The nature of the universal church is then affirmed, including the ordinance of baptism and the hope of the resurrection and life everlasting.

The articles found in these two creeds are considered to be foundational for Christians; they are the "non-negotiables" of the faith. The fundamental beliefs they express are subscribed to not only by Protestant churches, but also by Roman Catholic and Orthodox churches as well. But creeds were not just part of the early Christian church; nor, as we will see, did they even originate there. Rather, they began as an integral part of the nation of Israel and played a crucial role in the identification of the people of God throughout the Old Testament period. If Scripture is God's voice to humanity, then creeds, in turn, are humanity's response to God. *Credo*, "I believe."

2
THE OLD TESTAMENT
AS THE FORERUNNER OF CHRISTIAN CREEDS

We opened the first chapter with a discussion on the meaning of the word creed and looked at the both the Apostles' Creed and the Nicene Creed as examples. But as its title bears out, this book is interested in going even further back in history, to the first century AD, and to the earliest Christian creeds found in the New Testament. This study would be incomplete, however, if we neglected to examine the predecessor of the New Testament church: the nation of Israel. In this chapter, we will turn our attention briefly to the Old Testament,[1] as it is the precursor to the New Testament in God's progressive revelation.

The relationship between creeds and hymns are important because, as noted earlier, there is an organic association between the two. As we shall see, hymns in both the Old and New Testament implicitly carry within themselves creedal affirmations and so are inextricably tied together. Hymns may even be thought of as a form of creed put to song. Gordon Fee essentially captures the direction I hope to achieve and expand on in this book when he says, "Such songs [hymns] are by their very nature creedal, full of theological grist, and thus give evidence of what early Christians most truly believed about God and his Christ."[2] Hymns can also "include dogmatic, confessional, liturgical, or doxological material."[3] Throughout the years, Christians have often confessed what they believed theologically through the medium of song. For example, consider the well-known hymn, "Holy, Holy, Holy, Lord God Almighty" by Reginald Heber (1826). In the first and last stanzas of this hymn

---

[1] The term "Old Testament," or "Old Covenant," finds its roots within the New Testament text itself. It is explicitly used in 2 Corinthians 3:14. It is also implied elsewhere wherever the New Covenant is contrasted with the Old Covenant, as in Hebrews 8:13.

[2] Gordon D. Fee, *Pauline Christology* (Peabody: Hendrickson Publishers, 2007), 493. For a review of this book, see Tony Costa, "Pauline Christology: An Exegetical-Theological Study: Review" in *TJT* 24, no. 1 (2008): 110-111.

[3] Robert L. Reymond, *Jesus, Divine Messiah: The New Testament Witness* (Phillipsburg: Presbyterian and Reformed Publishing Company, 1990), 245 n.11.

we read the words "God in three persons, blessed Trinity!" This is a creedal statement if there ever was one. And just as we saw that confessions often overlap with creeds, so we shall see that there is a fine line between creeds and hymns. It is thus true that, according to Stauffer, "Many confessions were hymn-like and many hymns were creed-like."[4]

The contribution of the Old Testament is an invaluable resource as we seek a better understanding of the earliest creeds in the Christian community. Not only is it obviously the wellspring from which the Christian movement emerged, it is also the theological source and background to the creeds of the Christian community. When speaking of the Old Testament we also need to be aware that in the time of Jesus there were at least two versions of it—one in Hebrew, and the other in Greek—which came to be known as the Septuagint.[5] Most Old Testament citations in the New Testament come from the LXX (Roman numerals used to represent the Septuagint). And when we recall that Greek had become the *lingua franca* of the world during the first century AD, it is not surprising that the New Testament, also written in Greek, would cite the LXX as its primary Old Testament source.

A number of the main creeds contained in the Old Testament are later repeated and adapted by New Testament writers. In some cases, just as we saw in the evolution of later creeds in church history following the Apostles' Creed, they were also expanded with additional material. One of the most important creeds in the Old Testament is found in Deuteronomy 6:4-5.

Deuteronomy 6:4-5

One of the best-known creeds in the Old Testament is the *Shema*, which is a Hebrew word meaning "hear" or "listen." It appears in Deuteronomy 6:4-5, and reads, "Hear, O Israel: The LORD our God, the LORD is one. You shall love the LORD your God with all your heart and with all your soul and with all your might."[6] This creed establishes the unity and sovereignty of the God of

---

[4] Ethelbert E. Stauffer, *New Testament* Theology, trans. J. Marsh (London: SCM Press, 1948), 237.

[5] The version known as the LXX was produced by Jewish scribes who knew Greek, and presumably lived in Alexandria, Egypt. The accounts of its origin and formulation are given by Philo of Alexandria, the Epistle of Aristeas, and Josephus' own account. See C.K. Barrett, *New Testament Background: Selected Documents* (New York: Harper and Row, 1961), 209.

[6] The latter part of Deuteronomy 6:4 can also be translated variously as "the LORD our God, the LORD is one" and "the LORD is our God, the LORD is one" or as "the LORD is our God, the LORD alone."

Israel against all other gods and affirms unequivocally that Israel's God is one.[7] It goes on to state that only the LORD, or Yahweh, is worthy of full, heartfelt worship. We see here that the faith community of Israel was to couple their monotheistic confession with an unreserved love and devotion to Yahweh alone. In fact the *Shema* played such an important role in the life of Israel that it often appears in the New Testament, particularly in the Gospels. Jesus himself was aware of the *Shema* and would undoubtedly have recited it during his life. The *Shema* appears in all of the Synoptic Gospels (Matt. 22:34-40; Mark 12:28-34; Luke 10:25-28).[8]

It is interesting to note that while both Matthew and Luke record the section of the *Shema* concerning loving God with one's whole being (cf. Deut. 6:5), it is only in Mark 12:28-30 that we see a full citation of the *Shema*:

> And one of the scribes came up and heard them disputing with one another, and seeing that he answered them well, asked him, "Which commandment is the most important of all?" Jesus answered, "The most important is, 'Hear, O Israel: The Lord our God, the Lord is one. And you shall love the Lord your God with all your heart and with all your soul and with all your mind and with all your strength.'"

Here Jesus affirms that the *Shema* is the most important commandment of all because it is centred first and foremost on God himself. Note that this early creed begins first with belief in the oneness of God. It should also be noted that the *Shema* is theocentric; it centres on God and his unity, and our response of love and devotion to him. The identity of God and our love and commitment

---

[7] The word for "one" in Deuteronomy 6:4 is the Hebrew word *echad*, which many commentators have noted denotes a "composite unity" in God as opposed to the another Hebrew word, *yachid*, which implies an absolute, solitary unity. The use of *echad* to communicate a composite unity is seen in several places in the OT, such as in Genesis 1:5, where evening and morning are described as יוֹם אֶחָד (*yom echad*), i.e., one day. Notice that there are two events (evening and morning) which form one day. The same idea is seen in Genesis 2:24 where the ordinance of marriage is described as a man and woman becoming בָשָׂר אֶחָד (*basar echad*), i.e., one flesh. Again, there are two persons, the man and his wife, who become one flesh through the bond of marriage. Plurality in unity is what is envisioned here. The Hebrew word *echad* is by far the most common word used in the Old Testament when referring to God as "one." This use of *echad* for the oneness of God in Deuteronomy 6:4 is important as it demonstrates that the God of the Bible is not a unitarian being (one person in the Godhead), but rather a trinitarian being (a composite unity of three Persons in the Godhead).

[8] According to the Mishnah, *Tamid* 4:3; 5:1, the Shema was recited by the priests in the Second Temple, indicating that the practice existed before the destruction of the temple in AD 70. See Tony Costa, *Worship and the Risen Jesus in the Pauline Letters*, Studies in Biblical Literature, 157 (New York: Peter Lang, 2013), 376 n.113.

to him are central. This is a theme that runs throughout the Old Testament and here Jesus himself acknowledges this creed as the first and foremost commandment. This demonstrates both Jesus' commitment to monotheism, and his enthusiasm for the love and worship of God above all else.

An interesting transition takes place in the New Testament as the creeds become less theocentric and more Christocentric. This of course does not minimize the importance and centrality of God. On the contrary, God is revealed precisely in the New Testament through the person of Christ, who is the fulness of deity in bodily form (Col. 2:9). According to John 1:18, it is the Son himself who has fully explained, revealed, and exegeted (the actual word used in the original Greek of this text) the Father to us. But while God revealed himself in the Old Testament though a cloud of fire, or a bright shining cloud, or smoke which filled the temple, or in the burning bush, it is only in the Son where God is revealed *par excellence*. Though in times past God spoke through the prophets, in these last days he speaks through his Son (Heb. 1:1-2). This is why the creeds in the New Testament are primarily centred on Christ.

Jesus' reaffirmation of the *Shema* also reinforces the Christian emphasis on monotheism. The Christian affirmation of the *Shema* in its monotheistic emphasis is seen in several New Testament passages, such as Galatians 3:20 (God is one), Ephesians 4:6 (one God and Father of all), 1 Timothy 2:5 (for there is one God), and 1 Corinthians 8:4 (there is no God but one). When we examine the New Testament creeds in the next chapter, we will see how Paul revamps the traditional *Shema* from Deuteronomy 6:4 into a New Testament version.

Another interesting creed in the Old Testament is found in Deuteronomy 26:5b-9:

> A wandering Aramean was my father. And he went down into Egypt and sojourned there, few in number, and there he became a nation, great, mighty, and populous. And the Egyptians treated us harshly and humiliated us and laid on us hard labor. Then we cried to the LORD, the God of our fathers, and the LORD heard our voice and saw our affliction, our toil, and our oppression. And the LORD brought us out of Egypt with a mighty hand and an outstretched arm, with great deeds of terror, with signs and wonders. And he brought us into this place and gave us this land, a land flowing with milk and honey.

Old Testament

We see here that some creeds, while certainly affirming what people believe, also contain historical elements within them. For example, in the Apostles' Creed we see this historical statement: "He [Jesus] suffered under Pontius Pilate." This statement affirms that Jesus was condemned to be crucified under the orders of Pontius Pilate during the first century AD, an event that the Gospels bear out. Little did Pontius Pilate know that his name would go down in infamy and be immortalized in the creeds of the Christian church!

The creed of Deuteronomy 26:5b-9 is an important creed in that it is rooted in the history of the people of Israel. It contains four principle elements: the patriarchs—especially Jacob, the wandering Aramean nomad whose name was changed to Israel and from which his descendants obtained the same name—the enslavement in Egypt, the exodus, and the entry into the promised land. These elements are also found in Deuteronomy 6:20-24, Joshua 24:2b-13, and in Psalm 105. Though this creed recalls the identity of Israel and her history, the most important element it identifies is her relationship with God the Redeemer. The exodus also appears as a central theme in Israel's history as it remains the defining act of her redemption. Thus every annual observance of the Passover was intended to rehearse and remember the redemptive event of the exodus. The repeated imperative in the Old Testament, especially in the Pentateuch, is that the people of Israel are to *remember* Yahweh and what he did for them (Exod. 13:3; Num. 15:39-40; Deut. 7:18; 8:2,18; 15:15; 16:3,12; 24:18).

Out of all Ten Commandments, the one commandment which uses the verb "remember" is the command regarding the Sabbath, "Remember the Sabbath day, to keep it holy" (Exod. 20:8). This is the only commandment that has a time element connected to it, i.e., it could only be obeyed once a week, from Friday night until Saturday night. It could also only be broken once a week. All the other nine Commandments—adultery, blasphemy, murder, lying, and so on—could be broken any day of the week. The Sabbath was a weekly reminder for the people of Israel to rest one day in seven. Just as God created the heavens and the earth and rested on the seventh day, so his people should also enjoy rest from their labors (Exod. 20:9-11). On this day they were to remember that God is the Creator of all things, that all things come from his hand, and that work is honorable. They were also to look forward to the day when, through the person and work of the Messiah, the Sabbath rest would become permanent, and in the New Covenant we read that believers in Christ have already entered into that rest (Heb. 3:7–4:13).[9]

But there is another reason God gave the Sabbath to Israel. To find it, we must turn to another version of the Decalogue found in Deuteronomy 5, which is really a review of the Decalogue by Moses. Deuteronomy is the name given to the last book of the Pentateuch, which in Hebrew is called *Devarim* ("words"), but in the Greek version it literally means "second law." It was a review of the law given to Israel and the one which Moses rehearses to Israel just before his death (Deut. 34). In Deuteronomy 5:12, the command given is not to "remember" the Sabbath, but to "observe" (*shamar*; Hebrew) the Sabbath. While the reason given in Exodus 20 is to recall God as the Creator of all things and the giver of rest, the reason given in Deuteronomy 5:15 as to why Israel should observe the Sabbath is as follows:

> You shall *remember* that you were a slave in the land of Egypt, and the LORD your God brought you out from there with a mighty hand and an outstretched arm. Therefore the LORD your God commanded you to keep the Sabbath day (italics mine).

In Deuteronomy 5:15, we are told that another reason for Israel to keep the Sabbath was to help them remember that they had been freed from slavery in Egypt. By examining both Exodus 20 and Deuteronomy 5 together, we are then able to see the full purpose of the Sabbath: it reminded Israel that God was both their Creator and Liberator. And so we see that Jesus, as God's true Sabbath, gives his people rest (Matt. 11:28–30), but that he also comes to set his people free from their bondage to sin (John 8:32, 36). Unlike the earthly Sabbath, which came and went once a week, this will be a permanent rest. It will be a true and lasting freedom that believers experience in Christ (Gal. 5:1). The Sabbath, then, was a weekly time to remember God as both Creator and Liberator, and to assert those truths in either creeds or hymns.

Even after the Israelites had crossed the Jordan river, Joshua reminded them to "*remember* the word that Moses the servant of the LORD commanded you" (Josh. 1:13; italics mine). In the closing words of the Old Testament, we also read that God's final instructions to his people are to "*remember* the law

---

[9] For a full treatment of the Sabbath and its relation to the New Covenant, see Tony Costa, "The Sabbath and Its Relation to Christ and the Church in the New Covenant," *SBJT* 20, no. 1 (2015): 123–147.

of my servant Moses, the statutes and rules that I commanded him at Horeb for all Israel" (Mal. 4:4; italics mine). Recalling the past is crucial as it serves as a history lesson to those in the present. We also need to remember that history matters to God as it is the theatre wherein he works out his purposes in space and time for his eternal glory. The apostle Paul understood the importance of history and regularly reminded believers that the divine calamities which fell on Israel in times past were to serve as warnings to present day believers (1 Cor. 10:6), while at the same time providing instruction and encouragement that we might have hope (Rom. 15:4).

The New Testament ordinance of the Lord's Supper, which evolved from the original Passover meal, also contains within itself the imperative to remember and declare the Lord's death until he comes again (1 Cor. 11:23-26). The Lord's Supper, like the Passover, looks back to Christ's redemptive work as the new exodus in which his people are delivered from the bondage of sin and death to the freedom of new life.

The entrance into Canaan with Joshua is also recalled here. At the end of Joshua's life, he once again rehearses the people's ancestral history (like Moses did in Deuteronomy), and erects a stone in Shechem to serve as a tangible witness of their agreement to renew the covenant with Yahweh (Josh. 24:1-27). This act reinforces the point that the past is of utmost importance. It shows God to be the Lord of history, who is actively involved in time and space and works out his purposes for his glory. Creeds, then, are anchored in history and serve to recall important events—especially salvific ones like the exodus—or in the case of the Lord's Supper, the death and resurrection of Jesus, which inaugurates a new and better exodus.

The creed in Deuteronomy 26:5b-9 emphasizes how important it was for Israel to remember her relationship with God, which was the heart of the covenant. This is why covenantal language plays such an integral part in creeds. The very concept of covenant in the Old Testament can be communicated in two simple statements: "I will be your God, and you will be my people." In this most basic form, we see that a covenant is a relationship between God and his people.

The Old Testament also contain hymns in which creedal affirmations appear. As stated above, there is a fine line between creeds and hymns and often times they seem to overlap. One of the hymns found in the Old Testament is the Song of Moses in Exodus 15:1-18. This hymn recounts the triumph of Yahweh over the Egyptians and once again we see that the context is that of the exodus, the major salvation event in Israel's history. It also affirms the unique relationship of Yahweh with Israel and throughout the hymn he is described as the hero and Redeemer of his people. In addition, there are also beautiful anthropomorphisms such as, "At the blast of thy nostrils the waters piled up, the floods stood up in a heap" (Exod. 15:8, RSV); "Thou didst blow with thy wind, the sea covered them" (Exod. 15:10, RSV); and, "Thou didst stretch out thy right hand, the earth swallowed them" (Exod. 15:12, RSV). It then culminates with the triumphant statement, "The LORD will reign forever and ever" (Exod. 15:18, RSV).

Hymns also played a major role in the Old Testament and are usually applied to victories in battle, as in the case of the exodus. It is for this reason that the song listed in Exodus 15:3 describes Yahweh as a warrior, "The LORD is a man of war; the LORD is his name." Yahweh is the true warrior of Israel. War hymns are a common feature in the Old Testament as well as in Second Temple Jewish literature.

The word associated with "sing" in Hebrew is etymologically associated with the word for "battlecry." We see this correlation in the Song of Deborah in Judges 5 where once again it is Yahweh who is credited with granting Israel victory, "So perish all thine enemies, O LORD!" (Judg. 5:31, RSV). Prominent in these hymns and others is also the idea of theophany (visible manifestations of God), and he is often described as "appearing" to save his people. For example, "The mountains quaked before the LORD, you Sinai before the LORD, the God of Israel" (Judg. 5:5, RSV). Today we don't usually envision people going into battle while singing, but not too long ago armies would often wage war accompanied by the sound of trumpets or coronets.

Storm theophanies, where God's appearance is likened to the coming of a flashing and thunderous storm, are also prominent through the Old Testament and some hymns were put to song to conjure up this imagery about Yahweh. The shattering sound of thunder evoked for the Israelites what it would have been like to hear God utter his voice. The voice of Yahweh is like the sound of many waters falling or cascading (Ezek. 1:24; 43:2). To observe flashes of lightning would have evoked the imagery of fiery arrows darting through the sky and coming down from heaven upon the earth. Thus, in the Psalter, references to lightning are described as God's arrows which he shoots at his enemies (Ps. 18:14; 77:17; 144:6). The lightning is also associated with God's spear (Hab. 3:11). The imagery of thunder and lightning coming down from heaven was a metaphorical and phenomenological spectacle of God's role as a warrior bringing judgment against his enemies on the earth. Like their Ancient Near Eastern neighbours, Israel depended on rain showers to enliven their crops and maintain a balanced agriculture; it is therefore not surprising to find common elements between the Bible and the writings of their neighbours. One interesting example is found in Psalm 29:3, 5, 7-8, 10:

> The voice of the LORD is upon the waters;
> The God of glory thunders,
> The LORD, upon many waters ...
> The voice of the LORD breaks the cedars ...
> The voice of the LORD flashes forth flames of fire,
> The voice of the LORD shakes the wilderness of Kadesh.
> The LORD sits enthroned over the flood.

In this hymn, the glory of God is depicted in terms of storm imagery, and God is shown to be the one who brings the waters. It should also be noted that waters in the Old Testament were often a representation of chaos, and sometimes of the chaotic nations (Isa. 57:20).

Another beautiful storm theophany appears in Psalm 18:6-14, 17 (RSV), where David recounts how God delivered him from Saul and his men:

> In my distress I called upon the LORD;
> to my God for help.
> From his temple he heard my voice,
> and my cry to him reached his ears.
> Then the earth reeled and rocked;
> the foundations also of the mountains trembled
> and quaked, because he was angry.
> Smoke went up from his nostrils,
> and devouring fire from his mouth;
> glowing coals flamed forth from him.
> He bowed the heavens, and came down;
> thick darkness was under his feet.
> He rode on a cherub, and flew;
> he came swiftly upon the wings of the wind.
> He made darkness his covering around him,
> his canopy thick clouds dark with water.
> Out of the brightness before him
> there broke through his clouds
> hailstones and coals of fire.

> The LORD also thundered in the heavens,
> and the Most High uttered his voice,
> hailstones and coals of fire.
> And he sent out his arrows, and scattered them;
> he flashed forth lightnings, and routed them ...
> He delivered me from my strong enemy,
> and from those who hated me;
> for they were too mighty for me.

The Psalms were part of the hymn book of God's people.[10] Many of the them have to do with the praise and worship of God, although there were other types of psalms (lament, royal, etc.) as well. Thus, we see that from an early time, singing hymns in worship to God was a normative practice among the worshipping community. Even in present day Judaism, worship services are usually led or aided by a cantor (a *hazzan* in Hebrew) who chants or sings during worship services in the synagogue. Their function is to lead the congregation in prayers with song, not unlike how the biblical psalms would have been sung. The hymns we find in the Old Testament typically rehearse God's redemptive works in history but at the same time serve as creedal affirmations about what the people believed about God and his covenant with them. In other words, the Israelites confessed what they believed in song.

The use of hymns in worship to God and their relationship to creeds did not end with the closure of the Old Testament canon. During the intertestamental period—sometimes called the "silent years," and extending roughly 400 years between the book of Malachi and the writing of the New Testament—literature continued to be written. This literature is referred to as belonging to Second Temple Judaism. The rabbis had taught that the spirit of inspiration had departed from Israel after Malachi, thus signifying the termination of the writing of inspired Scripture.[11] The intertestamental literature, therefore, was not believed to be inspired as were the Old Testament books. However, they do give us valuable insight into what the Jews believed before God's voice would be heard once again through the ministry of John the

---

[10] On the psalms and their use in the worship of Israel see Bruce K. Waltke with Charles Yu, *An Old Testament Theology: An Exegetical, Canonical, and Thematic Approach* (Grand Rapids: Zondervan, 2007), 870-896; John Day, *Psalms*, Old Testament Guides (Sheffield: JSOT, 1992); Harvey H. Guthrie, Jr., *Israel's Sacred Songs* (New York: Seabury Press, 1966); Sigmund Mowinckel, *The Psalms in Israel's Worship*, 2 vols. (New York: Abingdon Press, 1962).

[11] *B. Sanh.* 11a.

Baptist (Luke 3:2).[12] Some of the collections from this time period are known as the Apocrypha and the Pseudepigrapha, and it is within these collections that we also encounter several hymns.

The Apocrypha collection comes from the books of the Second Temple Jewish period (ca. 515 BC–AD 70), and attests to the ongoing tradition within the Jewish community of employing the use of hymns in their worship. We see examples of such hymns in the apocryphal books of Judith 16:1-17 and Sirach 51:1-12. Judith 16:2 (RSV) states, "And Judith said, 'Begin a song to my God with tambourines, sing to my Lord with cymbals. Raise to him a new psalm; exalt him, and call upon his name.'" Note how the terms "song" and "new psalm" are used interchangeably here.

As in the Song of Moses and Deborah above, the context of Judith 16 is a battle, and credit for the victory is given to God, "For the Lord is a God who shatters war; he has pitched his camp in the middle of his people to deliver me from the hands of my enemies" (Jdt. 16:3).[13] The theme of theophany is also present in this hymn, "Should mountains topple to mingle with the waves, should rocks melt like wax before your face" (Jdt. 16:15). Notice again how God is credited as the true warrior of Israel, as we saw in Exodus 15:3.

In Sirach 51, which is structured like much of the wisdom literature in the Old Testament, there is a hymn of thanksgiving very similar to that found in the Psalms. First, we find an indirect allusion to the exodus in Sirach 51:11-12, "Then I remembered your mercy, Lord, and your deeds from earliest times, how you deliver those who wait patiently, and save them from the clutches of their enemies." Note again the importance of remembering what God has done in the past.

The Qumran community, sometimes identified as the Essenes, was an apocalyptic community that lived in the desert of Qumran awaiting the end of the world and the final battle. They were a hermitic community who believed that the priestly establishment of Jerusalem was corrupt and illegitimate and that they alone were the sons of light and could serve God in truth. As a community they held to various rules, including rules for worship, among which were also found several hymns. What is interesting about the hymns found in

---

[12] That the Word of God was heard anew through John the Baptist is seen in the very Semitic wording of Luke 3:2, "the word of God came to John the son of Zechariah in the wilderness." This was the typical OT language of revelation which would come to the prophets (Jeremiah 1:2; 2:1; Ezekiel 1:3; Hosea 1:1 et al.).

[13] References to the Apocrypha in this section are taken from *The Jerusalem Bible* (New York: Doubleday, 1968).

EARLY CHRISTIAN CREEDS AND HYMNS

Qumran is that they seemed to be intended more as individual hymns than communal. Geza Vermes points out that,

> I have counted twenty-five compositions similar to the biblical Psalms. They are all hymns of thanksgiving, individual prayers as opposed to those intended for communal worship, expressing a rich variety of spiritual and doctrinal detail. But the two fundamental themes running through the whole collection are those of salvation and knowledge.[14]

As already stated, hymns often contain creedal elements within themselves, and the biblical Psalms are examples of this. Hymns are flexible in that they can be appropriated by both the individual and the community, much like the biblical Psalms were. For example, while the Psalms reflect the prayers of David and others, they were also utilized by the larger faith community who could personally identify with the psalmist in their prayers to God. The Qumran hymns also focus on the importance of the covenantal relationship which an individual shares with God. The backdrop to this covenantal language is, once again, the Old Testament, in which Israel was to live in covenant relationship with God. The Qumran hymns also present God as the Deliverer and Redeemer of his people, the same theme which was noted in the exodus motif. In addition, the Qumran community also had among its collection of Dead Sea Scrolls a number of hymns, such as the Thanksgiving Hymns in 1QH.[15]

This point is clearly seen in Hymn 6 from the Dead Sea Scrolls:

> I thank Thee, O Lord,
> For Thou art as a fortified wall to me,
> And as an iron bar against all destroyers ...
> Thou hast set my feet upon a rock ...
> That I may walk in the way of eternity
> And in the paths which Thou hast chosen.[16]

In the Pseudepigrapha collection, the book of *1 Enoch*—with language borrowed from Daniel 7:13-14—envisions an eschatological time when the "son of man," who is identified as the Messiah, will bring about the universal praise

---

[14] Geza Vermes, *Dead Sea Scrolls* (London: Penguin Books, 1968), 149.
[15] Richard N. Longenecker, *New Wine Into Fresh Wineskins* (Peabody: Hendrickson Publishers, 1999), 7.
[16] Vermes, *Dead Sea Scrolls*, 160.

of God, "He [the son of man] shall be the hope of those whose hearts are troubled. All, who dwell on earth, shall fall down and worship before him; shall bless and glorify him, and sing praises to the name of the Lord of spirits [God]" (*1 Enoch* 48:4). At this time, all who dwell on the earth shall worship and "sing praises." Here too we see cosmic worship being realized through singing.

Thus, the Old Testament shows us the importance of the use of creeds and hymns among the people of God. They were a way for the people of Israel to remember God and his redemptive works. We also see how important the creed of the *Shema* was in grounding the people in their conception of Yahweh as the one and only God whom they should love with their whole being.

Hymns were also an important part of the Old Testament community. One of the first places we see Israel breaking into a hymn is at the crossing of the Red Sea: the defining event of the exodus that will go on to shape the redemption and identity of Israel. In this hymn, sung by Miriam, creedal statement are made about God as Protector, Redeemer, and King. We also saw that hymns played a significant part in the military triumphs of Israel in those psalms where God is credited as the true Warrior and Protector of his people. We then saw that hymns did not end with the closing of the Old Testament canon, but continued on into the intertestamental period as recorded in the Apocrypha, Pseudepigrapha, and the Dead Sea Scroll community in Qumran. From this we must conclude that the people of God in the Old Testament were both a confessional and a singing community. Both creeds and hymns were integral to the identity of the worshipping community of Israel. In the next chapter we will see how these same identity markers go on to define the New Testament worshipping community.

3
CREEDS IN THE NEW TESTAMENT

Being that they are grounded in the person of Jesus Christ, we find that creeds and hymns are much more prevalent in the New Testament. As discussed above, the creeds, especially in early Christianity, functioned to keep insiders and outsiders distinctive.

In Mark 4:11 for instance, referencing his parables, Jesus delineates between those who hear and *can* understand his parables (the insiders), and those who hear but *cannot* understand the same parables (the outsiders). It is interesting to note that following the destruction of the Second Temple in AD 70 and towards the end of the first century, the Jews had a creedal confession referred to as the "Eighteen Benedictions" whereby they weeded out Jewish Christians from their synagogues or religious gatherings. In this case, those who were weeded out were most likely Christians. The early Jewish followers of Jesus would have probably continued to attend synagogue worship in the earliest and formative years of the Christian movement, albeit as secret believers. We know from the book of Acts that the apostles continued to go to the temple to worship and pray (Acts 2:46; 3:1, 3; 5:42; 22:17) until they were finally evicted.

In the "Eighteen Benedictions" (*Shemoneh 'Esreh* in Hebrew) as they have come to be known, theological swords were drawn towards the end of the first century AD. In Benediction 12, also known as the "Cursing of the Heretics" (*Birkhat ha-Minim*; Hebrew) it states:

> For the renegades let there be no hope, and may the arrogant kingdom [perhaps a reference to Rome] soon be rooted out in our days, and the Nazarenes and the *minim* [heretics] perish as in a moment and be blotted out from the book of life and with the righteous may they not be inscribed. Blessed art thou, O Lord, who humblest the arrogant.[1]

---

[1] Quoted in C.K. Barrett, *The New Testament Background: Selected Documents* (New York: Harper and Row, 1961), 167.

There is some question as to whether "the Nazarenes" (*ha-notzrim*; Hebrew) in the text above was part of the original benediction; some claim it may have been expunged during the Medieval period due to Christian sensitivities and suspicion.[2] Early Church Fathers, such as Justin Martyr in his *Dialogue with Trypho the Jew*, and Jerome seemed to be aware of these curses directed at Christians in the synagogue prayers.[3] In the New Testament, we find the title "Nazarenes" given to the early Christians (Acts 24:5) who were followers of Jesus, who was himself a Nazarene (Mark 14:67). It is clear, however, that the *minim*—the heretics—were clearly being referred to here and would no doubt have included Jewish Christians as well. The push to remove Jewish followers of Jesus from the synagogue was already evident in the life and ministry of Jesus, as is shown in John 9:22, "For the Jews had already agreed that if anyone should confess Jesus to be Christ [the Messiah], he was to be put out of the synagogue." Even in Matthew there is a perceived tension between the followers of Jesus and the unbelieving Jews.[4]

The *minim* in Benediction 12 referred to sects that were deemed heretical by Judaism. This particular benediction was used, according to Barrett, "as a 'test benediction'; it was one which no heretic could pronounce ... and therefore had the effect of banning heretics from the synagogue."[5] The strong opposition with which Judaism reacted to new sects like Christianity is also evident in rabbinic literature. For instance, Rabbi Akiba writes, "Also he that reads the heretical books, that have no share in the world to come."[6] This would refer to any books considered to belong in the category of *minim*. It is possible that this may also have been referring to certain parts or books of the New Testament, including its contained Christian creeds and hymns.

---

[2] *Encyclopedia Judaica*, s.v. "Birkat Ha-Minim," (accessed March 31, 2020, www.jewishvirtuallibrary.org/birkat-ha-minim). The validity of this reference to Jewish Christians seems to be sound and certain, "The Palestinian texts of the Amidah preserve an early form of the Benediction against Heretics which includes both minim, Jewish Christians, and nozerim, Gentile Christians. The Benediction's recitation was intended to bring about the separation of Christians from the synagogue." Center for Online Judaic Studies. n.d. "The Eighteen Benedictions-The Benediction Against the Heretics." (Accessed March 31, 2020. http://cojs.org/eighteen-benedictions-benediction-heretics).

[3] Justin Martyr, *Dial* 16; Jerome, *In Esaiam* 52.5, *Ep.* cxii. 13.

[4] Matthew presents the real tension between early Jewish Christians and the unbelieving Jewish religious leaders of his day in a "we" vs. "they" dichotomy. We see this in phrases such as "*their* synagogues" (Matthew 4:23; 9:35), "*your* synagogues" (23:34), "*their* scribes" (7:29), "*their* city" (22:7) and "*the Jews* to this day" (28:15). Italics are mine for emphasis.

[5] Barrett, *New Testament Background*, 167.

[6] Barrett, *New Testament Background*, 166.

New Testament

The creeds in the New Testament focus primarily on the person and work of Jesus. They also express a relationship between the believing individual and the believing community and attempt to describe what God has done for them through Jesus of Nazareth. Jesus is always described as the unique agent through whom God has brought his plans to fruition; we also frequently encounter terminology such as "through Christ" and "in Christ" throughout many New Testament creeds.

How do we know where to find the creeds of the New Testament? How can we extrapolate them from the text? I will address these questions in the next chapter as we examine various scriptural passages. Here I will only say that in our search to find the earliest creeds in Christianity we need to start by examining the earliest texts in the New Testament. Unfortunately, the New Testament texts do not come with a publication date, which makes their precise dating difficult. The general consensus of the vast number of New Testament scholars maintains that the earliest documents are the letters of Paul; others would also include the letter of James. If pressed, most scholars would agree that 1 Thessalonians is likely our earliest text. The dating of the New Testament books has been an ongoing debate for years, with some such as liberal scholar A.T. Robinson arguing that all the books of the New Testament were written before AD 70.[7] Other scholars, especially liberal scholars, would place some of them, including the Gospels, after AD 70. None of these dates are conclusive, and, for at least some scholars advocating for a later dating of Matthew, Luke, and John, their methods seem shaped more by worldview than anything else. Take Jesus' prediction in the Gospels about the destruction of the temple in Jerusalem, which occurred in AD 70 (Matt. 24, Mark 13, Luke 21). Due to an anti-supernaturalistic worldview that sees such prophecies as impossible, many scholars attempt to push the authorship of Matthew and Luke to AD 70 or later. However, they are constrained to keep Mark a little earlier (AD 66) because most assume that Mark wrote his gospel first, which was then copied by Matthew and Luke; they also believe that both Matthew and Luke utilized a hypothetical source called "Q" (from the German word *Quelle* meaning "source").

All this to say that apart from one's philosophical presuppositions, there is no good reason why the Gospels could not have been written earlier than these

---

[7] John A.T. Robinson, *Redating the New Testament* (London: SCM Press, 1976), 3, 342-348. W.F. Albright took the position that no book of the NT was written beyond AD 80. William F. Albright, *Recent Discoveries in Bible Lands* (New York: Funk and Wagnalls, 1955), 136.

scholars suggest. And though it is true that Christians also have their own philosophical presuppositions, it is important to note that the New Testament was written by believers and eyewitnesses, or at least by those who had access to eyewitnesses (Luke 1:1-4). In other words, these were people who saw and heard Jesus and were convinced that he had been raised from the dead and witnessed alive by his earliest followers. A resurrection from the dead obviously demands a supernatural explanation, which would imply the existence of God. In early Christian apologetics, it was the argument for the resurrection of Jesus which served as the bedrock argument for not only the truth about Jesus, but also the truth that it was the God of Israel, the biblical God who raised Jesus from the dead. As stated above, the central focus of the Christian creeds is the person and work of Jesus, in conjunction with his resurrection from the dead.

The three main confessional titles ascribed to Jesus in the New Testament are the following: Lord, Christ, and Son of God. We will look at each of these titles in the context of creeds, but first, it is important for us to examine what is believed to be the earliest Christian creed that Christians would have recited and confessed. We now turn our attention to 1 Corinthians 15:3-4.

4
THE EARLIEST CHRISTIAN CREED
1 CORINTHIANS 15:3-4

As we begin our examination of the earliest Christian creed, I will supply the surrounding context of 1 Corinthians 15:1-4 while placing the creedal portion in bold lettering. The text reads as follows:

> Now I would remind you, brothers, of the gospel I preached to you, which you received, in which you stand, and by which you are being saved, if you hold fast to the word I preached to you—unless you believed in vain. For I delivered to you as of first importance what I also received: **that Christ died for our sins in accordance with the Scriptures, that he was buried, that he was raised on the third day in accordance with the Scriptures.**

Paul begins this part of the letter by reminding the believers at Corinth about the good news of the gospel—the same gospel that was preached by Paul and received by the Corinthians, and upon which they took their stand (verse 1). Paul reminds them that it is by this gospel alone that they are saved; providing they hold fast to what Paul preached to them and demonstrate the fruit of their salvation in good works. Otherwise they would have believed in vain (verse 2). After Paul makes these preliminary remarks, he moves on to describe the passing on, or transmission, of various content that he had received. This is important for several reasons. First, Paul is not taking credit for the information he was about to pass on, otherwise he would not have spoken of receiving it. Second, it is also important to note that Paul refers to this information as being of "first importance." Here Paul uses the Greek word *protois*, which is a plural masculine adjective meaning "among the first" and "most important things."[1] This reminds us that the gospel is of first importance to the believer. Third, Paul goes on to state that he passed on, or delivered, what he received,

---

[1] W. Bauer, F.W. Danker, W. Arndt, and F.W. Gingrich, *A Greek-English Lexicon of the New Testament and Other Early Christian Literature*, 3rd ed. (Chicago: University of Chicago Press, 2000), 893. Hereafter *BDAG*.

EARLY CHRISTIAN CREEDS AND HYMNS

which implies that he got it from someone else. The language Paul uses here of delivering and receiving is especially important. The specific Greek words—παρέδωκα (*paredoka*), meaning "delivered," and παρέλαβον (*parelabon*), meaning "received,"—are technical words describing the transmission of source tradition. 1 Corinthians was written probably between AD 50-AD 55, which would place it about twenty years after the death and resurrection of Jesus. This is a relatively short period of time. It would mean that the events of the death, burial, and resurrection of Jesus would still be verifiable by eyewitnesses who were still alive when Paul penned 1 Corinthians. Paul implies this in his reference to the 500+ brethren who saw the risen Christ, most of whom he wrote, were still alive (1 Cor. 15:6).

Notice that Paul precedes each clause in the creed with the Greek conjunction ὅτι (*hoti*), "that," which often indicates that someone, or something, is being quoted: in this case, a creed.[2] Dana and Mantey state that the conjunction *hoti* "does not need translation, for it is practically equivalent to our quotation marks."[3] In Greek grammar this is also known as a *recitative hoti*.[4] Here is verses 3 and 4 again: "That Christ died for our sins in accordance with the Scriptures, that he was buried, that he was raised on the third day in accordance with the Scriptures."

So how do we know that this passage is, in fact, a creed? Several factors indicate that it is. First, Paul admits that he has received and passed on this material; it is not his own. Secondly, the creed is *that* Jesus died for our sins, *that* he was buried, and *that* he rose again on the third day. Even the grammar of the phrases "died for our sins," "was buried," and, "was raised on the third day," is significant. The first two phrases—he "died for our sins," and, "was buried,"—are aorist verbs. Wallace notes that the aorist "usually indicates *past* time with reference to the time of speaking" and is like "taking a snapshot of the action" in the past.[5] The last word, "raised," is a perfect passive verb.

---

[2] Louw and Nida point out that this conjunction and its cognates serve as "markers of discourse content, whether direct or indirect." J.P. Louw and E.A. Nida, eds., *Louw-Nida Greek-English Lexicon of the New Testament Based on Semantic Domains*, 2nd ed. (New York: United Bible Societies, 1988), 90.21.

[3] H.E. Dana and Julius R. Mantey, *A Manual Grammar of the Greek New Testament* (Toronto: The Macmillan Company, 1955), 252.

[4] Daniel B. Wallace, *The Basics of New Testament Syntax: An Intermediate Grammar* (Grand Rapids: Zondervan, 2000), 302.

[5] Daniel B. Wallace, *Greek Grammar Beyond the Basics: An Exegetical Syntax of the New Testament* (Grand Rapids: Zondervan, 1996), 555 (italics in original).

The earliest Christian creed

The perfect tense usually refers to "an event accomplished in the past ... with results existing afterwards ... it describes an event that, completed in the past ... has results existing in the present time."[6] So, when the creed speaks of Jesus being raised from the dead, the perfect verb is used to communicate an event that, though completed in the past, *continues to have ongoing results*. The resurrection of Jesus and its efficacy continues to bear results in the present day in the on-going redemption of God's elect.[7] Notice Paul also states that Jesus' death and resurrection were "in accordance with the Scriptures." The death, burial, and resurrection of Jesus were in accordance with the Scriptures as they were part of God's divine plan, progressively revealed it in the Old Testament.

How old is this creed? James Dunn states that "this tradition [1 Cor. 15:3-4], we can be entirely confident, *was formulated as tradition within months of Jesus' death.*"[8] That is a fantastic claim by Dunn. It should also be noted that this creed would probably have been confessed orally long before being set down in writing, which would move the date even farther back. There is nothing in all the writings of antiquity that even approaches this kind of early attestation. To have a creed come into existence a mere number of months after the event it witnessed took place is absolutely unprecedented. Gerd Lüdemann, a sharp critic of the New Testament, places the latest point this creed could have been formulated to be "not later than three years ... *the formation of the appearance traditions mentioned in I Cor.15.3-8 falls into the time between 30 and 33 CE.*"[9] N.T. Wright similarly concurs, "This is the kind of foundation-story with which a community is not at liberty to tamper. It was probably formulated within the first two or three years after Easter itself, since it was already in

---

[6] Wallace, *Greek Grammar Beyond the Basics*, 572-573.

[7] In John 19:30, Jesus cries out τετέλεσται ("it is finished"). This verb (finished) is also in the perfect tense and means "to bring an activity to a successful finish—'to complete, to finish, to end, to accomplish'" (Louw and Nida, *Greek-English Lexicon*, 68.22). When Jesus declared that his redemptive work was finished, the idea being communicated by the perfect verb is that the work of Christ has been completed in the past with ongoing results. Jesus' death, because it was perfect and "once for all" (Hebrews 7:27; 9:26; 10:10), continues its saving efficacy to the present in the salvation of God's people. In this respect we can speak of the perfect work of Christ on the cross on grammatical grounds.

[8] James D.G. Dunn, *Jesus Remembered: Christianity in the Making* (Grand Rapids: Eerdmans, 2003), 854-855 (italics in original).

[9] Gerd Lüdemann, *The Resurrection of Jesus*, trans. John Bowden (Minneapolis: Fortress, 1994), 171-172 (italics in original).

formulaic form when Paul 'received' it."[10] The early dating of the creed in 1 Corinthians 15:3-4 seems to be well recognized by New Testament scholars.[11]

Related to this early tradition is the claim some scholars make of the so-called "pre-Markan passion narrative." I only bring up this theory in terms of possibility, much like the arguments scholars have made for Q.[12] The creedal source material in 1 Corinthians 15:3-4 already suggests that Christians began confessing their belief in the death, burial, and resurrection of Jesus at an extremely early period when. However, scholars who believe that there was a "pre-Markan passion narrative," also argue that there was an account of the suffering and death of Jesus that existed even before Mark wrote his Gospel. This source, if existent, would point to an even earlier date of composition. In a previous work I noted that,

> Some scholars have also suggested that prior to the writing of the gospel of Mark, there was a pre-Markan Passion Narrative, an account which is believed by some to date *before* [AD] 37 ... and is believed to have covered the materials found in Mark 14-16. There is some dispute about the exact parameters of the materials that are part of the pre-Markan Passion Narrative in Mark 14-16. Some hold that the pre-Markan Passion Narrative also included the narrative of the burial of Jesus. If

---

[10] N. T. Wright, *The Resurrection of the Son of God* (Christian Origins and the Question of God. Vol. 3; Minneapolis: Fortress, 2003), 319.

[11] On the early dating of the creed in 1 Corinthians 15:1-5 see also Michael Goulder, "The Baseless Fabric of a Vision" in Gavin D'Costa, ed., *Resurrection Reconsidered* (Oxford: Oneworld, 1996), 48; A.J.M. Wedderburn, *Beyond Resurrection* (Peabody: Hendrickson, 1999), 113-114.

[12] Q (from the German word *Quelle* meaning "source") is a hypothetical source of sayings believed to be used by both Matthew and Luke. Q is believed to be represented in places where Matthew and Luke use the same "sayings of Jesus" material as in Matthew 11:27 and Luke 10:22.

this is the case, then there is further evidence of an even earlier source that existed before Mark completed his gospel.[13]

According to some of these scholars, this pre-Markan passion narrative is believed to date *before* AD 37. If this is indeed the case, then we have material in the Gospel of Mark (Chapters 14-16) that take us back to the formative years of the Christian movement. One of the indicators that this material is so early is the fact that certain people are mentioned by name, almost as if Mark expected his readers to know who they were. These, in fact, may well have been members of Mark's own church family. For example, "And they compelled a passerby, Simon of Cyrene, who was coming in from the country, the father of Alexander and Rufus, to carry his [Jesus'] cross" (Mark 15:21). Here Simon

---

[13] Tony Costa, "The Burial of Jesus and Its Relation and Importance to the Gospel Message," *AJBT* 20 no. 11 (March 2019): 102 (italics mine). For further reading on the pre-Markan passion narrative and the AD 37 date see Rudolf Pesch, *Das Markusevangelium*, 2 vols. (Freiburg: Herder, 1977); Richard Bauckham, *Jesus and the Eyewitnesses* (Grand Rapids/Cambridge: Eerdmans, 2006), 183-201; Kirk R. MacGregor, "1 Corinthians 15:3b-6a,7 and the Bodily Resurrection of Jesus," *JETS* 49 no. 2 (2006): 225-234; Marion L. Soards, "The Question of a Pre-Markan Passion Narrative," in Raymond E. Brown, *The Death of the Messiah*, 2 vols. (New York: Doubleday, 1994), 2:1492-1524. One of the examples that Bauckham cites for proof of a pre-Markan passion narrative is the theme of protective anonymity, where certain members of the early Christian community were not named, possibly to protect them from danger from the Jewish religious leadership in Jerusalem. An example is Mark not mentioning the name of the high priest Caiphas, whom he only refers to as "the high priest" (Mark 14:53), while the other Gospel writers mention him by name (Matthew 26:57; Luke 3:2; John 18:13-14, 24). The high priestly office of Caiphas and Annas was held until AD 42 and the family remained in power thereafter. They also persecuted the Jerusalem church, as evidenced in the early chapters of the book of Acts. Bauckham comments that it was "diplomatic for the Christian traditions formed in Jerusalem in that period not to refer explicitly to the name of Caiphas in an account of the death of Jesus" (Bauckham, *Jesus and the Eyewitnesses*, 186-187). Another area where protective anonymity is seen is in the striking of the high priest's servant's ear in the garden of Gethsemane. Mark records, "But one of those who stood by drew his sword and struck the servant of the high priest and cut off his ear" (Mark 14:47). Mark is very vague here and it should be noted that he does not directly identify who it was that struck the servant's ear. Matthew (26:51) and Luke (22:50) also do not mention the assailant's name. We only know it was Peter because John 18:10 tells us. John is also the only one who tells us the name of the servant, Malchus. Bauckham argues that the reason John identifies Peter as the assailant is because Peter had already died at the time of his writing and thus there was no need for protective anonymity (Bauckham, *Jesus and the Eyewitnesses*, 195).

Bauckham also notes that Pontius Pilate lost his office in AD 37 and is explicitly named by Mark and blamed for the death of Jesus (187). In other words, Pilate was already out of the picture and had returned to Rome after which it is believed he was exiled to southern France. H.W. Hoehner, s.v. "Pontius Pilate," in Joel B. Green, Scot McKnight and I. Howard Marshall, eds., *Dictionary of Jesus and the Gospels* (Downers Grove/Leicester: InterVarsity Press, 1992), 616. According to church historian Eusebius, Pilate committed suicide due to his involvement in the trial, or mistrial, of Jesus (Eusebius, *Hist. Eccl.* 2.7).

of Cyrene is referred to as "the father of Alexander and Rufus." But which Alexander and Rufus? Alexander was a common name in the Greco-Roman world. The assumption here is that Mark's readers already knew Alexander, Rufus, and their father Simon—who was a direct eyewitness to Jesus' suffering![14] If Jesus died in AD 33, this passion narrative was probably composed between that time and AD 36, a mere three years later. This would place the source material in the same time frame as the creed in 1 Corinthians 15:3-4, which, according to Dunn, may even be earlier, being confessed to "within months" of the death and resurrection of Jesus.

Returning to 1 Corinthians 15:3-4, Paul clearly does not take ownership of this creed as he claims that he "received" and "delivered" it to the Corinthians, language indicating the formal passing on of traditional material.[15] A careful examination of this creed shows a summary, in capsule form, of the passion and resurrection accounts in the Gospels. The passion narratives in the Gospels deal with the death, burial, and resurrection of Jesus, but also with his post-mortem appearances (Matt. 27-28, Mark 15-16; Luke 23-24, John 19-21), which also follow the creed in 1 Corinthians 15:5-8. For the purposes of this book, we will confine our focus to verses 3-4, which are generally accepted as part of the creed. The references to Jesus' post-mortem appearance in verses 5-8 are accepted by some scholars as part of the creed, but not all.[16]

---

[14] Paul also knew a "Rufus" in the church of Rome. He writes, "Greet Rufus, chosen in the Lord; also his mother, who has been a mother to me as well" (Romans 16:13). Is this the same Rufus mentioned in Mark 15:21? It is not impossible. It is interesting to note, however, that Mark is believed to have written his Gospel under Peter's direction while he was in Rome, the same city that the Rufus whom Paul mentioned lived in. The second century AD Church Father Irenaeus writes, "Peter and Paul proclaimed the gospel in Rome and founded the community. After their departure [death], Mark, the disciple and interpreter of Peter, handed on his preaching to us in written form" (Iranaeus, *Adversus Haereses* 3.1). The Gospel of Mark was so closely associated with Peter that it was sometimes referred to as Peter's Gospel. Another second century AD Church Father Justin Martyr, who was active in Rome wrote, "It is said that he [Jesus] changed the name of one of the apostles to Peter; and it is written *in his memoirs* that he changed the names of others, two brothers, the sons of Zebedee, to Boanerges, which means 'sons of thunder'" (Justin, *Dial* 106.3 [italics mine]). The only Gospel that records John and James being called "Boanerges" is Mark (3:17).The Latin Father Tertullian agrees "that [gospel] which Mark published may be affirmed to be Peter's whose interpreter Mark was" (Tertullian, *Against Marcion* 4.5).

[15] Joachim Jeremias, *The Eucharistic Words of Jesus*, trans. Norman Perrin (Philadelphia: Fortress Press, 1981), 101; William F. Orr and James A. Walther, trans., *1 Corinthians: A New Translation* (Garden City: Doubleday, 1976), 320; Willi Marxsen, *The Resurrection of Jesus of Nazareth*, trans. Margaret Kohl (Philadelphia: Fortress Press, 1970), 80.

[16] There is debate among scholars as to which verses in 1 Corinthians 15:3ff constitute creedal material. Some have argued that the creed extends to 1 Corinthians 15:7, while most hold that it

THE EARLIEST CHRISTIAN CREED

Also, Paul's own testimony of the appearance of the risen Jesus in verse 8 is his own material and thus would not be part of the creed that he received and passed on.

Here we have the heart of what Paul meant by "the gospel" in 1 Corinthians 15:1: the death, burial, and resurrection of Jesus. Any self-proclaimed gospel which does not contain these cardinal points of the creed, is not the gospel of Christ. For this reason the gospel message is also called "the word of the cross" or "the message of the cross" (NIV) in 1 Corinthians 1:18. This is why Paul would not boast in anything but in the cross of the Lord Jesus Christ (Gal. 6:14).

What we can gather from this early creed in 1 Corinthians 15:3-4 is that from the earliest traceable times, Christians were already affirming and confessing not only that Jesus had died for sins in general, but that his was a vicarious death on behalf of his people. Note the importance placed on the Old Testament Scriptures in the creed; Christ died for our sins "in accordance with the Scriptures." The idea of Christ dying for our sins is also reflected in Romans 4:24-25,[17] which is taken by some scholars to also be pre-Pauline. Larry Hurtado comments, "I propose that the formulaic expressions in Paul about Christ/the Messiah's death 'for our sins/us' (eg. Rom. 4:24-25; 1 Cor. 15:3) are probably traditional 'pre-Pauline' expressions which originated in Judean Christian circles."[18] **Note again the source of these formulaic expressions; they are to be found within *Judean* Christian circles, i.e., among the original Jewish Christian disciples of Jesus.**

The vicarious death of Jesus was understood by most to have been prophesied about in various Old Testament Scriptures such as Isaiah 53.[19] We also see the burial of Jesus is referred to in this creed. Why? One of the reasons might be that it was part of the passion narrative tradition in the Gospels. It could also have been mentioned to reaffirm that Jesus had truly died (Mark

---

ends with 1 Corinthians 15:5. See William Lane Craig, *Assessing the New Testament Evidence for the Historicity of the Resurrection of Jesus* (Lewiston: Edwin Mellen, 1989), 6-7.

[17] "It will be counted to us who believe in him who raised from the dead Jesus our Lord, who was delivered up for our trespasses and raised for our justification."

[18] Larry W. Hurtado, *Lord Jesus Christ: Devotion to Jesus in Earliest Christianity* (Grand Rapids/Cambridge: Eerdmans, 2003), 187.

[19] The fourth century AD Church Father Athanasius, in speaking about the suffering and death of Jesus, cites passages from Isaiah 53 which he saw as a very clear prophecy, "Nor is even His death passed over in silence: on the contrary, it is referred to in the divine Scriptures, even *exceeding clearly*" (Athanasius, *De incarnatione* 34).

Early Christian Creeds and Hymns

15:44-45; John 19:33-35).[20] This was not a swoon event where Jesus somehow feigned his death; only dead people are buried.

Another reason for the mention of the burial may also point to the empty tomb. Paul generally does not mention the burial of Jesus in his letters other than when mentioning the believers' burial with Christ in the metaphorical language of baptism (Rom. 6:4; Col. 2:12). In fact many critics maintain that Paul knew nothing about the empty tomb for this very reason. So why does Paul mention it here? Remember, this is not Paul's material. This is a creed that Paul is passing on, which means the ones who passed it on to Paul were either eyewitnesses themselves or had contact with the eyewitnesses who discovered the empty tomb. The mention of the burial of Jesus in the creed implies that the tomb was occupied with the Lord's body and then was empty after he was raised on the third day. It is important to realize that Paul would have understood this as a clear reference point to the resurrection of the body. It is worth noting that Paul himself was a member of the Pharisees (Phil. 3:5; cf. Acts 23:6; 26:5), a Jewish group that believed in the resurrection of the body (Acts 23:8).

The next part of the creed states that Jesus was raised on the third day in accordance with the Scriptures. We should note that the phrase "in accordance with the Scriptures" in the creed is connected to the death of Jesus and his resurrection. It is for this reason that the death and resurrection of Jesus become the two main focal points in the preaching of the gospel, with the burial of Jesus being connected with his death and subsequent resurrection. Another strong indicator that this creed is not Paul's is the reference to Jesus rising "on the third day." Paul, in fact, never mentions the resurrection of Jesus as being "on the third day" in any of his letters. This is not typical Pauline language and reinforces the idea that Paul is passing on material that is not his own.[21] However, we find the third day reference found throughout the gospels, including on the lips of Jesus as he spoke of the day he would rise from the dead (Matt. 16:21; 17:23; 20:19; Mark 8:31; 9:31; 10:34; Luke 9:22; 18:33; John 2:19). This creedal reference to the resurrection of Jesus on the third day suggests that the creed originated with the earliest disciples of Jesus in Jerusalem, as it was the place where the church began (Acts 2), and where the events of

---

[20] For a fuller treatment on the burial of Jesus see Costa, "The Burial of Jesus and Its Relation and Importance to the Gospel Message," 95-122.

[21] Jeremias, *The Eucharistic Words of Jesus*, 101-102.

The Earliest Christian Creed

the crucifixion and resurrection also occurred. Now we are getter warmer in tracing the origin of this creed in 1 Corinthians 15:3-4.

There are some other creedal indicators if we look at the material regarding the witnesses in verses 5-8. In 1 Corinthians 15:5, Paul cites the appearance of the Lord to Cephas, and then the twelve. We also know from Luke 24:34 of the appearance of the risen Jesus to Simon Peter,[22] who was probably the first apostle to see the risen Jesus.[23] It is interesting that Paul knows Peter by his Aramaic name "Cephas" which also means "rock," just like its Greek equivalent "Peter." His Hebrew name was "Simon." When Jesus called Simon to follow him, he gave him the Aramaic name "Cephas" (John 1:42), and in so doing, acted in a divine fashion. Who changed the name of Abram to Abraham (Gen. 17:5)? Who changed the name of Jacob to Israel (Gen. 35:10; cf. 32:28)? It was God himself. Now Jesus changes Simon's name to Cephas, as he was to be one of the New Testament patriarchs, so to speak, alongside James and John. These were to be the "pillars" of the early church (Gal. 2:9).[24] So we see from Luke 24:34 that the appearance of the risen Jesus to Cephas came from an early tradition.

There is also reference to the fact that Jesus appeared to the "twelve;" an event which is corroborated in the Gospels (Matt. 28:16-17; Mark 16:7;[25] Luke 24:36-53; John 20:19-29; 21:1-25). It should be noted here that even

---

[22] It is worth noting that whenever Peter is called "Simon" in the gospels, he is in a backslidden state. He has not yet been restored by the Lord at this point (see Luke 22:31-32).

[23] Reymond, *Jesus*, 285-286.

[24] The word for "pillars" in Galatians 2:9 comes from the Greek word *stulos*, which, while sometimes referring to physical pillars, can also refer to "one who is a leader of a group, with the implication of strategic responsibility" (Louw and Nida, *Greek-English Lexicon*, 36.7). It is interesting that in the transfiguration narrative, Jesus refers to Peter, James, and John as "some standing here" who would see his glory and a foretaste of the kingdom of God when he was transfigured before them (Matthew 16:28; Mark 9:1; Luke 9:27). The idea of "standing" also conjures up the imagery of a pillar which is intended to hold up the roof of an edifice (cf. 1 Timothy 3:15 where it refers to the church). We sometimes refer to buildings or towers as "free standing" structures or, after an earthquake, refer to a building that is no longer "standing" due to its collapse. It is interesting that Jesus uses this language of Peter, James, and John, and that Paul refers to Cephas (Peter), James, and John as "pillars." It should also be noted that the "James" Paul refers to in Galatians 2:9 is not the first James who followed Jesus, as he was the brother of John, and son of Zebedee. He was executed by Herod Agrippa I (Acts 12:1-2). The James that Paul refers to is the Lord's brother (Galatians 1:19; cf. Matthew 13:55).

[25] I am of the conviction that Mark ended his gospel at 16:8 and do not take the "longer ending" usually found at Mark 16:9-20 to be part of the original Gospel. Rather, I am of the view that it was a later addition to the text, and thus not to be considered as inspired Scripture. It appears to be a patchwork of endings taken from Matthew, Luke, John, and Acts.

Paul's reference to the "twelve" in 1 Corinthians 15:5 is not a typical Pauline word, but only appears in this creedal portion. This is likely another case of *hapax legomenon*, just as we saw with the "third day" reference above. Usually when Paul refers to the early disciples of Jesus, he uses the term apostles. After citing the appearance to Cephas, he also cites the appearance to James and then to all of the apostles (1 Cor. 15:7). This is the only reference in the New Testament to an appearance of the risen Jesus to James, the brother of the Lord (Gal. 1:19; cf. Matt. 13:55). Though the gospels do not contain a reference to this appearance it is certainly part of the earliest source tradition of the early Christians.[26] According to John 7:5, the brothers of Jesus did not believe in him and even sought to frustrate his ministry. There would have been no reason for James to believe in Jesus as the Messiah until he had seen the risen

---

[26] In the apocryphal work, *The Gospel of the Hebrews*, which is no longer extant but has been preserved in a number of quotations from several church fathers, there is one quotation Jerome cites in *De Viris Illustribus* 2 which records an appearance of the risen Jesus to James: "Also the Gospel according to the Hebrews, lately translated by me into Greek and Latin speech, which Origen often uses, tells, after the resurrection of the Saviour: 'Now the Lord, when he had given the linen cloth unto the servant of the priest, went unto James and appeared to him (for James had sworn that he would not eat bread from that hour wherein he had drunk the Lord's cup until he should see him risen again from among them that sleep),' and again after a little, 'Bring ye, saith the Lord, a table and bread,' and immediately it is added, 'He took bread and blessed and brake and gave it unto James the Just and said unto him: My brother, eat thy bread, for the Son of Man is risen from among them that sleep.'" Source cited from http://www.earlychristianwritings.com/text/gospelhebrews-mrjames.html (accessed July 27, 2020).

This quotation is fraught with difficulties. Jesus gives the "linen cloth," presumably his burial shroud, to the servant of the high priest as if to testify to his resurrection. This presumes the Jews and probably the Romans were guarding the tomb of Jesus (much like as in the apocryphal *Gospel of Peter*). James is also referred to as one who had eaten the last supper with Jesus and swore to go on a "strike fast" until he saw Jesus risen from the dead. The glaring problem here is that James, the Lord's brother, was *not* at the Last Supper, and that he and his other brothers did *not* believe Jesus to be the Messiah before his resurrection (John 7:5). The James mentioned in this text is "James the Just," which was a title used of the Lord's brother. In this apocryphal text Jesus also refers to James as "My brother." The author of this apocryphal text seems to be confusing James the son of Zebedee with James the Lord's brother; the former was at the Last Supper, the latter was not. The reference to Jesus blessing and breaking bread in declaration of his resurrection seems to be a re-working of the canonical story of Jesus and the two disciples on the way to Emmaus where he blessed and broke the bread with them (Luke 24:30-31). This apocryphal story seems to be built around the historical appearance of Jesus to James (1 Corinthians 15:7) and presumes this event to be historical fact. Philipp Vielhauer and Georg Stecker rightly comment, "It is clear that the account of Easter given in the [*Gospel of the Hebrews*] departed considerably from those of the canonical Gospels ... as literature and in substance [it] differs considerably from the canonical Gospels ... Its stories and sayings scarcely permit of their being understood as developments of synoptic or Johannine texts" (Philipp Vielhauer and Georg Stecker, *The Gospel of the Hebrews*, rev. ed., vol.1, *Gospels and Related Writings*, quoted in *New Testament Apocrypha*, ed. Wilhelm Schneemelcher, trans. R. McL. Wilson, rev. ed. [Louisville: John Knox Press, 1990], 172).

Jesus. Even a liberal scholar like Hans Grass remarked that the appearance of the risen Jesus to James was "one of the surest proofs" of the resurrection of Jesus.[27] We do know from Acts 1:14 that all of Jesus' brothers eventually come to faith in him as they lingered in the upper room awaiting the coming of the Holy Spirit. We also know that another brother of Jesus, Judas, or Jude (Matt. 13:55), became a believer as he also composed one of the New Testament letters and even identifies himself as "the brother of James" (Jude 1). The fact that Jude did not have to explain who this "James" was to his readers implies that he was a well-known authority figure in the early Christian movement. The letter of James found in the New Testament was written by the Lord's brother, the first to see him after the resurrection. The prominence of James in the early Christian community is also seen in the fact that he was the leader the Council of Jerusalem in about AD 50 (Acts 12:17; 15:12-21; 21:18).

The mention of the specific names of those who saw Jesus in 1 Corinthians 15:5-8 is significant. Though Paul includes himself in 15:8, the two prominent names are Cephas (15:5) and James (15:7) — two pioneering leaders in the Jerusalem church as we can see from the book of Acts. We have already discussed the antiquity of the creed in 1 Corinthians 15:3-4, with Dunn suggesting its origin as possibly within months of the death and resurrection of Jesus. Since Paul claims to have received this creed and passed it on, the question naturally arises: when did Paul obtain this creed? And did he receive it directly from the Lord, as when he claims regarding the Lord's Supper that, "I received from the Lord what I also delivered to you, that the Lord Jesus on the night when he was betrayed took bread" (1 Cor. 11:23)?

Paul uses the exact same language of having "received" and "delivered" as he does in 1 Corinthians 15:3, except that in this instance he claims to have received it directly "from the Lord." This could mean either that the Lord directly revealed this source tradition to Paul, or that he received it via one or several of the apostles who were with Jesus at the last supper. Either view would seem acceptable. Do we have evidence of Paul meeting with the original disciples of Jesus to learn and obtain information about Jesus from them? We do. Galatians 1-2 provides a valuable source of biographical information as it is here that Paul mentions that after his calling by the risen Jesus, he withdrew into Arabia and then later returned to Damascus (Gal. 1:17). Paul's hiatus in

---

[27] Hans Grass, *Ostergeschehen und Osterberichte*, 4th ed. (Göttingen: Vandenhoeck & Ruprecht, 1970), 102.

Arabia was no doubt a time for him to absorb what had just happened to him, to be alone with the Lord, and to study. Paul then tells us that after three years he went to Jerusalem to meet with Cephas (Peter) and remained with him for fifteen days (Gal. 1:18). The word Paul uses in Galatians 1:18 to describe how he went to "visit Cephas" is interesting and its nuance is sometimes missed in English translations. The word for "visit" in Galatians 1:18 comes from the Greek root word ἱστορέω (*historeo*), which means "to visit with the purpose of obtaining information— 'to visit and get information.'"[28] This word is also where we get our English word "history" from. It only appears here in the New Testament and is therefore yet another instance of *hapax legomenon*. Paul, much like an investigative reporter, was on a research trip to Jerusalem in order to obtain information about Jesus.

While staying with Peter for two weeks, Paul did not see any of the other apostles, except James, the Lord's brother (Gal.1:19). Notice the two apostles with whom Paul first had contact with, Peter and James, were the same two apostles he mentions by name in 1 Corinthians 15:5,7. Again, Paul includes himself in 1 Corinthians 15:8, so that we have Cephas (Peter), James, and Paul—the three persons also mentioned in Galatians 1:18-19 (Paul is including himself). If Paul spent fifteen days with Peter, and met James as well, what were they discussing during this time? The New Testament scholar C.H. Dodd, in speaking about this fifteen day visit of Paul with Peter, famously quipped "We may presume they did not spend all the time talking about the weather."[29] It would likely have been during this visit that Paul received information about Jesus' ministry, miracles, death, burial, and resurrection. He would also likely have received the creed that was being confessed in the early Jerusalem church—that Jesus died for our sins, was buried, and raised the third day. In other words, it would most likely have been during this visit that Paul obtained the early creed found in 1 Corinthians 15:3-4 from Peter and James. How else could Paul have known this creed and heard of the appearance reports of the risen Jesus to Peter and James?

---

[28] Louw and Nida, *Greek-English Lexicon*, 34.52. Louw and Nida also note here, "In rendering 'to get information from him' it may be more satisfactory to say 'to learn something from him' or 'to have him tell me what I needed to know.'" Some translations try to capture this idea: "to get to know" (HCSB), "become acquainted with" (NASB; cf. NIV), "get information" (NET), "to enquire" (YLT).

[29] C.H. Dodd, *The Apostolic Preaching and its Developments* (New York: Harper and Brothers, 1960), 16.

This was not Paul's only visit to Jerusalem. He would make a second visit to Jerusalem fourteen years later, which he refers to in Galatians 2:1 while discussing his outreach mission to the Gentiles. In his second visit, Paul would not only meet again with Peter and James, but with John as well (Gal. 2:9). It is also instructive that in Galatians 2:9 he mentions the three apostolic pillars as "James and Cephas and John." The order is significant. Paul mentions James first in his list, presumably because James was the leader of the Jerusalem church. This would also explain why the creed in 1 Corinthians 15:3-4 is considered by scholars to be the earliest Christian creed; it traces right back to the early disciples of Jesus to Jerusalem itself, the starting place of Christianity, and where the events of the death, burial, and resurrection of Jesus took place. Jerusalem would therefore be the best candidate for the place where the creed originated.[30]

As this creed traces back to the early disciples of Jesus, it is sometimes referred to as a pre-Pauline text.[31] Another argument for this creed predating Paul is that its original language is believed to have been Semitic, most likely Aramaic, which was the language Jesus and his apostles would have spoken. I. Howard Marshall has argued that "the Semitic background of the tradition [1 Cor.15:1-7] is beyond doubt."[32] In other words, this creed reflects the core beliefs of the earliest Christians in Jerusalem. The reference to the "third day" and to Peter as "Cephas" (his Aramaic name), also seems to point to an Aramaic source. Joachim Jeremias argues that this creed "comes from the Aramaic-speaking earliest community."[33] Paul, of course, had written the creed in Greek to the Corinthians. On a side note, it is interesting that the Corinthians also seemed to have been exposed to at least some Aramaic, as indicated by the Aramaic phrase, "Maranatha," in a prayer at the end of the letter in 1 Corinthians 16:22.

---

[30] A.M. Hunter, *Jesus Lord and Savior* (London: SCM Press, 1976), 99-100.

[31] For a list of pre-Pauline texts in the Pauline letters see Costa, *Worship and the Risen Jesus*, 284 n.40.

[32] I. Howard Marshall, *The Origins of New Testament Christology* (Downers Grove: Inter Varsity Press, 1976), 93.

[33] Jeremias, *The Eucharistic Words of Jesus*, 103. The arguments for a Greek original to the creed and a rebuttal to Jeremias' position on a Semitic original can be found in Joseph Kloppenborg, "An Analysis of the Pre-Pauline Formula 1 Cor. 15:3b-5 in Light of Some Recent Literature," *CBQ* 40, no. 3 (July 1978): 351-367. Even if the creed was originally written in Greek, this still would not preclude it coming from Jerusalem, as Greek was also spoken there. Kloppenborg in this work admits that the earliest form of the creed came "from the Palestinian church" (p. 357).

EARLY CHRISTIAN CREEDS AND HYMNS

There is one final point I would like to address before closing this chapter. Some critics have tried to find a contradiction between Paul's delivery of the creed in 1 Corinthians 15:3-4 and his words in Galatians 1:11-12, 15-17:

> For I would have you know, brothers, that the gospel that was preached by me is not man's gospel. For I did not receive it from any man, nor was I taught it, but I received it through a revelation of Jesus Christ ... But when he who had set me apart before I was born, and who called me by his grace, was pleased to reveal his Son to me, in order that I might preach him among the Gentiles, I did not immediately consult with anyone; nor did I go up to Jerusalem to those who were apostles before me, but I went away into Arabia, and returned again to Damascus.

Here Paul points out that the gospel he preached is not man's gospel. It did not come from a human source. Rather, he states to have received it by, or through, a revelation of Jesus Christ and that it was God who set Paul apart before he was born (cf. Jer. 1:5) and revealed his Son to him. Paul here also claims that he did not consult anyone, nor did he go to the apostles, but went into seclusion in Arabia. Critics allege that Paul's words here contradict his words in 1 Corinthians 15:3-4, where he says that he had received and delivered the creed. So did he receive the gospel from men, such as the apostles in Jerusalem? Or did he receive it directly from Christ? The answer here is that there is no real contradiction at all. Paul does not deny that he *later* consulted with the apostles in Jerusalem, in fact he explicitly mentions that he met with Peter and James in Galatians 1:18-19 and visited them again after fourteen years (Gal. 2:1). The point that needs to be distinguished here is that in Galatians 1:11-12, Paul is speaking about the *content* of the gospel, which is God's saving work by grace through his Son. In 1 Corinthians 15:3-4, however, Paul is citing the *formal creed* of the gospel, which does not contradict but rather confirms what he had already received. This is why Paul points out that the gospel he preached was the very same gospel the Jerusalem apostles preached (1 Cor. 15:11). Paul even goes so far as to lay out the gospel he was preaching to the Jerusalem apostles to ensure that he had not been "running" in vain (Gal. 2:2). In other words, Paul wanted to know if he was on the "same page" as the Jerusalem apostles, who in response gave him "the right hand of fellowship" and their blessing. The gospel they preached to the Jews was the same gospel Paul was preaching to the Gentiles (Gal. 2:7-9).

In this chapter we have seen that the earliest creed in the New Testament is found in 1 Corinthians 15:3-4. It is a creed that likely dates to within months of the death and resurrection of Jesus, or at least within the proceeding three years. The language that is used in this creed also hints at an early dating. We also saw that the earliest Christians confessed that Jesus died for their sins as a vicarious atonement, was buried, and was raised again the third day. The death and resurrection of Jesus were the focal points of the gospel; without the resurrection, there can be no Christianity (1 Cor. 15:14). Any gospel message that does not have the death, burial, and resurrection of Jesus is no gospel at all but is rather "another gospel" which comes under the anathema of God (Gal. 1:6-9). A title of Jesus which is closely associated with his resurrection, and which quickly became a creed in the early Christian movement, is that of "Lord" to which we now turn our attention.

5
The Shortest Creed: "Jesus is Lord"

We often hear the phrase "Jesus is Lord" in many evangelical circles. Where did it come from? What does it even mean? Does it convey what the English mean when they speak about the "House of Lords" in the Parliament of the United Kingdom, or something else? More importantly, what did it mean to the earliest Christians? And why were they imprisoned or executed for simply making such a statement during the early years of Christianity?

We need to begin by defining what the term "Lord" even means in this context. The word comes from the Greek word κύριος (*kyrios*) and has a wide semantic range. For example, the master of a household could be addressed by such a title, as could emperors and kings, including the Roman emperor Caesar himself. It was also used to communicate the equivalent meaning of our English word "sir," and was seen as a respectful way of addressing someone in authority.[1] It can also refer to transcendent beings, including pagan deities (1 Cor. 8:5), and occasionally as a substitute term for the name "Yahweh" in the Hebrew text of the Bible.[2] There are also places in the New Testament where the name Yahweh is quoted as it appears in the Old Testament, but since it quotes mostly from the LXX, wherever the Divine Name appears, "Lord" is used in its place.[3] What makes this subject even more interesting is that it seems the New Testament writers understood the Old Testament references to Yahweh as equally referring to Jesus.[4] Since the word has such a wide

---

[1] Henn, *One Faith*, 47.

[2] See *BDAG*, 576–579; Louw and Nida, *Greek-English Lexicon*, 12.9; 57.12; 37.51; 87.53.

[3] There are a few exceptions to this rule. In some early manuscript fragments of the LXX, especially those of the second century AD in Hellenistic Jewish writers like Aquila, Symmachus and Theodotion, we find the Divine Name written into the text using paleo-Hebrew letters, an old form of Hebrew writing. Among the collection of the Dead Sea Scrolls found in Qumran Cave 4, we find a fragment from the book of Leviticus, which also contains the Divine Name written with Greek letters IAO—an attempt at a transliteration of the name Yahweh.

[4] For a full treatment on this subject see David B. Capes, *Old Testament Yahweh Texts in Paul's Christology* (Waco, TX: Baylor University Press, 2017).

Early Christian Creeds and Hymns

semantic range, however, the only way we can conclusively determine what it means is by paying close attention to the surrounding context.

The application of the title "Lord" to Jesus is perhaps one of the oldest Christian creeds and was commonly confessed among the earliest Christians. The confession "Jesus is Lord" is made up of two words in Greek—κύριος Ἰησοῦς (*kyrios Iesous*)—and we find it used in passages such as Romans 10:9, 1 Corinthians 12:3 (cf. 2 Cor. 4:5), and Philippians 2:11. As can be seen, this phrase appears in what is believed to be one of the earliest texts of the New Testament: the letters of Paul. This short creed, however, just like the earliest creed we saw in 1 Corinthians 15:3-4, may find its origins not in Paul, but in the early Aramaic Christian community.[5] I mentioned earlier that 1 Corinthians was written between approximately between AD 50 and AD 55—a mere twenty years after the death and resurrection of Jesus. This is quite early and means that the eyewitnesses to Jesus were likely still alive, as Paul himself implies in 1 Corinthians 15:6.

When early Christians made the confession "Jesus is Lord," this entailed a number of assumptions. First, it carried an obvious, anti-imperialist sentiment.[6] In the Roman empire, the only confession a citizen could make was Καῖσαρ κύριος (*Kaisar kyrios*/"Caesar is Lord"). But because Jesus is the Lord of lords, including "lord" Caesar (Rev. 17:14; 19:16), Christians refused to make this confession and instead confessed that "Jesus is Lord." This was, according to *Lex Majestatis* ("the law of treason"), an act of high treason against the emperor.[7] One can now see why Christians came under such severe persecution. The earliest Christians, unlike many modern-day professing Christians, would not compromise their allegiances.

This anti-imperialist theme is seen throughout the New Testament. When Jesus was born, the angels told the shepherds that they came with the good news that in the city of David, a Savior was born, who was Christ the Lord (Luke 2:10-11). Each of these descriptions are chock-full of imperialist overtones. Though "good news" was usually reserved for imperial announcements by Caesar or the birth of a successor, it is here being used of the birth of a new king and emperor who would be an occasion of great joy for all people.

---

[5] Costa, *Worship and the Risen Jesus*, 158-159.

[6] On anti-imperialism in the NT see Richard A. Horsley, *Jesus and Empire: The Kingdom of God and the New World Disorder* (Philadelphia, PA: Fortress Press, 2003).

[7] John Dominic Crossan, *God and Empire* (San Francisco, CA: Harper San Francisco, 2007), 28.

The Shortest Creed: "Jesus is Lord"

The angelic announcement of peace on earth (Luke 2:14) was a rival statement against the *pax romana* ("peace of Rome"), which Rome imposed by force and subjugation. This newborn king, on the other hand, would bring peace through his gospel. Titles such as "Savior," "Christ," "King," and "Lord" (*kyrios*), were all titles that were reserved for the Roman emperor, who in this case was Augustus Caesar (27 BC–AD 14).[8] John Dart notes that,

> To many in the empire, Roman civilization brought stability and wealth. And the people were urged to have "faith" in their "Lord," the emperor, who would preserve peace and increase wealth. "In the Roman imperial world, the 'gospel' was the good news of Caesar's having established peace and security for the world," wrote Richard A. Horsley in *Jesus and Empire*. Christians gave secular words associated with the empire a new meaning.[9]

In other words, Luke 2:11 is stating that the child who would be born would be the true Savior, King, and Lord (*kyrios*). Titles like these and others were employed by the Roman emperor to appropriate divine status to himself.[10]

The following passages show us the uses of this early, one-clause creed, which are in bold for clarity:

---

[8] According to Crossan, other titles that the Roman emperor took to himself included, "'Divine,' 'Son of God,' 'God,' and 'God from God,' ... 'Redeemer,' [and] 'Liberator.'" Crossan, *God and Empire*, 28. The title "God from God" is an interesting one as the Nicene Creed also says of the Son that he is "God of God."

[9] John Dart, reply to "Up Against Caesar," SBL Forum, April 2005, http://sbl-site.org/Article.aspx?ArticleID=388.

[10] The Roman emperor didn't just stop at appropriating to himself divine titles like "Lord." Some emperors, like Domitian (AD 51–AD 96), went even further and demanded to be addressed by the title "dominus et deus noster", i.e., "our lord and god." See Barrett, *New Testament Background*, 19-20; Suetonius, *Domitian* 13. On the use of divine titles and emperor cult see S.R.F. Price, "Gods and Emperors: The Greek Language of the Roman Imperial Cult," *Journal of Hellenic Studies* 104 (November 1984): 79-95.

If we take the view that the Gospel of John was written towards the end of the first century AD then this would place it near the time in which Domitian died in AD 96. It is interesting that in John 20:28, as Jesus appears to the disciples and invites Thomas to touch his wounds, that Thomas says to Jesus, "My Lord and my God!" The Latin Vulgate reads, "Dominus meus et Deus meus," using the same titles Domitian used of himself: "dominus" and "deus." In this case, John 20:28 can also be seen as an anti-imperialist confession in the same vein as Luke 2:10-11. Jesus Christ is Lord and God, not Caesar (Domitian). The titles "Lord" and "God" are also applied to Yahweh in Psalm 35:23, "Awake and rouse yourself for my vindication, for my cause, my God and my Lord!" The language of Psalm 35:23, especially in the LXX, is strikingly parallel with John 20:28, the only difference being that the titles are used in reverse.

If you confess with your mouth that **Jesus is Lord** and believe in your heart that God raised him from the dead, you will be saved" (Romans 10:9).

Therefore I want you to understand that no one speaking in the Spirit of God ever says "Jesus is accursed!" and no one can say "**Jesus is Lord**" except in the Holy Spirit (1 Corinthians 12:3).

And every tongue confess that **Jesus Christ is Lord**, to the glory of God the Father (Philippians 2:11).

We will now examine each of these passages in turn.

Romans 10:9

The passage in Romans 10:9 seeks to answer the question: what must one do to be saved? We are familiar with this question, as it is the same one which the jailer asked of Paul and Silas in Acts 16:30. The response given to him was, "Believe in the Lord Jesus, and you will be saved, you and your household" (Acts 16:31). What does this process look like? Romans 10:9 shows us. We know that the phrase "Jesus is Lord" is a creed because the language in Romans 10:9 demonstrates this.

The first step is verbal confession, "If you *confess* with *your mouth* that Jesus is Lord, you will be saved" (italics mine). The word "confess" here is ὁμολογέω (*homologeo*) which, as we saw in the first chapter, literally means "to say the same words." To confess is to declare what one believes. In Romans 10:9, a true believer is one who makes the confession, "Jesus is Lord." Notice this is something that must be confessed to with the "mouth." In Romans 10:10 Paul goes on to stress the confessional nature of this creed by stating, "With the mouth one confesses [*homologeo*] and is saved." Paul also uses the conjunction ὅτι (*hoti*), or "that," in Romans 10:9, which, as already noted above, functions as a quotation marker. The lordship of Christ is paramount here. After the confession that Jesus is Lord, one must also believe that God raised him from the dead. The confession of the lordship of Jesus is connected to a belief in his resurrection and, as such, serves as a verbal manifestation of what is believed already in the heart. Earlier in Romans 1:3-4, Paul pointed out that Jesus was declared to be the Son of God with power by the resurrection from the dead. This early confession "Jesus is Lord" revolves around the person of Jesus Christ; his resurrection is the confirmatory event that he is

The Shortest Creed: "Jesus is Lord"

both Lord and Redeemer of his people (Acts 2:36). In Chapter 2 I noted that there is a noticeable shift in the New Testament from a theocentric view to a Christocentric view. This particular creed is evidence of this shift and demonstrates once again that the earliest creeds are centred on Jesus.

Paul also connects the confession of Jesus as Lord with one's salvation. While it isn't wrong to see the term "Lord" in Romans 10:9 as referring to Jesus as Master and Ruler over all, to view this as the only definition would be unfair reductionism. Paul, in fact, defines what he means by Jesus being "Lord," and does so by quoting from Joel 2:32. In the Hebrew Bible this verse states, "And it shall come to pass that everyone who calls on the name of the LORD shall be saved."[11] Whenever we see the word "Lord" in capitals in the Old Testament, it is an indicator that the Hebrew text contains the Divine Name of God: Yahweh. This way, it can be properly translated, "Then everyone who calls on the name of Yahweh will be saved" (HCSB). However, Paul is not citing the Hebrew text of Joel 2:32, but the LXX, where it says, "And it shall come to pass *that* whosoever shall call on the name of the Lord [κύριος/*kyrios*] shall be saved." The LXX uses the word "Lord" for Yahweh, the same word Paul applies to Jesus in Romans 10:9. Whose name then, the believer is to call upon as Lord in order to be saved, according to Romans 10:9, 13? Jesus himself!

Here we have an extraordinarily strong testimony to the deity of Christ. Hopefully we can see that the term "Lord," when applied to Jesus, means much more than simply saying that he is Ruler or Master; it is saying that he is Yahweh himself.

In Romans 10:12, Paul also refer to Jesus as "Lord of all." This title was used by Greek poets such as Pindar (d. 438 BC), who said of Zeus that he is, "Zeus the lord of all."[12] The Israelites made the same confession of Yahweh as Lord (Psalm 8:1; 30:8; 35:23), and in Second Temple Jewish literature, God was also called, "Lord of all" (2 Macc. 14:35).[13] The very language of "calling upon the name of the Lord" is an idiomatic expression for invoking a deity in

---

[11] In the Masoretic Text of the Hebrew Bible, the text of Joel 2:32 appears in Joel 3:5. The difference is due to a different structuring of the verses in the Masoretic Text.

[12] Pindar, *Isthm* 5.53.

[13] Also see Acts 10:36 where Jesus is also called "Lord of all." For similar language used of God in the Dead Sea Scrolls and Josephus, see Costa, *Worship and the Risen Jesus*, 382 n.172.

worship.¹⁴ That this invocatory language is used of Jesus is clearly seen in 1 Corinthians 1:2, where Christian believers are identified as those "who in every place *call upon the name* of our Lord Jesus Christ, both their Lord and ours" (italics mine). The confession "Jesus is Lord" would also no doubt have been part of the baptismal services of the early church in which the new believer would make an allegiance to Jesus as Lord and be identified with him in his death and resurrection (Rom. 6:4).¹⁵ The act of swearing allegiance to the gods by invoking their names was not foreign to Greco-Roman society but, "appears similar to the Roman military practice of making a *sacramentum*, which was an oath that soldiers made by invoking the gods, and thereby binding themselves to loyalty and obedience."¹⁶ In confessing "Jesus is Lord," early Christian believers were essentially binding themselves to their Lord with promises of loyalty and obedience. If Jesus is Lord, there can be no rivals. Even if there are some who call themselves "lords," Jesus is still "King of kings and Lord of lords." So we see in Romans 10:9 that salvation is dependent on the confession that "Jesus is Lord" and the belief that God raised him from the dead. This is Lordship salvation at its finest.

1 Corinthians 12:3

In 1 Corinthians 12:3, Paul states that the one who confesses "Jesus is Lord" can only do so under the influence of the Holy Spirit. Here we see Jesus' promise to send a Comforter, who would testify about and glorify him (John 15:26; 16:14), fulfilled. The lordship of Jesus was understood and affirmed spiritually by the agency of the Holy Spirit. It is the ministry and work of the Holy Spirit to reveal Christ as the divine Lord who is supreme over all (cf. Rom. 1:3-4; 1 Cor. 1:2). The role of the Holy Spirit is always to point to Christ, and to teach and guide Christian believers and bring to their remembrance what Jesus

---

[14] I would direct the reader to my treatment of this idiomatic expression of worship in Costa, *Worship and the Risen Jesus*, 147-169.

[15] On baptism and its association with early Christian worship and confessions see Costa, *Worship and the Risen Jesus*, 219-224. Philip Schaff also notes, "[S]o the confession of faith, or the creed, was *orally* taught and transmitted to the catechumens, and professed by them at baptism, *long before* it was committed to *writing*." Schaff, *The Creeds of Christendom*, 1:5 (italics mine). Schaff's observation is important. The creed or confession of faith, much like the one in 1 Corinthians 15:3-4, would likely have been orally taught to early Christians preparing for baptism, and would then have been professed by them at the actual event. This reinforces my argument that creeds arose in an oral context before being written down and appears to be consistent with what we see in the New Testament.

[16] Costa, *Worship and the Risen Jesus*, 159. The Latin word *sacramentum* is where we get our English word "sacrament" from and carries notions of allegiance and binding loyalty.

The Shortest Creed: "Jesus is Lord"

himself taught (John 14:26). The early Christian community believed themselves to be in fellowship with the Holy Spirit (2 Cor. 13:14), and thus were recipients of the revelation God had delivered to them by the apostles.

How we define "Lord" is very important because many heretics of the past, such as Arius of Alexandria in the 4th century, could deny the deity of Christ and still happily confess that "Jesus is Lord." Modern cults like the Jehovah's Witnesses and Mormons would also affirm that "Jesus is Lord" while at the same time rejecting his deity. Are heretics and cultists speaking by the Holy Spirit when they say such? Absolutely not. In his second letter, Paul warns the Corinthians about those who preach "another Jesus" when in fact they are no more than false apostles and deceitful workers (2 Cor. 11:3-4,13-15). We need to recall, as we did in our treatment of Romans 10:9, that when Jesus is called "Lord," it does not only convey that he is Ruler and Master, but also that he is Yahweh.[17] The term "Lord," as we have seen, is used as a substitute for Yahweh (Rom 10:13). Thus, properly understood, the confession of Jesus as "Lord" also carries with it a confession of his deity. Conversely, one cannot be inspired by the same Spirit to curse Jesus.

Who would say that Jesus is accursed? There are a few possible answers. This might be referring to the unbelieving Jews or Gentiles who viewed Jesus as a Messianic pretender, or as a new god who would demand sole obedience and the renunciation of their other gods. It may also be that such anathemas were demanded of Christians who refused to claim Caesar as Lord. Paul himself, at the end of his first letter to the Corinthians, brings down such a curse on anyone who does not love the Lord Jesus, "If anyone has no love for the Lord, let him be accursed [*anathema*]" (1 Cor. 16:22). Paul uses this same word in 1 Corinthians 12:3 and Galatians 1:6-9 during his denunciations of those who preach "another gospel."

It is possible that some professing Christians may have called Jesus accursed under threat of persecution. We also know from passages like Matthew 10:17-20 that Jesus himself had already promised the inspiration of the Holy Spirit to the disciples during such times. Roman sources indicate that Christians were often forced to curse Jesus in the process of being forced to renounce their faith. In a letter from the Roman governor Pliny the Younger to

---

[17] The rabbinic literature even admits that the Messiah bears God's name, "What is the name of the Messiah King?" Rabbi Abba Bar-Kahana said: 'The Lord' is his name, and that is the name by which He will be called, The LORD, Our Righteousness (Jeremiah 23:6)." *Midrash Eichah Rabbah* 1.

EARLY CHRISTIAN CREEDS AND HYMNS

the Emperor Trajan around AD 111–AD 113, he recounts a trial of Christians which he oversaw, and he reports that,

> After they had worshipped thy image [Caesar's] with incense and wine, and besides *cursed Christ (maledicerent Christo) ... none of which those who are really Christians can, it is said, be forced to do* ... All worshipped thy image and the images of the gods, and *cursed Christ (Christo maledixerunt)*.

We see a similar account in the martyrdom of Polycarp (AD 69–AD 155), who was a church father in the early second century and also known to be a personal disciple of the apostle John.[18] When asked to curse Christ at his trial, Polycarp responded, "How could I *curse* my King, who has saved me?"[19] What is instructive in the letter of Pliny is that the litmus test for weeding out Christians under suspicion is to have them curse Christ, "none of which those who are really Christians can, it is said, be forced to do." Pliny, however, does go on to mention a number of Christians who, when pressed, admitted that they had recanted their Christians faith:

> Others, whose names were given me by an informer, first said that they were Christians and afterwards denied it, declaring that they had been but were so no longer, some of them having recanted many years before, and more than one so long as twenty years back. They all worshipped your image and the statues of the deities, and cursed the name of Christ.[20]

Cursing the name of Christ would be the exact opposite of declaring, with the creed, that "Jesus is Lord." It is also interesting to note that Pliny provides what is perhaps the earliest extra-biblical description of a Christian gathering in the early second century AD:

> On a stated day they had been accustomed to meet before daybreak and to *recite a hymn among themselves to Christ, as though he were a god*, and that so far from binding themselves by oath to commit any crime, their

---

[18] D.F. Wright, "Polycarp," in *New International Dictionary*, 791.

[19] *Martyrdom of Polycarp* 9:3 quoted in Oscar Cullmann, *The Earliest Christian Confessions* (London: Lutterworth Press, 1949), 29 n.3 (italics mine).

[20] Pliny the Younger, *Letters* 10:96.

The Shortest Creed: "Jesus is Lord"

oath was to abstain from theft, robbery, adultery, and from breach of faith, and not to deny trust money placed in their keeping when called upon to deliver it.[21]

While I will return to this passage when we deal with early hymns in the Christian movement, it is worth noting here that according to Pliny's report, early Christians came together on a "stated day." We are not sure whether that was a Sunday or not, but we know that on this day they would recite a hymn "to Christ, as though he were a god." In the Roman empire it was permissible to worship other, even non-Roman, gods; the problem with early Christians is that they refused to acknowledge any other god or lord, including Caesar himself. Even the imperial official who ordered Polycarp's martyrdom asked him, "What then is so terrible in saying Καῖσαρ κύριος (Caesar is Lord) and in sacrificing?"[22] But it was precisely the Christians' refusal to acknowledge any other "Lord" but Jesus that doomed them to death.[23] We also see from this report that Jesus was *already* worshipped by early Christians since they sang to him "as to a god."[24] Jesus was viewed by early Christians as an object of worship, a detail which is also confirmed by the New Testament. As Christianity was relatively new to the Roman Empire, it was under suspicion by the Roman authorities of being a *religio illicita* (illicit religion), and such anti-imperial practices were punishable by the state.[25]

There are instances of Christians throughout history who, under pressure, did deny Christ and then later returned to the church. We know that Peter

---

[21] Pliny the Younger, *Letters* 10:96 (italics mine).

[22] *Martyrdom of Polycarp* 8:2.

[23] The Latin Church Father Tertullian also states, "Do you believe that it is permitted to a Christian to add an oath made before a man to an oath made before God, and to engage himself to yet another lord after he has once engaged himself to Christ?" Tertullian, *De Corona Militis* II.

[24] Another extra-biblical source which confirms that Jesus was worshipped by the earliest Christians is seen in the attacks by the second century Platonic philosopher, Celsus (AD 177–AD 188). His writings, known as "The True Doctrine," are no longer extant but have been preserved in Origen's work, *Contra Celsum*. Celsus argues, "It is easy to convict them [Christians] of worshipping not a god, not even demons, but a dead person" (Origen, *Contra Celsum* 7.68). As can be seen here, Celsus also mocks the resurrection of Jesus. Celsus goes on to further denounce Christians, "While you pronounce imprecations upon those others that are recognised as gods, treating them as idols, you yet do homage to a more wretched idol than any of these, which indeed is not even an idol or a phantom, but a dead man" (Origen, *Contra Celsum* 7.36).

[25] Jews also refused to pay homage to Caesar as a god and would not worship his image. Rome had given Judaism an exemption as a *religio licita* (a legal religion) because of its antiquity, for which the Romans had a deep respect. See Bruce W. Winter, *Seek the Welfare of the City: Christians as Benefactors and Citizens* (Grand Rapids: Eerdmans, 1994), 133–135.

himself denied Jesus three times and wept bitterly afterwards for what he did (Luke 22:62), and how he was also later reinstated by the Lord Jesus (John 21:15-19). During the fourth to sixth century AD, a significant controversy arose in regards to barring those who had denied Christ and were therefore viewed as traitors to the faith. Those who barred the admission of these "traitors" back into the church were known as the Donatists, and were later vociferously opposed by Augustine, the bishop of Hippo. That subject, however, is outside the scope of this book.[26]

The idea of saying Jesus was accursed could also have come from within Jewish circles. Earlier in his letter, Paul pointed out that the preaching of the cross was a stumbling block to the Jews (1 Cor. 1:23). Why would the preaching of the cross be a stumbling block? The reason was that the Jews saw crucifixion, or the act of being hung on a tree,[27] as a sign of God's curse on a criminal, based on Deuteronomy 21:22-23 (italics mine):

> And if a man has committed a crime punishable by death and he is put to death, and *you hang him on a tree*, his body shall not remain all night on the tree, but you shall bury him the same day, for *a hanged man is cursed by God*. You shall not defile your land that the LORD your God is giving you for an inheritance.

Paul knew about this passage, and no doubt the Christian veneration of a Messiah who died the death of a cursed criminal may have led to his persecution of Christians. Paul himself alludes to this passage in Galatians 3:13, "Christ redeemed us from the curse of the law by becoming a curse for us—for it is written, 'Cursed is everyone who is hanged on a tree.'" The key point in this passage is that Christ redeemed us from the curse of the law by becoming a curse *for us*. Christ himself was not cursed, but *became a curse* on behalf of his people so that he takes their place and imputes his righteousness to them. This is the great exchange. He bore our transgression, took the curse of sin upon himself, and endured God's wrath. Centuries before Jesus, Isaiah had prophesied about the rejection of the Messiah by his people and their mistaken

---

[26] Quote from *Martyrdom of Polycarp* 9:3 in Cullmann, *The Earliest Christian Confessions*, 29 n.3 (italics mine). On the Donatist Controversy see Richard Miles, ed., *The Donatist Schism: Controversy and Contexts* (Liverpool: Liverpool University Press, 2018).

[27] Deuteronomy 21:22-23 was applied by Jews to crucifixion, at least by the Qumran community. See J.A. Fitzmyer, "Crucifixion in Ancient Palestine, Qumran Literature, and the New Testament," *CBQ* 40, no. 4 (October 1978): 493-513.

perception that he was smitten and cursed by God, "Surely he has borne our griefs and carried our sorrows; *yet we esteemed him stricken, smitten by God*, and afflicted" (Isa. 53:4; italics mine). The idea of a crucified Messiah was an oxymoron to Jewish ears. What made it even more scandalous was the Christian idea that God, in the person of Jesus, hung on a cross. Martin Hengel captures this shocking image when he states, "A crucified Jewish martyr, a martyred innocent, a second Socrates could have appealed to Jews and Greeks as an edifying example; a crucified God was for every educated person in antiquity a shameless impertinence, indeed an absurdity."[28]

Justin Martyr's *Dialogue with Trypho the Jew* (written AD 150–AD 160) also bears witness to such doubts among the Jews regarding the idea of the Messiah's suffering. The Jewish aversion to Jesus is also seen in the way the rabbinic writings and a medieval anti-Christian Jewish parody called the *Toledot Yeshu* ("Life of Jesus") refers to him not by his Aramaic name *Yeshua*, but by the name *Yeshu*, which stands for "may his name and memory be blotted out."[29] When this prevailing mentality is taken into consideration, we can see how an unbelieving Jew would consider Jesus to be cursed. Already in the New Testament gospels we see hints of this opposition when the Jews denounce him as being a Samaritan and having a demon (John 8:48), and calling into question his parental legitimacy (John 8:41), a point the Babylonian Talmud also raises.[30]

The Gospel of John's third person reference to the "the Jews" is taken by some critics as an example of antisemitism in the New Testament, but this is an overstretch and completely false. The Gospel of John bears witness that Jesus was himself a Jew (John 4:9), and that he claimed that "salvation is from the Jews" (John 4:22)—hardly a statement from an antisemitic document. Surprisingly, the Gospel of John may be the most Jewish of all the gospels.[31]

---

[28] Martin Hengel, *Studies in Early Christology* (London/New York: T&T Clark, 1995), 383.

[29] Joseph Klausner, *Jesus of Nazareth*, trans. Herbert Danby (New York, NY: Macmillan, 1946), 53. See also George Howard, *Hebrew Gospel of Matthew* (Marcon, GA: Mercer University Press, 1995), 207. The Babylonian Talmud also refers to Jesus as *Yeshu* in *b. Sanh.* 43a.

[30] *b. Sabb.* 104b; *b. Sanh.* 67a. Origen also records Celsus, a third century AD critic of Christianity as agreeing with the claims recorded in the Babylonian Talmud of Jesus being illegitimate. Origen, *Contra Celsum* 1.28. Celsus claims that Jesus himself made up the virgin birth story.

[31] Dr. Israel Abrahams, a reader in Rabbinics at the University of Cambridge and an orthodox Jew, startled the learned world by remarking in a paper read to the Theological Society that, "to us Jews the Fourth Gospel [John] is the most Jewish of the four." Quoted in Stephen Neill, *The Interpretation of the New Testament* (London: Oxford University Press, 1966), 315.

The term "the Jews" from Ἰουδαῖοι (*Ioudaioi*), "may refer to the entire Jewish people, the residents of Jerusalem and surrounding territory, the authorities in Jerusalem, or merely those who were hostile to Jesus."[32] Context is key here, and a number of commentators take this reference to the "Jews" in John to refer to Jewish leaders or authorities who were "hostile to Jesus."[33] The creed "Jesus is Lord" would also be perceived as blasphemous to an unbelieving Jew because of the association of "Lord" with the Divine Name Yahweh. We know that the deity of Jesus was a source of tension between early Christians and Jews. A third century AD Jewish teacher, Rabbi Abbahu from Caesarea in northern Israel, said, "If a man says to you 'I am God,' he lies. 'I am the Son of man' [a human being], he will be sorry at the end [he will die]. 'I will go up to heaven' he says so, but will not fulfill it."[34] Scholars are persuaded that these words are directed at Christian beliefs and show just how early a belief in the deity of Christ was.[35] The claims to being God (John 8:58-59; 10:30-33), being the son of man (Mark 14:61-64),[36] and that he would return to heaven (John 20:17; cf. Acts 1:9-11) were also all made by Jesus. Another famous Rabbi, Akiba, said of those Jews who "read the heretical books" that they did not have a "share in the world to come."[37] What were these so-called heretical books? Could they have been the Gospels, or other texts from the New Testament? This seems to be the case according to the Jewish rabbinic text *Tosefta*, which states about the heretics (the "*min*" in Hebrew), "Their books are the books of diviners."[38] This would have been another driving wedge between those Jews who believed in Jesus and those who did not.

It is also possible that Jewish believers would be faced with persecution and that some would even have been forced to curse Jesus or be put to death. Jesus even predicted that those who would kill his followers would think that they were offering service to God, "They will put you out of the synagogues.

---

[32] John 20:19, NET n.34. The NET translates the word Ἰουδαῖοι (*Ioudaioi*), or "Jews," in the Gospel of John as "the Jewish leaders" when the authorities are in view.

[33] See R.G. Bratcher, "'The Jews' in the Gospel of John," *BT* 26, no. 4 (October 1975): 401-409.

[34] Jerusalem Talmud, *Taanit* 65b.

[35] For an academic treatment of the deity of Christ see Murray J. Harris, *Jesus as God: The New Testament Use of Theos in Reference to Jesus* (Grand Rapids, MI: Baker, 1992); Robert M. Bowman, Jr. and J. Ed Komoszewski, *Putting Jesus in His Place: A Case for the Deity of Christ* (Grand Rapids, MI: Kregel Publications, 2007).

[36] On the title Son of Man, its origins, and how it was applied to Jesus, see Appendix 2.

[37] Mishnah, *Sanhedrin* 10.1.

[38] *t. Hul.* 2:20-21.

The shortest creed: "Jesus is Lord"

Indeed, the hour is coming when whoever kills you will think he is offering service to God" (John 16:2).[39] The putting out of the synagogues seems to suggest that Jewish believers are clearly in view here. The word for "service to God" is also one that carries connotations of worship. In other words, the killing of Jewish followers of Jesus would have been seen as an act of worship to God.

We also get a sense of Jewish opposition against Jewish believers in the letter to the Hebrews. The audience is undoubtedly a Jewish audience who are facing pressure to go back to Judaism and its religious systems. As we have seen above, it is clear from the Gospels that Jesus was opposed by most of the Jewish authorities. Throughout the book of Acts, almost immediately after the church begins, the main antagonists to the gospel are the Jewish religious authorities; their influence extends even beyond the land of Israel as we see in their opposition to Paul as he preaches to the Gentiles. The Jewish persecution was so intense that Paul wrote in 1 Thessalonians 2:14-16,

> For you, brothers, became imitators of the churches of God in Christ Jesus that are in Judea. For you suffered the same things from your own countrymen as they did from the Jews, who killed both the Lord Jesus and the prophets, and drove us out, and displease God and oppose all mankind by hindering us from speaking to the Gentiles that they might be saved—so as always to fill up the measure of their sins. But God's wrath has come upon them at last!

We must realize that Paul is not speaking about all Jews in this passage, as he himself was a Jew (Acts 21:39; 22:3), and there were also a number of Jewish believers in his day, as there are today. Rather, he is referring to the unbelieving Jewish leaders who opposed the gospel message. The Christians in the city of Smyrna were also persecuted by the Jews in that city, as the risen Jesus relates through John, "I know your tribulation and your poverty (but you are rich) and the slander of those who say that they are Jews and are not, but are a synagogue of Satan" (Rev. 2:9).

---

[39] We see the fulfillment of this prediction in the killing of both Stephen by the Sanhedrin (Acts 7:58-60), and James, the brother of John, by Herod Agrippa I (Acts 12:2-3). The death penalty for apostasy in Judaism is recorded in Deuteronomy 13:6-11. The examples of Phinehas in Numbers 21:1-15 and Mattathias (1 Maccabees 2:19-28) in killing apostates in Israel were also cited as justification to execute apostates. On John 16:2 and later rabbinic writings and Patristic sources on the killing of apostates in Judaism see Costa, *Worship and the Risen Jesus*, 318-319 n.30.

It was also in the city of Smyrna that the Church Father Polycarp—described as "a bishop of the holy Church which is in Smyrna"—was persecuted and later martyred.[40] The Jews in Smyrna were also instrumental in having Polycarp put to death and we are told that "the whole multitude both of Gentiles and of Jews who dwelt in Smyrna cried out with ungovernable wrath" against Polycarp and demanded he be burned alive—a task "the Jews more especially assisted in this with zeal, as is their custom."[41] The church in Philadelphia also faced persecution from the local Jews, who, like the local Jews in Smyrna, were also called a "synagogue of Satan" (Rev. 3:9).[42]

Philippians 2:11

The passage in Philippians 2:11 is part of a broader text that begins in 2:6-11. While I will address this passage more fully in the next chapter, I want to focus primarily on the creed that is embedded in this text, which is also believed to be part of a hymn called the *Carmen Christi*. The passage reaches its climax in verses 10-11 when it says that every knee in the tripartite universe (what is in heaven, on the earth, and under the earth) will bow, and that every tongue will confess that "Jesus Christ is Lord" which will redound to "the glory of God the Father." This creed is set in a cosmic scale where there will be a universal allegiance made to the exalted Christ as Lord, both now and in the future. It is no surprise that Paul mentions this point in his letter to the Philippians, as the city of Philippi was known to be a very loyal and pro-imperial city with a long history of emperor devotion.[43] Paul highlights the fact that Jesus, not Caesar, is the Lord of all, and by implication that Caesar must also bow the knee to Christ. We need to recall that the term "Lord," as we have seen in Romans 10:9-13 (cf. Joel 2:32), when applied to Jesus, does not just refer to Jesus as Ruler and Sovereign. It also refers to Jesus as the "Lord" which came to be used as a substitute for Yahweh, especially in the LXX. We see the same thing here. In Philippians 2:9 we read that God "bestowed on him [Jesus] the name that is above every name." Many Christians have mistakenly believed this "name" that is above every name to be the name of Jesus, but we need to

---

[40] *Martyrdom of Polycarp* 12:2; 16:2, 19:1; 22:2.

[41] *Martyrdom of Polycarp* 12:2; 13:1. The murderous anger against Polycarp by the Jews is also described in the same text in 18:1 where it refers to, "the opposition raised on the part of the Jews."

[42] In *Martyrdom of Polycarp* 19:1 there is a reference to the Christian believers in Philadelphia who also suffered martyrdom with Polycarp in Smyrna.

[43] Costa, *Worship and the Risen Jesus*, 236.

The Shortest Creed: "Jesus is Lord"

understand that Jesus was a common Jewish name in the first century AD. The name that is above every name, which God has bestowed on Jesus, is his very name—Yahweh—which is translated in the Greek New Testament as "Lord." This is why the confession is made that "Jesus Christ is Lord."

That the name "Lord" is the name in view here is further supported when we recognize that the background to Philippians 2:10-11 is Isaiah 45:23 where Yahweh says, "By myself I have sworn; from my mouth has gone out in righteousness a word that shall not return: '*To me every knee shall bow, every tongue shall swear allegiance*'" (italics mine). In Isaiah 45:23, it is to Yahweh that every knee will bow and every tongue will swear allegiance; in Philippians 2:10-11, however, it is to Jesus Christ that every knee will bow and every tongue confess to. Paul is clearly identifying the exalted Christ with Yahweh, who is also the Lord. This connection between Philippians 2:10-11 and Isaiah 45:23 is well recognized among scholars.[44] William Henn comments, "Philippians reaches a crescendo in the bestowal on Jesus of the name above every other name: 'Jesus Christ as Lord,' with an echo of [Isa. 45:23] suggesting that the same adoration which is there given to Yahweh is now also to be given to Jesus."[45] Oscar Cullmann also recognizes that the name "Lord" is the name above all names, because this passage "speaks of His [Jesus'] work as servant which culminates in His elevation to the rank of *Kyrios-Adonai,* a name which is above all names, since it formerly belonged to God alone."[46]

Thus, we see that the short, one-clause creed "Jesus is Lord," was viewed as a claim to the deity of Christ, as well as an affirmation of his status as Sovereign and Ruler of all. Christ is Lord not only now, but will someday be universally acclaimed and confessed, by both believers and unbelievers, to be Lord by all of creation.

So, we have seen that the shortest creed in the early Christian movement, "Jesus is Lord," was also a central one. It highlights both the sovereign rule of Jesus, as well as his status as Lord, as seen by it being used as a substitute term in the LXX for Yahweh. We also see several passages clearly identifying Jesus the Lord as Yahweh, such as in Romans 10:9-13 (cf. Joel 2:32) and Philippians 2:9-11 (cf. Isa. 45:23). The confession of Jesus as Lord was also a prerequisite

---

[44] On the connection between Isaiah 45:23 and Philippians 2:10-11 see Costa, *Worship and the Risen Jesus,* 240-245, 247-248, 276-277.

[45] Henn, *One Faith,* 49.

[46] Cullmann, *The Earliest Christian Confessions,* 55. See also Marshall, *Origins of New Testament Christology,* 106.

for salvation, along with the belief that God had raised him from the dead (Rom. 10:9-10), and may also have been verbally confessed at baptism. We also saw that to confess Jesus as Lord could only be prompted by the Holy Spirit (1 Cor. 12:3), and that there was evidence in early Christianity of some who opposed the Lordship of Jesus and cursed him instead and that the incentive to do so may have been engendered by persecution. We also saw how this creed was viewed as an anti-imperialist statement since Christians, in affirming Jesus as Lord, could not ascribe lordship to Caesar. As Jesus was "Lord of lords" there could be no rivals.

The lordship of Jesus, as reflected in these creeds above, was of utmost importance to the early Christians. It is no surprise that the most quoted passage in the New Testament is Psalm 110:1, "The LORD says to my Lord: 'Sit at my right hand, until I make your enemies your footstool,'" or, "Yahweh declared to my Lord, 'Take your seat at my right hand, till I have made your enemies your footstool'" (NJB). The latter translation, which is based on the Hebrew text, has been included to demonstrate the equivalence of the terms "Yahweh" and "Lord." However, as already noted, the New Testament quoted mainly from the LXX, which was the Greek version of the Old Testament. In the LXX of Psalm 110:1 it reads, "The Lord said to my Lord, Sit thou on my right hand, until I make thine enemies thy footstool." It looks like this in Greek: Εἶπεν ὁ **κύριος** τῷ **κυρίῳ** μου Κάθου ἐκ δεξιῶν μου, ἕως ἂν θῶ τοὺς ἐχθρούς σου ὑποπόδιον τῶν ποδῶν σου. In the LXX reading (Psalm 109:1 in LXX) you will notice that there are two persons who are referred to as "Lord," which I have made bold so you can see that they are related to each other. In the LXX, there is no difference with the first "Lord" and the second "Lord;" thus, when the New Testament quotes Psalm 110:1, you will notice it also speaks of two Lords (Matt. 22:44; Mark 12:36; Luke 20:42; Acts 2:34). In this text the Father (the first Lord), addresses the Son (the second Lord), and entreats him to sit at his right hand until his enemies are made his footstool.

This imagery evokes the risen and exalted Jesus as the Sovereign who sits at the right hand of the Father, a point that is affirmed in both the Apostles' Creed and Nicene Creed, which we saw in our first chapter. The title "Lord" was so closely linked to Jesus that it virtually became a standard term for him so that when one spoke about the Lord, they knew they were also speaking about Jesus.[47]

---

[47] In the Gospels the title "Lord" is used of Jesus most often in Luke, who uses the term some eighteen times as simply "the Lord." John uses the title "Lord" fifteen times in the resurrection chapters (20–21). Henn, *One Faith*, 48.

6
JESUS IS THE CHRIST

The first believers in Jesus were Jewish, not Gentile. With the beginning of the church at Pentecost, the Christian movement moved first among Jewish and then Gentile territory, just as Jesus predicted (Acts 1:8). As history advanced, however, this Jewish Messianic movement became increasingly and predominantly Gentile, as it is to this day.

The concept of the coming of the Messiah was an important part of Judaism. The word Messiah comes from the Hebrew and is better known in the New Testament by its Greek equivalent, "Christ." Both of these words mean "anointed one." This title was applied to three offices in the Old Testament: priests, such as the high priest (Lev. 4:3, 5, 16), prophets (Ps. 105:15), and kings (1 Sam. 2:10, 35; 2 Sam. 1:14; Ps. 2:2; 18:50)—all offices which Jesus incorporates into himself. The term was also used of the Gentile king Cyrus of Persia, who permitted the Jewish exiles to return to their homeland after the Babylonian Captivity (Isa. 45:1). In the New Testament this word is used as a title of Jesus, which designated him as *the* Messiah, the one promised by the prophets. Both Matthew 1:1-17 and Luke 3:23-38 provide genealogies of Jesus, tracing him back to king David and even farther in order to establish his Messianic credentials.

The importance of the Messianic status of Jesus, and the origin of the Christian movement from Jewish soil is not only evident in the gospels but reinforced in the Early Church Fathers. Early church tradition maintains that Matthew originally wrote his gospel in the Hebrew or Aramaic language to the Jews.[1] The first followers of Jesus, who, as noted already, were all Jews, came to believe that he was the long-awaited Messiah of Israel. Though in the context of their own day, there were many self-proclaimed messiahs and Messianic movements, none continued beyond the first century AD, except the movement of Jesus the Messiah.

---

[1] Eusebius, *Hist. Eccl.* 3.39.16. Eusebius in ca. AD 300 quotes from Papias ca. AD 125 who is credited with making this statement about Matthew's gospel.

EARLY CHRISTIAN CREEDS AND HYMNS

Another creed that arose from the Jewish matrix of the early Christian movement was "Jesus is the Christ," or "Jesus is the Messiah." Though it may not seem like it to us, such a creed would have been seen by many as polemical. This is because, though it was a statement of faith, it was also a statement against Judaism, which for the most part had rejected Jesus of Nazareth as the Messiah of Israel—a point the apostle Paul, with a heavy heart, addresses in Romans 9-11. This rejection of Jesus as Messiah by Israel was so painful to Paul that he wished he could be "accursed" (Greek, *anathema*) and "cut off" from Christ for the sake of his Jewish kinsmen if it would mean their salvation (Rom. 9:3). Paul never gave up longing to see the Jews saved, and neither should we. But this creed wasn't just meant as a polemic against Judaism; it also implicitly stood against the emperor and imperial Rome.

As noted above, the words "Christ" and "Messiah" carried within themselves regal connotations and overtones. The Messiah was believed to be a royal figure, a scion from David's regal lineage. Kings were anointed, and the Messiah, as the son of David, was *the* Anointed One of God, the King whom Yahweh has set on Mount Zion (Ps. 2:6-12), the one who will someday reign from "sea to sea" (Ps. 72:8). In other words, referencing Jesus as the "Christ" also means affirming him as the "King of kings" (Rev. 17:14; 19:16). Therefore, confessing "Jesus is the Christ" is just as much an anti-imperialist confession as confessing that "Jesus is Lord." This creed also carries within it implicit proof of the deity of Christ in that "King of kings" (Rev. 17:14; 19:16; cf. 1:5) is also a title ascribed to God himself (1 Tim. 6:15).[2]

---

[2] There are two human kings in the Bible that are also called "king of kings": the Persian king Artaxerxes (Ezra 7:12), and the Babylonian king Nebuchadnezzar (Ezekiel 26:7; Daniel 2:37). The context of these passages reveals two things about the circumstances of this title in terms of it being appropriated by human kings. First, we see that at the time they were the sole super powers of the ancient Near East; and second, God had given these kings their supremacy and authority. Thus, their title of "king of kings" was not theirs by nature but derived from God. This is clearly seen in Daniel 2:37-38, "You, O king [Nebuchadnezzar], the king of kings, *to whom the God of heaven has given the kingdom*, the power, and the might, and the glory, and *into whose hand he has given*, wherever they dwell, the children of man, the beasts of the field, and the birds of the heavens, making you rule over them all" (italics mine). Note that the authority God gave to Nebuchadnezzar reflects the dominion God had given to Adam and Eve as his image bearers (Genesis 1:26-27). This dominion was also promised to the Davidic king, but with the collapse of the Davidic monarchy in 586 BC this promise of dominion was transferred to the coming Son of David, the Messiah, who possesses it by divine right (Psalm 2:7-12). This accords with Paul's statement regarding governmental authorities that "there is no authority except from God" (Romans 13:1). Paul discusses this in full length in Romans 13:1-7.

JESUS IS THE CHRIST

In rejecting Jesus as the Christ, the Jewish leaders simultaneously rejected Jesus as King. In fact, they only used the connection between Christ and king to force Pilate to have Jesus crucified.[3]

Paul himself, shortly after his calling by the risen Christ, argued to his fellow Jews that Jesus was the promised Messiah: "But Saul increased all the more in strength, and confounded the Jews who lived in Damascus by proving that Jesus was the Christ" (Acts 9:22). In the letters of Paul, which were written primarily to a Gentile audience, he refers to Jesus as "Christ" 379 times.[4] "Jesus is Christ" would be a foreign creed to a Gentile audience, as would be the idea of a Messiah, as neither of these terms were part of their religious worldview, though the idea of kingship was not unknown to them. This creed, therefore, finds it origin on Jewish soil.

This creed was no minor point to quibble over either; rather, it became a test of orthodoxy, to ascertain whether one was in harmony with the Christian movement. To deny that Jesus was the Christ was to identify oneself as a liar and an antichrist, "Who is the liar but he who denies that Jesus is the Christ? This is the antichrist, he who denies the Father and the Son" (1 John 2:22). It should also be noted that affirming Jesus as the Christ is also closely associated with his identity as the Son of God, as we shall see more fully below. To deny that Jesus is the Christ is also to deny the Father and the Son, thus jeopardizing one's salvation.

---

[3] A claim to kingship, was an automatic frontal assault against the Roman emperor which was tantamount to treason under Roman law. The Jewish authorities declared, "Everyone who makes himself a king opposes Caesar ... Pilate said to them, 'Shall I crucify your King?' The chief priests answered, 'We have no king but Caesar'" (John 19:12, 15). Here we see the close association between Jesus' identity as Christ and king. The claim of the Jewish leadership that they had "no king but Caesar" is ironic; they charge Jesus with treason against the Roman emperor, and yet by claiming they have no king but Caesar, they commit treason against the true king, who is the Messiah, and by extension, God himself. The passion narrative is also full of irony. Even on the cross, the *titulus* that hung on the cross above the head of Jesus bore the inscription "King of the Jews" (Matthew 27:37; Mark 15:26; Luke 23:38; John 19:19-22). It should also be stated that in the apocryphal Gospel of Peter (4:11), this tradition of the *titulus* is also attested, "And when they had set up the cross, they wrote on it, 'This is the King of Israel.'" See Burton H. Throckmorton, *Gospel Parallels* (Nashville: Thomas Nelson, 1979), 182. The term, "King of the Jews" is also applied to Jesus in the infancy narrative of the Matthean gospel, "Where is he who is born king of the Jews?" (Matthew 2:2). There is a direct parallel here between "king of the Jews" in Matthew 2:2, and "Christ" in Matthew 2:4. In Matthew, Jesus is believed to have been king of the Jews from birth. The terms "King of the Jews" and "King of Israel" are used interchangeably, even in the gospels. For instance, Matthew 27:42 reads "King of Israel," while 27:37 has "King of the Jews."

[4] Henn, *One Faith*, 45.

EARLY CHRISTIAN CREEDS AND HYMNS

Even though the idea of "Messiah" was mainly a Jewish one, when the gospel went out to the Gentiles, it remained a part of who Jesus was. This is also why the title "Christ" is generally attached to the name of Jesus, as in the Apostles' and Nicene Creed.[5] In fact, the Messianic identity of Jesus was so central that he was sometimes referred to as "Christ Jesus" or even simply as "Christ." Thus, as we saw in the earliest creed in Christianity (1 Cor. 15:3), "Christ" is often used synonymously with Jesus. The followers of Jesus eventually came to be known as "Christians," a term which was first applied in Antioch (Acts 11:26; 26:28; 1 Pet. 4:16). The term "Christian" came to refer to the followers of the Christ or Messiah. We see the creed "Jesus is the Christ," and related statements in several passages in the New Testament. I have placed the creedal portion in bold letters:

Simon Peter replied, "**You are the Christ**, the Son of the living God" (Matt 16:16).

Peter answered him, "**You are the Christ**" (Mark 8:29).

And Peter answered, "[You are] **The Christ** of God" (Luke 9:20)

But these are written so that you may believe that **Jesus is the Christ**, the Son of God, and that by believing you may have life in his name" (John 20:31).

Everyone who believes that **Jesus is the Christ** has been born of God, and everyone who loves the Father loves whomever has been born of him (1 John 5:1).

John tells us in his gospel (20:31) that the purpose and reason why he wrote his gospel was that his readers would come to believe that "Jesus is the Christ" as well as the Son of God, so that they could have life in him. Again in John 20:31 we see the conjunction ὅτι (*hoti*), "that," before the creed "Jesus is the Christ," which, as we have seen, often acts as quotation mark indicators. Note that the confession "Jesus is the Christ" precedes the confession that he is the

---

[5] See Chapter 1.

JESUS IS THE CHRIST

Son of God. In 1 John 5:1, it is stated that the one who believes that Jesus is the Christ has been born of God, i.e., regenerated.

In the first three passages referred to above, which are taken from the Synoptic Gospels, we encounter what is called the Petrine confession. Jesus asks his disciples directly who they think he is and Peter, in Matthew's account, responds with the confession "You are the Christ, the Son of the living God" (Matt. 16:16). Peter's ability to make this confession, Jesus goes on to tell him, was not initiated by flesh and blood, i.e., from a human source, but rather by the Father in heaven (Matt. 16:17). In other words, the disclosure of the true identity of Jesus only comes as a gift of God the Father, the one who draws his elect to the Son (John 6:44). It is this confession that Jesus will go on to call "this rock" in Matthew 16:18, and on which he claims he will build his church.

The word "church" first appears here in Matthew 16:18 and only appears in the Gospel of Matthew twice (16:18; 18:17), and never in any of the other Gospels. This is not a verse establishing Peter as the first of many popes; on the contrary, the "rock" in this verse is the confession which Peter made.[6] As Schaff has also argued, "This is the fundamental Christian Confession, and the rock on which the Church is built."[7]

If we compare Matthew 16:18 with John 20:31 we will note a striking resemblance; in fact, the creeds are almost exactly the same. The apostle John, who heard the words Jesus communicated to Peter, understood very well which "rock" Jesus spoke of and inserted it towards the end of his gospel. In Mark 8:29 and Luke 9:20, which record the same event, the creed that Jesus is

---

[6] Augustine himself saw the *confession* of Peter as the "rock" upon which the church was built: "In a passage in this book, I said about the Apostle Peter: 'On him as on a rock the Church was built.' ... But I know that very frequently at a later time, I so explained what the Lord said: 'Thou art Peter, and upon this rock I will build my Church [Matt. 16:18],' *that it be understood as built upon Him whom Peter confessed* saying: '*Thou art the Christ, the Son of the living God*,' and so Peter, called after this rock, represented the person of the Church which is built upon this rock, and has received 'the keys of the kingdom of heaven.' For, 'Thou art Peter' *and not* '*Thou art the rock*' was said to him. But '*the rock was Christ*,' in *confessing* whom, as also the whole Church *confesses*, Simon was called Peter. But let the reader decide which of these two opinions is the more probable" (Augustine, *The Retractions* 1:20:1). (italics mine)

[7] Schaff, *Creeds of Christendom*, 2:4.

the Christ is emphasized with only slight nuances.[8] Only Matthew adds "the Son of God" to the confession, a point which I will address in the next chapter.

The creed "Jesus is the Christ" appears throughout the Gospels whenever Jesus' Messianic status is questioned and challenged. To confess Jesus as the Christ was already very risky during his earthly ministry, "For the Jews had already agreed that if anyone should confess Jesus to be Christ, he was to be put out of the synagogue" (John 9:22). We saw that this creed may have originated during the ministry of Jesus and appears to be a pre-Easter creed, which would make it a close rival with the earliest creed in 1 Corinthians 15:3-4. At the resurrection of Lazarus, Jesus asked Martha if she believed he was the resurrection and life (John 11:25-26) to which she responded, "I believe that you are the Christ, the Son of God, who is coming into the world" (John 11:27). Again, we encounter the same creed found in Peter's confession in Matthew 16:16, as well as at the end of John (20:31).

It is significant that immediately following Peter's confession of Jesus as the Christ in the Synoptic Gospels, Jesus begins to speak of his impending suffering, death and subsequent resurrection. The trigger seems to be Peter's confession. However, the idea that the Messiah would go on to die an ignominious death was so appalling that even Peter recoiled at it and rebuked Jesus for suggesting it, "And he [Jesus] said this plainly. And Peter took him aside and began to rebuke him" (Mark 8:32). In Matthew's version we hear Peter's adamant words, "And Peter took him aside and began to rebuke him, saying, 'Far be it from you, Lord! This shall never happen to you'" (Matt. 16:22).

---

[8] In John 6:69, there is a statement where Peter says to Jesus, "We have believed, and have come to know, that you are the Holy One of God." The title "Holy One of God" can be understood in a Messianic context (Acts 2:27; 3:14; 13:35; cf. Psalm 16:10). This verse has a number of variants in later manuscripts but the reading "the Holy One of God" is certainly the original reading as it appears in the earliest manuscripts of John. The variants in the manuscripts emerged as a result of scribal attempts at harmonizing this passage in John 6:69 with Peter's confession in Matthew 16:16. For example, John 6:69 (AV) reads, "And we believe and are sure that thou art that Christ, the Son of the living God." There is no need to harmonize John 6:69 to make it read the same as Matthew 16:16 as Peter could have said both statements. The creed that Jesus is the Christ and Son of God already appears in John 11:27. We see another confession in John 1:49 given not by Peter, but by another of Jesus' disciples, Nathaniel, who says to Jesus, "Rabbi, you are the Son of God! You are the King of Israel!" This confession also bears a resemblance to Matthew 16:16, where Peter confesses Jesus to be the Christ and the Son of God. Nathaniel confesses Jesus as the Son of God, but also implies Jesus is the Christ by calling him the "King of Israel," a title reserved for the Messiah (note the use of "king" and "son" used of the Messianic figure in Psalm 2:6-7).

Jesus responded by rebuking Peter, and Satan, who presumably was speaking through or influencing Peter (Mark 8:33; Matt. 16:23).

In Matthew 16:22 we see an example of what scholars call the criterion of embarrassment. Peter takes it upon himself to rebuke Jesus openly and tell him that he, being the Messiah, will most certainly not undergo such a humiliating death. Such conduct is completely out of line coming from a disciple towards his master, and the fact that Scripture even records it speaks of the authenticity of the event. The same principle would apply to Peter's triple denial of Jesus.

The identity of Jesus as the Messiah is closely related to his redemptive work and mission, which he will fulfill precisely because of who he is. The confession of Jesus as Christ is also an apostolic one, being confessed to by Peter (Matt. 16:16), Nathaniel (John 1:49), John (John 20:31), and Martha, the sister of Lazarus (John 11:27).[9] It even seems to have been understood by Jesus' antagonists, who, at his trial before the Sanhedrin, was asked whether or not he was the Christ and Son of God (Mark 14:61; Matt. 26:63; Luke 22:66-67). This would imply that this creed may already have been circulating in the early Christian movement, to the point that even its adversaries knew about it.

---

[9] This creed was also well-known to the Church Father Justin Martyr (*c.* AD 100–AD 165), "that Jesus is the Christ and the Son of God" (*First Apology*, 17–18, 54).

7
JESUS IS THE SON OF GOD

Another important creed that developed early in the Christian movement was "Jesus is the Son of God." What does it mean for Jesus to be the Son of God? Does it mean that he is one special son among many other sons of God? And if he is a son, does this mean that he came into existence at some point? These are all extremely important questions.

Right off the bat we must acknowledge that when Christians referred to Jesus as the Son of God, they did not mean that he was created; Scripture clearly teaches that the Son eternally existed within the Godhead (John 1:1-3). The Arian heresy, however, stated that the Son of God was created in time, as was stated in a popular song that Arius himself created, "there was a time when he [the Son] was not."[1] Note how even heretics, in this case Arians, used hymns or songs to promulgate their own teachings. Arianism was a view that the church vehemently rejected and condemned officially at the Council of Nicaea in AD 325.

As we shall see, the creed that affirms Jesus as the Son of God also rejects the idea that Jesus is just one among many sons of God. Rather, Jesus is uniquely the Son of God, the "one and only Son" (John 3:16 NIV, NET, HCSB), "his only Son" (RSV, NRSV, NJB), or as traditionally translated, "his only begotten Son" (AV, NKJV, NASB). But this raises another question. What does the phrase son of God mean when it is applied to other figures in the Old Testament? Here we need to remember that the definition of words is based on their usage in context and that the term son of God has a wide range of meaning throughout the Bible. Before addressing the creed "Jesus is the Son of God," it will be worthwhile to review how the idea of son or sons of God develops and is used in the Old Testament.[2]

---

[1] Schaff, *Creeds of Christendom*, 2:34.
[2] See the important work on this subject by Martin Hengel, *The Son of God* (Philadelphia: Fortress, 1976).

Adam

Adam was the first man and the progenitor of the whole human race. Both Adam and Eve share the unique status of being the only humans who had no parents. Adam was directly created by God from the dust of the ground and by the breath of life imparted by the Creator (Gen. 2:7). Adam was made in the image of God (Gen. 1:26) and had perfect fellowship with God prior to the Fall. He was also a prophet, as he spoke God's words; a priest, as he approached and walked with God; and a king, as he and his wife were given dominion over the whole earth and all its creatures (Gen. 1:28). All of these terms—image of God, prophet, priest, king—remind us of someone who is to come. In fact, Scripture tells us that Adam "was a type of the one who was to come" (Rom. 5:14). As such, Adam is also called "the son of God" (Luke 3:38) by virtue of being directly created by God.

The Heavenly Council and Heavenly Beings: Angels

The first time "sons of God" appear in Scripture is in Genesis 6:2,4 where "the sons of God" (the heavenly beings) come down and defile themselves with the "daughters of men."[3] Regardless of the various interpretations on this passage, both agree that the phrase "sons of God" first appear here. We see the "sons of God" also mentioned again in Job 1:6–12; 2:1–6, where they appear before God at the heavenly council, with *Satan* (adversary) is also mentioned as presiding among them. In Job 38:7 the sons of God also sing together and shout for joy when God lays down the foundations of the earth at creation and suggests that these heavenly beings pre-existed humankind.

We see the heavenly council again in Psalm 82:1–8 where the heavenly beings are called "sons of the Most High," and even "gods" (Ps. 82:6).[4] Though the majority of interpreters have taken this passage to refer to human judges,[5]

---

[3] This is the classical interpretation of the text. There are other evangelical scholars who are of the opinion that the sons of God here refer to the godly descendants of Seth, and the daughters of men are the apostate line of Cain. See Erickson, *Christian Theology*, 412. Erickson states that "neither view can be held dogmatically."

[4] On the heavenly council see Michael S. Heiser, "The Divine Council in Late Canonical and Non-Canonical Second Temple Jewish Literature," (PhD diss., University of Wisconsin-Madison, Madison, 2004). It is interesting that in Qumran, in a fragmentary text known as 11Q, Melchizedek is referred to as a heavenly being and even identified as the *Elohim* (God) of Psalm 82:1. See Hurtado, *Lord Jesus Christ*, 501.

[5] Although this list is not exhaustive, see for example Leon Morris, *The Gospel According to John*, NICNT, rev. ed. (Grand Rapids: Eerdmans, 1995), 468; John Marsh, *Saint John*, The

it is interesting to note that the language is similar to that of the book of Job. Sometimes such heavenly beings are also called the "sons of the mighty," as in Psalm 29:1 (NASB) and Psalm 89:6 (NASB). The heavenly beings, including angels, are called the "sons of God" because they are his direct creation and part of his heavenly council (see Deut. 32:8).[6]

The Corporate Nation of Israel

Another way the term son of God is applied is to the corporate nation of Israel. We see this in a number of biblical passages, for example, in Exodus 4:22, "Then you [Moses] shall say to Pharaoh, 'Thus says the LORD, Israel is my firstborn son, and I say to you, 'Let my son go that he may serve me.'" Moses also reminds the people of Israel, "You are the sons of the LORD your God" (Deut. 14:1). The idea of Israel as God's corporate son is also seen in the Prophets, "For I [God] am a father to Israel, and Ephraim [another term for Israel] is my firstborn" (Jer. 31:9); "When Israel was a child, I loved him, and out of Egypt I called my son" (Hos. 11:1). This passage is also cited in the New Testament in reference to Jesus in Matthew 2:15.

As a covenant nation, Israel was to understand and relate to God as their Father: "For you are our Father, though Abraham does not know us, and Israel does not acknowledge us; you, O LORD, are our Father, our Redeemer from of old is your name" (Isa. 63:16; see also Isa. 64:8; Mal. 2:10 where God is addressed as "Father"). Israel was chosen as a nation to be the son of God. It is clear that Israel was called the "son of God" because they were chosen from all the other nations to be the covenant people of God. As God's "firstborn son," Israel was not the first nation on the earth, but rather, she was the heir to the promises of God (cf. Rom. 9:1–5).

Pelican New Testament Commentaries (London: Penguin Books, 1977), 405; Amy-Jill Levine and Marc Zvi Brettler, eds., *The Jewish Annotated New Testament* 2nd ed. (New York: Oxford University Press, 2017), 200; B.F. Westcott, *The Gospel According to St. John: The Authorised Version with Introduction and Notes* (London: John Murray, Albemarle Street, 1882), 160; Reymond, *Jesus*, 91.

[6] There is a textual variant in Deuteronomy 32:8. The Masoretic Hebrew Text has "according to the number of the children of Israel" (see also AV, NKJV, NIV, NASB, HCSB), while others, like the LXX and the reading of Deuteronomy 32:8 in the Dead Sea Scrolls, have "according to the sons of God" (ESV, RSV, NET reads "according to the heavenly assembly" and NRSV "according to the number of the gods"). I take "according to the sons of God" to be the original reading as it is the more difficult one. It also appears in the earliest manuscripts and makes better textual sense, as Deuteronomy 32:8 is written about the scattering of the people into nations in Genesis 11.

The Davidic King

The anointed king of Israel in the Old Testament was also called the son of God. This title was used of David and of all who would descend from his royal lineage. But beyond David himself, such a title also pointed forward to the coming Son of David, who would be the Messiah.

We see the Davidic king referred to as God's son in several passages (2 Sam. 7:14; 1 Chr. 17:13; 22:10; 28:6; cf. Ps. 89:26-27). We also see this language in the royal psalms, "I will tell of the decree: The LORD said to me, 'You are my Son; today I have begotten you'" (Ps. 2:7). The title "son of God," as applied to David meant that he had been adopted by God and elevated to the status of a son with inheritance rights; he was to rule on earth in God's place as his vice-regent. The king was also the representative of the people of Israel so that in his person, all of Israel was represented,[7] a view that is carried over into the New Testament as Jesus Christ, the King and Son of David, represents his redeemed people before the Father. This is why Christian believers are commonly referred to as being "in Christ."

The concept of the monarchy's filial relationship to the divine was a common one throughout the ancient Near East. As we shall see, the ideal Son of David, the Messiah and true King to come, would be a much greater king than David and also a one-of-a-kind Son.

The Messiah

The Old Testament speaks of one who would come from the seed of Abraham, Isaac, and Jacob. He will come from the house of David and be a redeemer not only to Israel but also to the nations of the world. He will be a prophet, priest, and king. The title "Son" is also applied to the Messiah, but in a unique way. Several Old Testament passages bear this out, for example Isaiah 9:6, "For to us a child is born, to us a son is given; and the government shall be upon his shoulder, and his name shall be called Wonderful Counselor, Mighty God, Everlasting Father, Prince of Peace."[8] Notice in this passage that the child that is born is also a son who is given. This language is echoed in the New Testament in passages like John 3:16, which says that God loved the world so much

---

[7] This is seen in both 2 Samuel 24:1-17 and 1 Chronicles 21:1-17 where the nations of Israel suffers the consequences of David's sin against God.

[8] It is interesting how the three Persons of the Trinity are associated with peace. The Father is the God of peace (Romans 15:33), the Son is the Prince of Peace (Isaiah 9:6; cf. Colossians 3:15), and one of the fruits of the Holy Spirit is peace (Galatians 5:22). The Holy Spirit produces peace in believers because he is also the source of peace.

that he *gave* his only Son. If the Son is able to be given, it means that he already existed before coming into the world.

The pre-existence of the Messiah is found throughout the Old Testament (and in the inter-testamental writings such as the books of *1 Enoch* 37-71 and *4 Ezra*), especially in the prophecy of Micah 5:2, where the child who is to be born in Bethlehem is described as one "whose origin is from of old, from ancient days."[9] While the Messiah is sometimes spoken of in lofty terms in some of the literature of Second Temple Judaism—even being spoken of as pre-existent (*1 Enoch* 48:2-10),[10] he is never referred to in terms of a *personally* divine agent through whom all creation comes about. The names given to the Son in Isaiah 9:6, "Wonderful Counselor, Mighty God, Everlasting Father," are only used elsewhere in the Old Testament when referring to God alone. Clearly this Child, who is the Son, is someone very different from the human Davidic kings. Even the conception of this child is in itself a marvelous sign: "Therefore the Lord himself will give you a sign. Behold, the virgin shall conceive and bear a son, and shall call his name Immanuel" (Isa. 7:14; cf. Matt. 1:23). The name of this child, Immanuel, means "God is with us."

Another pertinent passage in the OT regarding the Messiah is the following: "Who has ascended to heaven and come down? Who has gathered the wind in his fists? Who has wrapped up the waters in a garment? Who has established all the ends of the earth? What is his name, and what is his son's name? Surely you know!" (Prov. 30:4). The answers to these rhetorical questions could only be God himself. Jesus spoke of himself as the one who descended or came down from heaven (John 6:38, 41-42, 51, 58; cf. Phil. 2:6-11). Jesus said no one ascended into heaven but he who descended from heaven (John 3:13). Notice that the language is strikingly similar to Proverbs 30:4. However, also notice that the transcendence of God is attached to "his name" and "his son's name." Notice the name of God's son is as equally

---

[9] Although not part of the Second Temple Jewish literature, there is an interesting statement in the Midrash, particularly its commentary on Genesis. In Genesis 1:2 it states that "the Spirit of God" was hovering over the primordial waters. In the third century AD text of Midrash *Genesis Rabbah* 1:2, it states, "The Spirit of God was moving over the surface of the waters." This was the Spirit of Messiah, as it is written, "The Spirit of the Lord will rest on him" (Isaiah 11:2). Other rabbinic literature also attests to the pre-existence of the Messiah, in identifying the light of creation (Genesis 1:3-4), as the light of the Messiah *Pes. R.* 36:1. The parallel with this rabbinic idea of the light of the Messiah, and Jesus' claim to be the light of the world (John 8:12) is striking. The NT also speaks about the Spirit of the Messiah/Christ (Romans 8:9; Philippians 1:19; 1 Peter 1:11), the Spirit of Jesus (Acts 16:7), and the Spirit of his Son (Galatians 4:6). The Majority Text reads "the Spirit" in Acts 16:7 whereas the Critical Text reads "the Spirit of Jesus."

[10] On this passage in *1 Enoch* see Appendix 1.

transcendent as God's name. The charge that the Old Testament does not teach that God has a son, or that there was no view among the Jews of a pre-existent Messiah, is demonstrably false.

It should also be noted that the prophecy in Psalm 2:7-12 of a king that would rule the nations with a rod of iron and that all the nations would surrender to was *never fulfilled by David or any other Jewish king*. Let us look at that passage again:

> I will tell of the decree: The LORD said to me, "You are my Son; today I have begotten you. Ask of me, and I will make the nations your heritage, and the ends of the earth your possession. You shall break them with a rod of iron and dash them in pieces like a potter's vessel." Now therefore, O kings, be wise; be warned, O rulers of the earth. Serve the LORD with fear, and rejoice with trembling. Kiss the Son, lest he be angry, and you perish in the way, for his wrath is quickly kindled. Blessed are all who take refuge in him.

The kings and rulers of the earth are warned to serve God with fear but also to "kiss the Son" who has the power both to save or destroy them. Did such a scenario take place in the life of any Davidic king? Never. This passage, then, is clearly speaking of the Messianic Son of David. As well, notice the promise for all those who take refuge in the Son. Even though God is only and always the object of refuge in the Old Testament (Ps. 5:11; 7:1; 11:1), here the Son is also portrayed as a place of refuge. In Jeremiah 23:5-6, the king to come from David's line will bear the name, "Yahweh our righteousness." Though only God may rightly bear that name, because the Messiah is also the Son of God, he is able to bear it equally with him.[11]

The Dead Sea Scrolls also demonstrate a familiarity with "son of God" language. For example, James Charlesworth, an expert in the Dead Sea Scrolls has argued, "We can no longer report that the Dead Sea Scrolls do not refer to God's Son or the Son."[12] One of the scrolls even mentions an unidentified

---

[11] Even in rabbinic literature it is admitted that the Messiah bears God's name: "What is the name of the Messiah King? Rabbi Abba Bar-Kahana said: 'The Lord' is his name, and that is the name by which He will be called, The LORD, Our Righteousness (Jeremiah 23:6)." *Midrash Eichah Rabbah* 1. Also see *Midrash Tehilim* on Psalm 21, "God calls King Messiah by His own name. But what is his name? Answer: YHWH is a man of war (from Exodus 15:3)."

[12] James H. Charlesworth, ed., *The Bible and the Dead Sea Scrolls* (The Scrolls and Christian Origins. Vol. 3; Waco: Baylor University Press, 2006), 113.

figure, "He shall be hailed (as) the Son of God, and they shall call him the Son of the Most High" (4QPs Dana). The similarity of this language with that of Jesus in the annunciation account to Mary is striking (Luke 1:32-35). Context as always is key in determining the various nuances of the term son of God.[13]

Christian Believers

Are believers also sons and children of God? Yes, but, as sons and/or children of God, we have been adopted into God's family. No one is a son in the same way that Jesus is. This is made clear in the following passages:

> For you did not receive the spirit of slavery to fall back into fear, but you have received the Spirit of *adoption* as sons, by whom we cry, "Abba! Father!" (Rom. 8:15; italics mine).

> But when the fullness of time had come, God sent forth his Son, born of woman, born under the law, to redeem those who were under the law, so that we might receive *adoption as sons*. And because you are sons, God has sent the Spirit of his Son into our hearts, crying, "Abba! Father!" (Gal. 4:4-6; italics mine).

Notice in the second passage that the Son and the Spirit of the Son are "sent" by God the Father. The Son was sent into the world to be born of a woman, which presupposes that the Son pre-existed. Recall Isaiah 9:6, where it says that the child that will be born is a Son who is *given*. Notice as well that "the Spirit of his Son" is sent into our hearts, who is spoken of here as the Holy Spirit (cf. Rom. 8:9). This is the language of deity.

Why did early Christians confess that "Jesus is the Son of God"? Such a creed arose from an early realization and acceptance of the teachings of Jesus. But where did Jesus use the term "Son" of himself? By the time of the New Testament, the Jews regarded themselves as God's children (John 8:41), the background of which, as we have seen, is the Old Testament (Exod. 4:22-23; Deut. 14:1). However, when Jesus spoke of himself as the Son of God and spoke of God as his Father, his hearers became angry and threatened to kill him. Why? The reason is that Jesus spoke of God as his Father in *a special and unique way*.

---

[13] For a treatment of the term son of God in the Apocrypha, Pseudepigrapha, the Targums, and rabbinic literature see Appendix 1.

God identified Jesus as his beloved Son both at his baptism (Mark 1:11), and at the transfiguration (Mark 9:7). The demons also recognized Jesus as the Son of God (Mark 1:34; 3:11), as did Satan (Matt. 4:3; Luke 4:3). Jesus spoke of God as "My Father" (John 5:17), and claimed several unique privileges, such as being able to raise the dead as the Father does, and giving eternal life to those who call upon him (John 5:21; 10:28-30). He even went so far as to say that all should honor the Son just as they honor the Father, indicating that both Father and Son were worthy of equal honor (John 5:23). There is clearly a different meaning in the way Jesus employs the word "Son." We can see this by observing the following passages: "All things have been handed over to me by my Father, and no one knows the Son except the Father, and no one knows the Father except the Son and anyone to whom the Son chooses to reveal him" (Matt. 11:27; cf. Luke 10:22);[14] and, "I and the Father are one" (John 10:30, 33, 36).

Jesus also claimed to possess intimate knowledge of the Father and reserved the sovereign right to reveal him to whom he willed. The use of this language has clearly transcended the kind of sonship language we saw with reference to Adam, angels, the nation of Israel, and David. Notice also how those who heard Jesus calling God his Father reacted: "This was why the Jews were seeking all the more to kill him, because not only was he breaking the Sabbath, but he was *even calling God his own Father, making himself equal with God*" (John 5:18; italics mine).

It is clear that Jesus understood his identity as the Son of God in a way that was unparalleled and that no one but himself could participate in. He is both the eternal Son of God and the eternal Word who pre-existed creation and voluntarily came into the world (John 1:1-3, 10, 14; 17:5). Unlike other temporal sons of God, who share a beginning in time, Jesus is the *eternal* Son. The word Son is meaningless without speaking about a Father, and vice versa, but when we speak of God, we must keep in mind that we are talking about an eternal

---

[14] The fact that Matthew 11:27 and Luke 10:22 read almost exactly the same in these passages bears witness, according to a number of scholars, to their dependence on Q, which we previously discussed. If this is so, this demonstrates that the idea of Jesus as the Son of God is very early, as Q is believed to be earlier than the composition of the gospels themselves, generally placed by scholars in the AD 50's. During this early period there was a unified view among early Christian believers on who Jesus was, contrary to what some critics say. Martin Hengel argues "that christological thinking between AD 50 and 100 *was much more unified in its basic structure* than New Testament research, in part at least, has maintained." Hengel, *Studies in Early Christology*, 383 (italics in original).

Jesus is the Son of God

Being who is tri-personal: Father, Son, and Holy Spirit. As we saw in our first chapter, Father-Son language in the context of the Godhead is not temporal, but eternal, i.e., the Father is *eternally* the Father in eternal relationship with the eternal Son and the Son is *eternally* the Son in eternal relationship with the eternal Father.[15] Within this unity there is also "the eternal Spirit" (Heb. 9:14). Jesus is the eternal Son of God, who has always been in an eternal relationship with the Father (John 17:5).[16] This eternal Son *became* human in the person of Jesus Christ (John 1:14). It is for this reason Jesus' Sonship far exceeds all other sons or sons of God.

Notice that during his trial, the Sanhedrin found Jesus guilty because of his claim to be the Son of God, "The Jews answered him [Pilate], 'We have a law, and according to that law he ought to die *because he has made himself the Son of God*'" (John 19:7; italics mine). In Mark 14:61-62 Jesus is asked, "are you the Christ, the Son of the Blessed?" To which Jesus gives the affirmative "I am." The high priest concludes that Jesus is guilty of blasphemy and worthy of death (Mark 14:63-64). We have seen already that the Jews had no problem with the term "son of God." So why did they take such offence to Jesus using that title? When Jesus refers to himself as the Son of God, it is clearly being used in a special way. Jesus is not just a Son of God like Israel, or the Israelite king, or Adam. Rather, he is the "unique" and "one and only" Son of God.

The New Testament underscores this point by using the Greek word μονογενής (*monogenes*) in reference to Jesus (John 1:14, 18; 3:16, 18; 1 John 4:9; cf. Heb. 11:17). This word is made up of two Greek words, *monos* ("one"), and *genos* ("kind"), and essentially means "one of a kind," "unique," or "only."[17] Jesus as the Son is unique because he shares in the

---

[15] This is the background to the statement in the Nicene Creed that states the Son is "begotten of the Father before all ages." As we speak about *eternal* Persons, keep in mind that this begetting is an *eternal* begetting, "before all ages," referring to the beginning of time. Jesus was the eternal Son when there was no time in existence. In other words, the Son is eternally begotten of the Father, and the Father eternally begets the Son. The language between Father and Son is that of begetting and being begotten. Origen, *Contra Celsum* 6.17 calls the Son the "unborn first-born." The Holy Spirit on the other hand eternally "proceeds" from the Father and the Son (John 15:26; 16:7). Confusion arises when one ignores the eternal aspect and brings time into this relationship. See the discussion on the Nicene Creed in Chapter 1.

[16] The use of the imperfect verb "I had" (*eichon*) in John 17:5 ties in with John 1:1 where the imperfect verb is also used to describe the Word who "was" and thus speaks of the eternal pre-existence of the Word. Costa, *Worship and the Risen Jesus*, 363 n.498.

[17] In John's gospel the word "Son" (*huios*) is *only* used of Jesus to describe his relationship with the Father as God's Son. Believers in John's Gospel are called *teknon*, "children" of God (John 1:12; 8:39; 11:52; 13:33; 21:5). We see the same pattern in the letters of John. Only Jesus

very nature of God (John 5:18; Phil. 2:6). After his resurrection, Jesus tells Mary Magdalene, "I am ascending to my Father and your Father, to my God and your God" (John 20:17). The inference here again is that Jesus shares a relationship with God that is different than others. Note the order, "My Father," and then, "your Father." Jesus could just as easily have said that he was ascending to "our Father." I believe this order is important and deliberate. God is, first and foremost, the Father and God of Jesus (cf. Eph. 1:3), and second, by virtue of our being "in Christ," God is also the Father and God of believers. In John 1:12-13, however, it is Jesus the Son who gives us the authority, right, and power to be children of God. The idea that Jesus is the Son of God is littered throughout the New Testament from beginning to end. He is Son of God at conception (Luke 1:35), and declared to be the Son of God by a Roman centurion at this death, "Truly this man was the Son of God!" (Mark 15:39;[18] cf. Matt. 27:54).[19]

---

is the "Son," whereas believers are "children." The King James Version unfortunately blurs this distinction in the Gospel and letters of John by translating *teknon* as "sons" instead of "children," as the vast number of Bible translations do. This distinction is unique to John's writings (except Revelation). Other New Testament texts use both "sons" and "children" to refer to believers (Romans 8:14; Galatians 3:26; 4:6).

[18] Many scholars take this confession by the centurion to be the climax of the Gospel of Mark. Some believe that it nicely closes the loop that started in Mark 1:1, "The beginning of the gospel of Jesus Christ, the Son of God."

[19] Luke 23:47 has, "Certainly, this man was innocent!" which can also mean, "Certainly this man was a righteous man" (AV; cf. NIV, HCSB). Some critics have tried to argue that there is either a contradiction or that the accounts in Matthew and Mark don't match with Luke's. However, there is no contradiction here, as one gospel does not say Jesus was the Son of God and another that he is not the Son of God. Rather, the most sensible approach is to accept that the Roman centurion said both that Jesus was the Son of God and that he was innocent. One reason Luke focuses on the innocence of Jesus here is due to the fact that this becomes a key theme in his gospel. Jesus is declared to be innocent by four figures in Luke 23: Pilate (23:4, 14-15, 22), Herod (23:15), the crucified criminal (23:41), and the centurion (23:47). The idea of a righteous or innocent person being identified as God's son was held to in some Jewish circles, as attested in the apocryphal book of Wisdom 2:10, 12-13, 16, 18-20. Wisdom 2:13, 17-20 (RSV; italics mine) appears to echo the scene of the taunting at the crucifixion of Jesus: "He professes to have knowledge of God, and calls himself *a child of the Lord* ... Let us see if his words are true, and let us test what will happen at the end of his life; for if *the righteous man is God's son*, he will help him, and will deliver him from the hand of his adversaries. Let us test him with insult and torture, that we may find out how gentle he is, and make trial of his forbearance. Let us condemn him to a shameful death, for, according to what he says, he will be protected."

JESUS IS THE SON OF GOD

It is from these sources that the creed "Jesus is the Son of God" arose in the early church. This creed would likely have been recited alongside the creed we saw in the previous chapter, "Jesus is the Christ." For example in John 20:31, we see how both these titles come together in a compound creed, "But these are written so that you may believe that Jesus is the Christ, the Son of God, and that by believing you may have life in his name." We saw this as well in Peter's confession in Matthew 16:16, "You are the Christ, the Son of the living God." Even prior to Peter's confession, the disciples, after seeing Jesus walking on the water, responded with worship and a confession, "And those in the boat worshiped him, saying, 'Truly you are the Son of God'" (Matt. 14:33). It is important to note that their confession of Jesus as Son of God is connected to their worship. In John 1:49, Nathaniel, after meeting Jesus, addresses him, "Rabbi, you are the Son of God! You are the King of Israel!" Here again we see the confession "Jesus is the Son of God," but this time compounded with the title "King of Israel,"—a title reserved for the Messiah.[20] We saw in the previous chapter how Paul, after being called by the risen Jesus, proclaimed him as the Christ to the Jews (Acts 9:22) but that he also proclaimed that Jesus was the Son of God, "And immediately he proclaimed Jesus in the synagogues, saying, 'He is the Son of God'" (Acts 9:20). This is the first time "Son of God" appears in the book of Acts.[21]

In Paul's opening in Romans 1:3-4, he also cites what is also believed to be a creedal formula, "Concerning his Son, who was descended from David according to the flesh and was declared to be the Son of God in power according to the Spirit of holiness by his resurrection from the dead, Jesus Christ our Lord." This confession, much like 1 Corinthians 15:3-4, is also believed to be

---

Wisdom 2:18 is instructive in terms of Luke 23:47. Note how "the righteous man" is identified as "God's son," so that righteous man equals the son of God. The word "righteous" in Wisdom 2:18 is δίκαιος (*dikaios*), which is the very same word used of Jesus in Luke 23:47, so that even in the confession of the centurion, in declaring Jesus to be "innocent" or "righteous," this would be the equivalent of calling him the Son of God. There is no reason that the centurion could not have said both. On δίκαιος (*dikaios*) see *BDAG*, 246-247.

[20] Note the use of "son" and "king" used of the Messiah in Psalm 2:6-7.

[21] While it is true that the title "Son of God" first appears in Acts 9:20 in application to Jesus, it is nevertheless already *implied* in Acts 2:33, "Being therefore exalted at the right hand of God, and having received from the Father the promise of the Holy Spirit." The use of the word "Father" here in relation to Jesus indirectly suggests a filial relationship. It should also be noted that Acts 2:33 is a trinitarian passage in which the three divine Persons are spoken of. The idea of the Sonship of Jesus in Acts is also reinforced by the fact that Luke, who is also the author of Acts, understands Jesus to be the Son of God throughout his gospel.

pre-Pauline and may have been received from the Jerusalem apostles. I. Howard Marshall notes, "This text has long been recognized as a pre-Pauline formula elaborated by Paul."[22] Martin Hengel has also argued that when Paul uses Son of God language of Jesus, "it was kept for exceptional usage, at the climax of certain theological statements."[23] Note also how Paul speaks here of the hypostatic union present in Jesus.[24] Jesus was truly man "according to the flesh," descended from David, and yet "was declared to be the Son of God in power according to the Spirit of holiness by his resurrection from the dead." The supreme declaration of Jesus as the Son of God in power was his resurrection from the dead. Here we see how closely connected Jesus' identity as Son of God is to the resurrection.

There may also be an anti-imperialist statement in Romans 1:3-4 as the word translated "declared" can also be translated as "appointed" (NET). This would be the language of the accession of an emperor to the throne, which would be the highest status in the empire. In other words, Paul may be employing imperialist language to show that Jesus has been appointed to the highest status in the cosmos. We saw in Chapter 5 how the confession of Jesus as Lord was based on his resurrection (Rom 10:9), but Paul shows us that the creed "Jesus is the Son of God" also rests on his resurrection.

In 1 John 5:1 it states that anyone who believes the creed that Jesus is the Christ has been born of God. In 1 John 5:5 he goes on to write, "Who is it that overcomes the world except the one who believes that Jesus is the Son of God?" Notice how these two creeds are mentioned in close proximity to one another. Again the second use of the word "that" in 1 John 5:5 is ὅτι (*hoti*) which, as we already noted, is an indicator that what follows—"Jesus is the Son of God"—is a quotation. The confession that Jesus is the Son of God is crucial because, in 1 John 4:15, it signals whether or not God abides in someone, "Whoever confesses that Jesus is the Son of God, God abides in him, and he in God." As we have seen, the creed "Jesus is the Son of God" points to his deity, but implicit in it is also the belief that the pre-existent Son was *sent* into the world. 1 John 4:14 states, "And we have seen and testify that the Father has sent his Son to be the Savior of the world." There are many other

---

[22] Marshall, *Origins of New Testament Christology*, 118.
[23] Hengel, *The Son of God*, 14.
[24] Passages like Romans 1:3-4; 9:5 and Philippians 2:6-11 may have anticipated the Chalcedonian Creed where the doctrine of the two natures of Christ in one person was formulated in AD 451.

Jesus is the Son of God

passages where Jesus speaks of having been sent from the Father (John 3:16-17), and how he "came down from heaven" (John 6:38, 41-42, 51, 58; cf. Phil. 2:6-11). This is clearly seen in Philippians 2:6-11, where Paul mentions how the pre-existent Son partook of human nature, suffered, died, and was highly exalted by God. As we shall see, Philippians 2:6-11 is also believed to be pre-Pauline, which brings this text even closer to the Jerusalem church and the apostles. This demonstrates that belief in Jesus as the pre-existent Son was already held by the earliest Christian community. Hurtado notes that, "the idea of Jesus' pre-existence was circulating among [Christian] adherents within the first decades of the Christian movement."[25]

There are early formulae in several New Testament passages where the title Son of God is associated with the pre-existence of Jesus and his having been sent into the world, such as Romans 8:3 and Galatians 4:4-6 (cf. Col. 1:15-20). As we noted, the Pauline letters are believed to be the earliest texts in the New Testament, a point that even liberal scholars will grant. These passages also speak of God *sending* his Son, a formula which presupposes the Son's pre-existence. Some critics have argued that these "sending" passages are only developed much later in the Gospel of John, but this view is certainly incorrect as we have already noted that they are present in the earliest New Testament texts. Simon Gathercole has shown that we already have the idea of the pre-existent Son being sent in the Synoptic Gospels of Matthew, Mark, and Luke.[26]

As we already saw anti-imperialist statements within the previous creeds, the same applies to the creed "Jesus is the Son of God." One of the titles that the Roman emperor appropriated to himself was that of "son of God." This practice began in the first century BC with Augustus Caesar: "When Roman law in 42 BC deified Julius Caesar, the status of Octavius, who took the name Augustus, was strengthened by adding the phrase 'son of God.'"[27] The Latin title *divi filius* ("son of God") was first used by Augustus Caesar, who ruled when Jesus was born (Luke 2:1). Temples were also erected to Augustus throughout the empire and he was even considered "a god" worthy to receive

---

[25] Hurtado, *Lord Jesus Christ*, 364-365.
[26] For a full treatment on this subject see Simon J. Gathercole, *The Pre-Existent Son: Recovering the Christologies of Matthew, Mark, and Luke* (Grand Rapids/Cambridge: Eerdmans, 2006).
[27] John Dart, "Up Against Caesar," SBL Forum, Society of Biblica Literature, http://sblsite.org/Article.aspx?ArticleID=388, accessed April 17, 2020.

sacrifice.[28] Even the Roman emperor Caligula (r. AD 37–AD 41) desired to be addressed as "Lord" and attempted to place his idol in the Jerusalem temple.[29] But when Christians confessed the creed "Jesus is the Son of God," it also constituted a rejection of Caesar as son of God. The Roman authorities would not have found it difficult to accept Jesus as a son of God insofar as Jesus was only one among many other sons of god. It was only the Christian's exclusive claim that Jesus was a Son of God over the emperor that resulted in their clash with Rome. The Romans did, however, have an awe for divine figures who were presumed to be the son or sons of a god.[30] Unlike the emperors who died and remained dead, however, Jesus was the true Son of God, who was raised and declared to be God's Son in power (Rom. 1:3-4).

The creed "Jesus is the Son of God," like the creed "Jesus is Lord," would have been confessed by early believers at their baptism. In the story of the conversion of the Ethiopian eunuch to the Christian faith we find an interesting twist. If you go to Acts 8:37, and have any modern translation, you will probably notice that verse 36 is immediately followed by verse 38. Some words may be italicized or there may be a footnote mentioning that some manuscripts have an addition in this place or some words may be italicized. In Acts 8:36, the eunuch, after hearing the good news about Jesus from Philip, desires to be baptized upon seeing a body of water. In verse 38, Philip goes into the water with the eunuch and baptizes him. What could be missing here? A good Baptist might respond—where is the eunuch's testimony and confession of faith in Christ? The fact is that no such confession exists in the original copy of Acts. This omission even seemed strange to later scribes who felt that the story seemed incomplete without a confession of some sort on the part of the eunuch. It is no surprise, then, that in later manuscripts we find that a confession or creed has been inserted in what is Acts 8:37. This later interpolation is found in some older translations such as the AV, "And Philip said, If thou believest with all thine heart, thou mayest. And he answered and said, I believe that Jesus Christ is the Son of God." Notice that in this addition to the text,

---

[28] Virgil, *Ecl.* 1.6-8.
[29] Costa, *Worship and the Risen Jesus*, 236.
[30] We get a glimpse of this idea in John 19:8-9. When Pilate heard that Jesus had claimed to be the Son of God (19:7), we read, "When Pilate heard this statement, he was even more afraid. He entered his headquarters again and said to Jesus, 'Where are you from?' But Jesus gave him no answer." It is interesting that Pilate asks about Jesus' origin, considering that Jesus may be a divine being or one of the sons of a god.

JESUS IS THE SON OF GOD

Philip tells the eunuch he may be baptized if he believes with all his heart, and the eunuch responds by confessing his belief in Jesus Christ as the Son of God. Note that both Christ and Son of God appear here, as we saw in John 20:31 and Matthew 16:16. This addition in verse 37 sounds like a creed and was most likely added sometime in the second century AD as it was known to several Church Fathers such as Irenaeus, Cyprian, Tertullian and other Christian writers.[31] It reflected a confession or creed that was already current in the second century when Christians were baptized. Already in the second century AD, we can see that belief in Jesus as the Christ and Son of God was a standard creed. Justin Martyr himself attests, "And we have been taught, and are convinced, and do believe ... that Jesus is the Christ and the Son of God."[32]

So, we have seen how the term son of God is used in various ways in the Bible and that context is crucial in determining its meaning. While it can refer to angels, the first man Adam, the nation of Israel as a corporate group, the Davidic king, and even to Christian believers, it is used in a unique way when referring to Jesus. The true and fullest expression of what it means to be son of God is found in Jesus who is the eternal and unique Son of God. And as the Son of God, he became human, so that through him, many more might also become sons of God (Gal. 3:26).

---

[31] F.F. Bruce, *The Book of the Acts*, NICNT, rev. ed. (Grand Rapids: Eerdmans, 1988), 178.
[32] Justin Martyr, *First Apology*, 10, 17–18, 54.

8
THE CHRISTIAN *SHEMA*
1 CORINTHIANS 8:6

In Chapter 2, we discussed the creeds in the Old Testament as a forerunner to the creeds of the New Testament. We looked at the *Shema* in Deuteronomy 6:4 which reads, "Hear, O Israel: The LORD our God, the LORD is one." As we saw, monotheism is at the heart of this creed as it affirms both the unity and sovereignty of God against all other gods. God is one. The *Shema* also appears in the Gospels. Jesus, himself a Jew, would likely have been familiar with it and would have confessed it during his earthly life. The *Shema* appears in all the Synoptic Gospels (Matt. 22:34-40; Mark 12:28-34; Luke 10:25-28).

In Mark 12:28-30, a scribe asked Jesus a question about the most important commandment:

> And one of the scribes came up and heard them disputing with one another, and seeing that he answered them well, asked him, "Which commandment is the most important of all?" Jesus answered, "The most important is, 'Hear, O Israel: The Lord our God, the Lord is one. And you shall love the Lord your God with all your heart and with all your soul and with all your mind and with all your strength.'"

Jesus affirms the *Shema* here as the most important commandment of all because it is centered first and foremost on God himself. We noted that the *Shema* is theocentric as it focuses on the unity of God and our love and devotion to him. The centrality of God and his unity runs throughout the Old Testament, and Jesus himself here acknowledged this creed as the first and foremost commandment. An interesting transition takes place, however, in the New Testament, where the creeds become more and more Christocentric. We have already seen this in the creeds we have examined above.

The New Testament affirms the *Shema* and its monotheistic emphasis by echoing its words on the unity of God. This can be seen in such passages as, "God is one" (Gal. 3:20), "one God and Father of all" (Eph. 4:6), "For there is one God" (1 Tim. 2:5), "there is no God but one" (1 Cor 8:4), and "You believe that God is one" (Jas. 2:19). The importance and the centrality of the *Shema* in Israel's history and identity cannot be overstated. It would have been confessed twice a day by every devout Jew, both in the morning and in the evening. The famous Rabbi Akiva, in the second century AD, while being tortured to death by the Romans for teaching the Torah, recited the *Shema*. His last word, which he uttered according to tradition, was the last word of the *Shema*: "one" (*echad*; Hebrew).[1]

In the New Testament, as we shall see, Paul renovates the *Shema* from Deuteronomy 6:4 into a kind of Christian version. It should be noted that Paul was well versed in the Torah, and often speaks of how he had advanced beyond many of his peers in Judaism, and was very zealous "for the traditions of my fathers" (Gal. 1:14). Paul also states, "[I was] educated at the feet of Gamaliel according to the strict manner of the law of our fathers" (Acts 22:3). Gamaliel was a "teacher of the law held in honor by all the people" (Acts 5:34) and is even recognized in rabbinic literature as "a highly esteemed first-century [AD] Jewish leader, scholar, and teacher."[2] It is interesting to note that at one point it is Gamaliel who calls for tolerance between the Jewish leaders and the new Messianic movement of the Christian church. His advice was to leave them alone (Acts 5:34-40). It seems this advice was not taken by one of his stellar students, Saul of Tarsus, also known as Paul. It would be fair to say that Paul

---

[1] *b. Brachot.* 61a.

[2] Levine and Brettler, eds., *Jewish Annotated New Testament*, 232. Reference is made to the rabbinic source in *m. Sot.* 9.15. There were a number of notable teachers by this name, but the one who taught Paul was Gamaliel I, also sometimes called "the Elder." He was also called Rambam Gamaliel, the title "Rambam" usually being reserved for highly influential and esteemed teachers. There are a number of interesting points about Gamaliel found in rabbinic literature which seemed to resonate in the character of Paul. Many disciples of Gamaliel were taught "Greek wisdom" (*b. Sotah.* 49b). This would explain Paul's knowledge of Greek literature which he cites in his sermons (Acts 17:28) and letters (1 Corinthians 15:33; Titus 1:12). Gamaliel is also recorded to have gone into a Greco-Roman bath house where a statue of the Greek goddess Aphrodite was present. When challenged, Gamaliel defended his action by claiming the statue was merely for decorative purposes and that the statue was not dedicated to the goddess (*m. Avodah Zarah* 3:4). This appears to have some similarity with what Paul says about what some in Corinth were saying about idols such as "an idol has no real existence" (1 Corinthians 8:5). While Paul agrees, in part, that an idol has no real existence, he also later warns them that what is offered to idols is in fact offered to demons (1 Corinthians 10:19-20). Paul seems to be primarily concerned with the kind of interaction between man and idol. A modern example would be a Christian going to a Chinese restaurant where there are Buddhist or Chinese idols, or an Indian restaurant with pictures of Hindu gods. Would it be permissible for a Christian to eat there? Most would say "yes" because one is eating and giving God thanks and not worshipping the idols present there. Entering a temple to worship such idols and eat food offered to them would be idolatry and this seems to be the issue Paul is addressing in 1 Corinthians 8-10. On food offered to idols see Costa, *Worship and the Risen Jesus*, 129-140.

was trained by one of the best teachers available to him and would have been qualified to speak on a central Jewish tenet such as the *Shema*. He does so in 1 Corinthians 8:6, "Yet for us there is one God, the Father, from whom are all things and for whom we exist, and one Lord, Jesus Christ, through whom are all things and through whom we exist."

In 1 Corinthians 8, Paul begins by addressing the issue of idols and whether it was permissible to offer food to them. He points out to them the truth that there is "no God but one" (1 Cor. 8:4). Paul moves on to distinguish the one true God and Lord over against the polytheistic gods and lords of the Greek world. In the Greco-Roman world of his day, it is true that Paul acknowledged, "For although there may be so-called gods in heaven or on earth—as indeed there are many 'gods' and many 'lords'" (1 Cor. 8:5). Yet he then proceeds to argue in contrast that "for us there is one God, the Father, from whom are all things and for whom we exist, and one Lord, Jesus Christ, through whom are all things and through whom we exist" (1 Cor. 8:6). This passage is also a creed. It contains a two-clause, or bipartite, creedal statement as opposed to a single, simple-clause creed like "Jesus is Lord" because it addresses two persons: the Father and the Son. This creed affirms the Christian belief in the oneness of God and, at the same time, the oneness of the Lord Jesus in contrast to the many gods and lords of the Greco-Roman world (1 Cor. 8:5).

Paul states that to the Christian believer there is one God, who is the Father, and one Lord, who is Jesus. The use of "one" before God and Lord should not be missed. In Paul's letters the word "God" is generally used of the Father, and the word "Lord" is generally used of the Son.[3] It should also

---

[3] There are clearly exceptions to this rule. Paul sometimes refers to Jesus as "God," as seen in Titus 2:13 and most probably in Romans 9:5 The issue in Romans 9:5 is not so much a textual-critical one, but rather a question of punctuation. See Costa, *Worship and the Risen Jesus*, 323 n.71; Raymond E. Brown, *An Introduction to New Testament Christology* (New York: Paulist Press, 1994), 182-183. For a full treatment and assessment of Romans 9:5 and alternative translations of this text see Harris, *Jesus as God*, 143-172; Reymond, *Jesus*, 272-277. I agree with Harris, Reymond, and other scholars that Jesus is clearly called "God" in Romans 9:5. For a differing position see Fee, *Pauline Christology*, 272-278. Paul refers to Jesus as "deity" in Colossians 2:9. The witness of the Apostolic Fathers in the early second and mid-second century regarding the deity or Christ is undoubtedly clear. It should be noted that Ignatius died in AD 110, over 200 years before the Council of Nicaea in AD 325. Ignatius writes, "Being united and elected through the true passion by the will of the Father, and Jesus Christ, our God ... There is one Physician who is possessed both of flesh and spirit; both made and not made; God existing in flesh; true life in death; both of Mary and of God; first passible and then impassible, even Jesus Christ our Lord ... For our God, Jesus Christ, was, according to the appointment of God, conceived in the womb by Mary, of the seed of David." Ignatius, *Letter to the Ephesians*, Greeting; 7:2; 18:2.

be noted that the terms "God" and "Lord" are both divine titles used in Deuteronomy 6:4, especially in the LXX, which is what Paul mostly quotes in his letters. Recall that the Greek word for "Lord" is used in the LXX in place of the Divine Name, Yahweh. Deuteronomy 6:4 (LXX) reads, "Hear, O Israel, The Lord our God is one Lord." Notice that the word "God" appears once, and "Lord" twice. We also see the word "one." Even though Paul is speaking of two divine Persons here, he maintains a strict monotheism. I have argued in an earlier work that "it would seem inconceivable for Paul as a monotheist (1 Cor. 8:4–6; Gal. 3:20; cf. 1 Tim. 2:5) to place Jesus alongside of God as another god. Paul conceives of the risen Jesus as being *included* within the divine identity not *added* to the divine identity."[4]

The same terms used for deity in Deuteronomy 6:4 are also used by Paul in 1 Corinthians 8:6 so that Paul appears to be identifying "God" in the *Shema* with the Father, and "Lord" with Jesus the Son.[5] In all this it should be noted that there is no sense in which monotheism is being undermined. Fee correctly notes that "such worship obviously includes Christ in the divine identity, while always maintaining unwavering monotheism."[6]

In the first clause of 1 Corinthians 8:6, Paul states that from the Father "are all things and for whom we exist." This is the language of source; all things come "from" the Father and all things, including creation, exist "for" him. All that exists has its source in God the Father. It is for this reason that the Apostles' Creed begins with the words, "I believe in God, the Father almighty, creator of heaven and earth," and the Nicene Creed begins with, "We believe in one God, the Father almighty, Maker of heaven and earth, of all things visible and invisible."

In the second clause, Paul states that the Son is "one Lord, Jesus Christ, through whom are all things and through whom we exist." Notice that Paul speaks of the Son here as the "Lord, Jesus Christ." We see in his name the titles "Lord" and "Christ"—words that are also part of the single-clause creeds confessed by early Christians that we saw in Chapters 5 and 6. Paul also states of the Son that in him "are all things and through whom we exist." The language now is that of agency, seen in the word "through." All things came

---

Justin Martyr in his *Dialogue with Trypho the Jew* also testifies, "that Christ is called both God and Lord of hosts ... as deserving to be worshipped, as God and as Christ ... He who is both God and the Angel, sent by the Father." Justin Martyr, *Dial.* 36, 63, 126.

[4] Costa, *Worship and the Risen Jesus*, 384 n.189 (italics in original).
[5] Fee, *Pauline Christology*, 49, 445, 551.
[6] Fee, *Pauline Christology*, 493.

THE CHRISTIAN *SHEMA*

into existence *through* the Lord Jesus Christ, and it is *through* him that we exist. It is important to note a strong confession here of the deity of Christ, especially in his role as Creator of all things. We already addressed the pre-existence of the Son, and logically he would have to be if he is also the Creator of all things. Scripture repeatedly speaks of God as the Creator of "all things" (Isa. 44:24; 66:1-2).[7] The language of agency is generally used of the Son in his role in creation. We see this elsewhere in the New Testament where it is through the Word that all things are made (John 1:1-3,10), and through the Son that God that the universe came into being (Heb. 1:2b). Paul also uses it in Colossians 1:15-20, a passage which speaks of the Son as the Creator of all things and has been called "the summit" of Pauline Christology.[8] It is also *through* the Son that believers exist. In short, all things are made and come *from* the one God, Father, and through the one Lord, Jesus Christ.[9]

As we saw in the first chapter, the language of agency as it pertains to the Son is attested to in the Nicene Creed when it says of Christ, "through whom all things were made." What Paul has done to the *Shema* is adapted it into a kind of Christianized version, where the "Lord" and "God" from Deuteronomy 6:4 are taken to be the Father and Son of the Godhead. The absence of the Holy Spirit here, of course, does not undermine the doctrine of the Trinity, and Christians also need to take the rest of Scripture into consideration. In another letter, Paul also writes that "there is one body and *one Spirit*—just as

---

[7] In Isaiah 44:24 it states, "Thus says the LORD, your Redeemer, who formed you from the womb: 'I am the LORD, *who made all things*, who alone stretched out the heavens, who spread out the earth by myself'" (italics mine). In the LXX of Isaiah 44:24 the word "Lord" is used, the same word Paul uses in 1 Corinthians 8:6 for Jesus. Note in this passage how the Lord "made all things," but that he also stretched out the heavens "alone" and spread out the earth "by myself." This language safeguards the unity of God, just as Paul does by using the word "one" of both the Father and the Son.

[8] A. Feuillet, *Le Christ: Sagesse de Dieu, d'après les épîtres Pauliniennes* (Paris: J. Gabalda et Cie, 1966), 271.

[9] Philo of Alexandria, a contemporary of Paul, also used this language of God, "for you will find that God is the cause [*aitios*] of it [the world], by [*hupo*] whom it was made ... that the instrument is the word of God, by means [*dia*] of which it was made." Philo, *Cher.* 1.127. Philo uses the Greek word *aitios* for God which means "reason, cause, source," Louw and Nida, *Greek-English Lexicon*, 89.15. He then mentions the "word of God" in relation to the means by which the world was made and uses the preposition *dia*, which denotes agency or means and is also communicated by the word "through." Paul uses this particular preposition in 1 Corinthians 8:6 in relation to the Son. It is interesting how Paul also sees the "word of God" as the instrumental means by which the world was created. The word *aitios* ("cause" or "source") is also used of Jesus as the source of eternal salvation in Hebrews 5:9, "And being made perfect, he became the source of eternal salvation to all who obey him."

you were called to the one hope that belongs to your call—*one Lord*, one faith, one baptism, *one God and Father of all*, who is over all and through all and in all" (Eph. 4:4-6; italics mine). Note the repeated use of the adjective "one." Even in 1 Corinthians, when Paul speaks of various gifts and services, he acknowledges that they all come respectively from "the *same* Spirit ... the *same* Lord ... the *same* God" (1 Cor 12:4-6; italics mine).[10]

The "Christian *Shema*," as presented in 1 Corinthians 8:6, is revolutionary in theological thinking. Here, Paul places Jesus of Nazareth on the same level of divine identity as God himself, and it was Jesus himself who challenged his hearers and followers to see this very truth in his identity, ministry, and life. Even though 1 Corinthians is an early letter, written some twenty years or so after the death and resurrection of Jesus, we already see the ascribing of divinity to Jesus. This demonstrates that the deity of Christ was not a late invention, but rather accepted very early on in the Christian movement. What we see in 1 Corinthians 8:6 and other passages like this, is a very early high Christology.[11] The centrality of this doctrine was so emphasized that Philip Schaff comments:

> This doctrine [the divinity of Christ] was the kernel of all the baptismal creeds, and was stamped upon the entire life, constitution and worship of the early church. It was not only expressly asserted by the fathers against heretics, but also professed in the daily and weekly worship, in the celebration of baptism, the eucharist and the annual festivals, especially Easter. It was embodied in prayers, doxologies and hymns of praise. From the earliest record Christ was the object not of admiration which is given to finite persons and things, and presupposes equality, but of prayer, praise and adoration which is due only to an infinite, uncreated, divine being. This is evident from several passages of the New Testament.[12]

The classical historian James O'Donnell also summarizes this point well when he states,

---

[10] Both 1 Corinthians 12:4-6 and Ephesians 4:4-6 are examples among others of "triadic passages" in the Pauline letters. Costa, *Worship and the Risen Jesus*, 316-317 n.18.
[11] On early high Christology, see Hurtado, *Lord Jesus Christ*.
[12] Philip Schaff, *History of the Christian Church* (New York: Charles Scribner's Sons, 1910), 1:530.

It is characteristic of Christian doctrine to hold ... that *the worship of Jesus Christ*, the Son of God, is ... *the only way* to salvation ... this insistence on the exclusivity [of their beliefs] more than an annoyance; it threatens the whole basis of the peaceful coexistence of religious cults in society.[13]

While early Christians remained completely dedicated to monotheism and would even die for such a belief, they nevertheless came to see monotheism through the lenses of the incarnation of the Son and the outpouring of the Holy Spirit. They came to understand that within the Godhead, there was a plurality of Persons. While the immediate context of 1 Corinthians 8:6 addresses two of these Persons—the Father and the Son—the whole witness of Scriptures attests to the Triune nature of God as Father, Son, and Holy Spirit.

---

[13] James O'Donnell, "The Demise of Paganism," *Traditio* 35 (1979): 45-88.

Part 2
Hymns

9
WHAT ARE HYMNS?

I have defined a hymn as follows:

> A song or hymn is not worship itself, but it functions as a vehicle or level of action whereby worship is expressed vocally by the [Christian] faith community and takes on a communicative aspect in that God or the risen Jesus are the implied referents. In this respect a song or a hymn functions as a subset of worship.[1]

The use of hymns or spiritual songs as identity markers in a religious context can be probably understood when one considers the purpose of one's national anthem. I am not claiming that hymns and national anthems are the same thing or that they are synonymous with one another, rather, they both function as identity markers. A national anthem asserts one's identity within their nation to show solidarity with their country. The national anthem of a given people express what they believe about themselves as a nation. National anthems can also contain historical references, such as the American "Star-Spangled Banner" which recounts the historical attack on Fort McHenry in Baltimore Harbour by British forces in the war of 1812.

Most of us are familiar with traditional church hymns such as "Amazing Grace" and "Blessed Assurance." Such hymns are an attempt to declare in song what Christians already believe in their minds and hearts. Hymns sometimes can function as creeds put to music, as both hymns and creeds can be in many cases interchangeable with each other. In this way, hymns often function as creeds, as Stauffer has argued, "Many hymns were creed-like."[2] I have also argued that "hymns thus appear to function as prayers put to music."[3] Augustine is reputed to have said (although the origin of this saying is debated), that "he who sings, prays twice." We especially see this dual function at work throughout the Psalter.

---

[1] Costa, *Worship and the Risen Jesus*, 217.
[2] Stauffer, *New Testament Theology*, 237.
[3] Costa, *Worship and the Risen Jesus*, 207.

EARLY CHRISTIAN CREEDS AND HYMNS

What do we do with ancient hymns? We know from the superscripts of many of the Psalms that song played a crucial part in the worship of God's people. For example, "To the choirmaster: with stringed instruments" (Ps. 4, 6, 76); "To the choirmaster: the flutes" (Ps. 5); "To the choirmaster: according to the gittith (probably a musical instrument) (Ps. 8); and "A song at the dedication of the temple" (Ps. 30). There are many others. Psalms 120–134 are also called the "Song of Ascents" which were probably sung during festival times. Are these superscripts inspired? Some would debate this, but Old Testament scholar Bruce Waltke believes they are indeed part of the sacred text and argues that scribes "neither alter nor omit them. No ancient version or Hebrew manuscript omits them."[4] The problem we moderns face is that unlike the masterpieces of Mozart, Bach, and Beethoven, the Bible supplies us with no such musical notations for its hymns.

As we saw in Chapter 1, we know that the people of God often put what they believed into song. God instructed Moses, "Now therefore write this song and teach it to the people of Israel. Put it in their mouths, that this song may be a witness for me against the people of Israel" (Deut. 31:19). Notice how this song was to be written down and taught to the people of Israel, which Moses later did (Deut. 31:22; cf. 31:30; 32:44). We also find the Song of Moses contained in Exodus 15:1–18, and the Song of Deborah in Judges 5. David also sang a song to Yahweh after being delivered from his enemies (2 Sam. 22:1) and placed men in charge of the service of song in the house of Yahweh (1 Chr. 6:31; cf. 2 Chr. 29:27).[5] One of the books in the Bible is also known as The Song of Solomon, which opens with the words, "The Song of Songs, which is Solomon's" (Song. 1:1). Even God is spoken of as singing over his people, "The LORD your God is in your midst, a mighty one who will save; he will rejoice over you with gladness; he will quiet you by his love; he will exult over you with loud singing" (Zeph. 3:17). Revelation 15:3 speaks about the saints singing "the song of Moses" and "the song of the Lamb" before God. Both the songs of Moses and the Lamb appear to connect the people of God in the Old Testament with the people of God in the New Testament. These songs, or hymns, demonstrate that the people of God are organically connected with one another through history. Unfortunately, what these songs would have sounded like when put to music is lost to us.

---

[4] Waltke with Yu, *Old Testament Theology*, 872.
[5] This is also attested in the Apocrypha (1 Maccabees 4:54; 2 Maccabees 1:30; Sirach 50:18).

WHAT ARE HYMNS?

We also know that members of the Qumran community had songs in their worship services. They believed that whenever they sang in worship, they were joining with the heavenly choirs in glorifying God. Geza Vermes, commenting on the worship practices of the Qumran community states:

> According to the Bible, the first duty of the heavenly beings—the Seraphim of Isaiah, the Cherubim of Ezekiel, and the angels of Psalm 148—is the praise and worship of God; and so it was for the followers of the Teacher of Righteousness [leader of the Qumran community]. They were to join their voices to those of the Angels of the Presence raised in prayer and blessing in the celestial Temple.[6]

In the New Testament, we also find hymns in the first chapter of the Gospel of Luke, such as the songs of Mary (Luke 1:46-55),[7] and Zechariah (Luke 1:67-79).[8] After Jesus shared the Passover meal with his disciples, they sang a hymn (Matt. 26:30; Mark 14:26) which may have been one or more of the *Hallel* (praise) psalms.[9] There are also a string of hymns offered to God and the victorious Lamb in Revelation 4-5, 7, and 15.

We know from extra-biblical sources that when Christians gathered for worship, they would often sing. Recall the letter which Pliny the Younger wrote to the Roman emperor Trajan in around AD 111-AD 113, which we examined above. Here he writes that Christians,

> On a stated day [Sunday?] they had been accustomed to meet before daybreak and to *recite a hymn among themselves to Christ, as though he were a god,* and that so far from binding themselves by oath to commit any crime, their oath was to abstain from theft, robbery, adultery, and

---

[6] Vermes, *Dead Sea Scrolls*, 42.

[7] Mary's song is called the Magnificat, taken from the Latin which means to magnify.

[8] While Zechariah is said to prophesy over the infant John the Baptist, the language in these verses is that of a hymn, sometimes called in Latin, the *Benedictus*, "Blessed be ..." (Luke 1:68). See Robert H. Stein, *Luke*, The New American Commentary (Nashville: B&H Publishing, 1992), 99. The *Gloria in Excelsis Deo* ("Glory to God in the Highest") became a well-known hymn in the second and third centuries AD and was based on Luke 2:13-14. The text does not explicitly say that the angelic hosts sang, but that they were "praising God." It was, nevertheless, taken later by Christians as a hymn of praise.

[9] The *Hallel* psalms were comprised of Psalms 113-118. See Costa, *Worship and the Risen Jesus*, 206-207.

from breach of faith, and not to deny trust money placed in their keeping when called upon to deliver it.[10]

The early date of this document is important. It was written at the beginning of the second century AD, probably more than a decade after the death of John the apostle. Here Pliny clearly describes Christians reciting a hymn among themselves, which shows that from an early period, Christians were already in the habit of singing hymns in their worship gatherings. The fact that they chose to "recite a hymn among themselves" seems to indicate they had already learned this hymn and all knew the words. That they recited this hymn to Christ "as though he were a god" demonstrates, as has been shown, that Jesus was already worshipped in the earliest Christian communities. In a sense, this adoration could be called a *Carmen Christi*, or hymn to Christ.

Several hymns of the earliest Christian movement can also be found in the New Testament. While there are several passages that explicitly mention hymns and songs, others are more embedded in the text. How do we know when there is a hymn in the text? There are grammatical indicators which scholars have detected that reveal signs of such hymns. As we will see, hymns were a central feature of Christian worship. In fact, they were so central that Larry Hurtado has argued that they "are a characteristic feature of early Christian worship."[11] Hymns were generally sung and seemed to be intended for use in a communal setting.[12] We already see the practice with Paul and Silas when they were imprisoned in Philippi, "About midnight Paul and Silas were praying and singing hymns to God, and the prisoners were listening to them" (Acts 16:25). Notice how they are "praying and singing hymns to God," which shows that Christian worship was already characterized by these two actions. Notice as well that the singing of hymns here is communal, it was *both* Paul and Silas who were singing, which may even have been learned in Christian worship settings. We see the same combination of prayer and singing in James 5:13, "Is anyone among you suffering? Let him pray. Is anyone cheerful? Let him sing praise." Again, here we see that praying and singing go together. We can deduce from these passages how important singing hymns

---

[10] Pliny the Younger, *Letters* 10:96 (italics mine). On Pliny's letter and how it relates to hymns see Costa, *Worship and the Risen Jesus*, 208-209.

[11] Hurtado, *Lord Jesus Christ*, 146.

[12] Costa, *Worship and the Risen Jesus*, 205.

WHAT ARE HYMNS?

were to the earliest Christians. We now turn our attention to some New Testament passages that clearly mention hymns in the church.

10
Hymns Edify the Church
1 Corinthians 14:26

In 1 Corinthians 14:26 Paul addresses the subject of Christian worship and spiritual gifts within the wider context of 1 Corinthians 12-14. In it he writes, "What then, brothers? When you come together, each one has a hymn, a lesson, a revelation, a tongue, or an interpretation. Let all things be done for building up." It is important to note the phrase "when you come together." This is an expression Paul uses when referring to the gathering of Christian believers, and does so only in 1 Corinthians (see also 1 Cor. 11:17-18,20,33-34). In an age where many immature Christians think that coming together for worship is not mandated in Scripture, passages like this one, and Hebrews 10:25, stand as an important rebuke. It is also important to realize that, "[t]he underlying tenor in Paul's wording here is the importance of the communal gathering of the faith community where in such a context, worship is supposed to occur."[1] The order Paul presents here is that of "a hymn, a lesson, a revelation, a tongue, or an interpretation." It is interesting to note that Paul mentions a hymn first in the list, especially in light of the fact that most of our church services today begin with a greeting or prayer and then move on to singing before the preaching of the Word.[2] Though we can't be sure if the list Paul provides is a definite order of worship, it is clear that singing was integral to Christian worship.

The language also indicates that there may have been more than one hymn sung in the church. While the ESV, NIV, RSV, NRSV have "hymn" in this passage, other translations—namely the AV, NKJV, ASV, NASB, HCSB, and NJB—have the word "psalm," and the NET even translate it as "song." The actual Greek word Paul uses in 1 Corinthians 14:26 is ψαλμός (*psalmos*), which means "psalm"; this is the only place in Paul's letters where he mentions it in the singular. It is because of passages like 1 Corinthians 14:26 that historic Reformed churches have made the singing of Psalms a substantial part

---

[1] Costa, *Worship and the Risen Jesus*, 210.
[2] I am thinking mainly of churches in the evangelical and Protestant traditions.

of their worship service, with some even arguing that *only* the Psalms should be sung in church. This tradition of singing Psalms has deep roots among Reformers such as John Calvin, who saw the Psalms as inspired songs to be sung by God's people.[3] The sole use of the singular *psalmos* (psalm) in 1 Corinthians 14:26 is yet another example of a *hapax legomenon*. According to Louw and Nida, the *psalmos* in 1 Corinthians 14:26 means "a song of praise."[4] It is probably from this understanding that the translators of the ESV, NIV, RSV, and NRSV translated this word as "hymn."

There is a specific Greek word for "hymn," and it is ὕμνος (*hymnos*); it is also used elsewhere by Paul and will be examined in the next chapter.[5] The differing translations here suggests that the translators saw the terms "psalm" and "hymn" as synonymous.[6] Philo of Alexandria (ca. 20 BC-ca. AD 50), a Hellenistic Jew and a contemporary of the apostle Paul, also spoke of the Psalms as "hymns."[7]

Paul sees the use of hymns, or psalms, in the church as having an end goal: "Let all things be done for building up." While hymns have a vertical dimension—we worship God through them—they also have a horizontal dimension—we edify each other as we sing with one voice to God. Another point needs to be made here. Only the Triune God is the rightful recipient of hymn singing; we sing to *God* and no one else in our worship gatherings. A man who courts a woman may serenade her, but he does not sing a hymn or psalm in worship of her. Hymns are ultimately aimed to glorify God.

---

[3] John Calvin in his *Preface to the Genevan Psalter* stated: "Wherefore, although we look far and wide and search on every hand, we shall not find better songs nor songs better suited to that end than the Psalms of David which the Holy Spirit made and uttered through him. And for this reason, when we sing them we may be certain that God puts the words, in our mouths as if Himself sang in us to exalt His glory."

[4] Louw and Nida, *Greek-English Lexicon*, 33.112; *BDAG*, 1096.

[5] Costa, *Worship and the Risen Jesus*, 211.

[6] Costa, *Worship and the Risen Jesus*, 414 n.562.

[7] *Plant.* 1.29; *Fug.* 1.59; *Conf.* 1.39; *Mig.* 1.157.

11
HYMNS SUNG TO THE LORD JESUS AND GOD THE FATHER
COLOSSIANS 3:16 AND EPHESIANS 5:19

In 1 Corinthians 14:26, Paul mentions hymns and songs being used in the worship gathering of the church. We will now see to whom these hymns were addressed by looking at two passages: Ephesians 5:19, and Colossians 3:16. We will set them side by side as the language in both of these letters is very similar.

> Let the word of Christ dwell in you richly, teaching and admonishing one another in all wisdom, singing psalms and hymns and spiritual songs, with thankfulness in your hearts to God (Col. 3:16);

> Addressing one another in psalms and hymns and spiritual songs, singing and making melody to the Lord with all your heart (Eph. 5:19).

Many scholars have noticed the similarity in language and content between the Ephesians and Colossians passages.[1] In fact, it is possible that the letter sent to the Ephesians was actually an encyclical letter meant to be circulated throughout the churches of Asia Minor (modern-day Turkey). One of the reasons for thinking this is that Paul mentions in Colossians 4:16 that he wants them to circulate his letter and also to read "the letter from Laodicea" that he wrote. Where is this so-called "letter to the Laodiceans"?[2] Some believe that this letter is what we know today as the letter to the Ephesians. This is a possibility. If you look at Ephesians 1:1 and have a critical apparatus with footnotes in your Bible, you will notice that the best and earliest manuscripts of Ephesians do

---

[1] D.A. Carson and Douglas Moo, *An Introduction to the New Testament* (Grand Rapids: Zondervan, 2005), 520–521.

[2] There is actually an apocryphal text called "The Epistle to the Laodiceans" presumed to be written by Paul. It is believed to date back to the fourth century AD and is a clear forgery. The source for the writing of this apocryphal text is the reference in Colossians 4:16. On the Epistle to the Laodiceans see Philip L. Tite, *The Apocryphal Epistle to the Laodiceans: An Epistolary and Rhetorical Analysis* (Leiden / Boston: Brill, 2012).

not contain the phrase "in Ephesus."[3] This may be a hint that this letter was originally meant to be an encyclical letter. Nevertheless, it has come down to us as the letter to the Ephesians and we will refer to it as such. After all, it is the body of the letter itself which the church accepted as inspired, not necessarily the title, which would have been added later.[4]

As we examine both of these passages, we notice that Paul actually provides us with an open window into a first century AD worship service. Let's look at the Colossians passage first. Notice the importance of the "word of Christ" dwelling in believers "richly" (Col. 3:16), thereby placing an emphasis on the importance of God's Word in the life of a believer. The reason the word of Christ should naturally dwell in believers is because Christians already have Christ dwelling in their hearts through faith (Eph. 3:17). The peace of Christ is also supposed to rule in the hearts of believers (Col. 3:15), which are to be blameless in holiness before God (1 Thess. 3:13) and "in every good work and word" (2 Thess. 2:17). Christ is also to be regarded as holy, and as Lord of our hearts (1 Pet. 3:15).[5]

---

[3] On the textual variant "in Ephesus," see Donald Guthrie, *New Testament Introduction* (Downers Grove: InterVarsity, 1970), 508-511. Bruce M. Metzger comments, "The words [in Ephesus] are absent from several important witnesses ... as well as from manuscripts mentioned by Basil and the text used by Origen. Certain internal features of the letter as well as Marcion's designation of the epistle as 'To the Laodiceans' and the absence in Tertullian and Ephraem of an explicit quotation of the words [in Ephesus] have led many commentators to suggest that the letter was intended as an encyclical, copies being sent to various churches, of which that at Ephesus was chief." Bruce M. Metzger, *A Textual Commentary on the Greek New Testament*, 2nd ed. (Stuttgart/New York: Deutsche Bibelgesellschaft/United Bible Societies, 2002), 532.

[4] A case in point is the letter to the Hebrews. We do not know who the author is as he is not mentioned in the opening verse. Editors of the AV considered Hebrews as an epistle of Paul and thus the superscript read, "The Epistle of Paul the Apostle to the Hebrews." Again, while the body of the letter to the Hebrews is inspired, the title is not.

[5] The reference to Christ as "Lord" in 1 Peter 3:15 is also an attestation of his deity. As we have seen, the word "Lord" (*kyrios*) is a Greek substitute for the Divine Name Yahweh. Peter is alluding to Isaiah 8:13 which speaks of Yahweh, "But the LORD of hosts, him you shall regard as holy. Let him be your fear, and let him be your dread." That Peter was indeed alluding to Isaiah 8:13 is seen in the AV translation of 1 Peter 3:15, "But sanctify the Lord God in your hearts." Metzger comments, "In place of [Christ] the Textus Receptus substitutes [God], with the later uncials (K L P) and most minuscules. The reading [Christ], however, is strongly supported by early and diversified external evidence ... as well as by transcriptional probability, the more familiar expression [Lord God] replacing the less usual expression [Lord Christ]." Metzger, in *Textual Commentary*, 621-622.

The reading from the AV is also found in the Byzantine Majority Text. Unfortunately, the NKJV preserves the AV reading but this is mostly due in part to the fact that the NKJV is following the Majority Text as its base text. The earlier reading "Christ the Lord" is to be preferred as it better attested and is the harder reading. As already noted, the earliest reading is a strong

HYMNS SUNG TO THE SON AND FATHER

We have already looked at the importance of the title "Lord" when applied to Jesus. The focus on the heart is to show that worship, rather than being merely a ritual, must be something that proceeds from our innermost being. It is for this reason that believers are called to worship the Lord "from a pure heart" (2 Tim. 2:22),[6] and why Jesus said that God can only be worshipped in spirit and truth, for these are the kind of worshippers the Father seeks (John 4:23-24). There is no doubt that during the early days of the church, the word of Christ would have been preached, heard and memorized. Notice also in the Colossians passage that Paul places an emphasis on "teaching and admonishing." This again shows the centrality not only of God's Word, but of the teaching of his Word to others and the admonishing of one another. Notice this is a reciprocal action, and is to be done for "one another," and, "in all wisdom."[7] God's Word is not to be taken out of context, abused, distorted, and used for one's own interests; rather it is to be rightly divided (cf. 2 Tim. 2:15, AV).

It is important to stress the much-ignored aspect of reading and studying God's Word as part of our worship. This is surely why Paul includes it before going on to discuss "the singing [of] psalms and hymns and spiritual songs." Notice that Paul speaks in the plural here: psalms, hymns, and spiritual songs. The earliest Christian movement was a singing, worshipping community. Which psalms, hymns, and spiritual songs is Paul specifically referring to? We are not told. In the following chapters we will examine some passages in the New Testament which are believed to be hymns. The psalms may have been taken from the Old Testament, as may have some of the hymns, or early Christians may have appropriated the biblical psalms and reinterpreted them in a Christological context.[8] Spiritual songs may have included songs that an individual or group in the church had composed. We cannot be fully certain, but we do know that singing was an integral part of early Christian worship. What

---

attestation and proof of the deity of Christ in identifying him as Yahweh. As a side note, it is also interesting to note that that in 1 Peter 3:15, Peter writes about always being ready to give a reason to those who inquire about the hope that Christian believers have in Christ. Peter is known for denying Jesus *three times*, an event no doubt that would have followed Peter all his life. He was restored and reaffirmed by Jesus when he confessed *three times* that he loved Jesus (John 21:15-19). The Peter in this letter is a changed man, and now urges that all believers should always be ready to give answers for their faith when confronted or challenged.

[6] On the purity of heart in Christian worship see Costa, *Worship and the Risen Jesus*, 59-61.

[7] Wallace comments, "Here [Eph. 5:19] is a rare instance of the reflexive pronoun used like a reciprocal pronoun." Wallace, *Greek Grammar Beyond the Basics*, 351.

[8] Hurtado, *Lord Jesus Christ*, 508.

should also be noticed is the object of these psalms, hymns, and spiritual songs; they are sung "in your hearts *to* God" (italics mine). Though God is *implied* as the object of Paul's hymn in 1 Corinthians 14:26, here in Colossians 3:16, God is explicitly identified as the object of worship. Another thing to notice is that these songs are sung *in* the hearts of believers to God and reminds us once again that worship comes from the heart.

Paul also exhorts that these psalms, hymns, and songs should be sung "with thankfulness in your hearts." A major component of hymns, even in our modern experience, is the giving of thanks to God. The Psalms, too, are filled with references of giving thanks.[9] Giving thanks to God in all circumstance is also stated to be the will of God for us (1 Thess. 5:18). An absence of thanks to God is characteristic of an unbelieving heart, as Paul points out in Romans 1:21, "For although they knew God, they did not honor him as God or give thanks to him." Even the unregenerate seem to understand that it is rude not to give thanks. And yet such rudeness has continued on a cosmic scale since the beginning of human history as we refuse to give thanks to God for the air we breathe, the food we eat, and the heart that continues to beat in our chests. This behavior emerges from an unrepentant heart and Paul identifies these as "haters of God" (Rom. 1:30).

Because thanksgiving so natural aligns with prayer in the Scriptures, it should come as no surprise that many of our prayers begin with or include the word "thanks" (1 Thess. 1:2). Even Jesus included thanksgiving in his prayers to the Father (Matt. 11:25; Luke 10:21; John 11:41). It is also not surprising that the ordinance of the Lord's Supper is called "the Eucharist" in some denominations, which is a word derived from a Greek word which means to give thanks, as Jesus did when he broke the bread and took the cup at the Last Supper. In Colossians 3:16 we see again that spiritual songs, being expressions of worship, may only be ascribed to God, as God alone is worthy of worshipped.

When we look at Ephesians 5:19 we note a strikingly similar wording to Colossians 3:16. Here Paul writes about "addressing one another in psalms and hymns and spiritual songs, singing and making melody to the Lord with all your heart." Notice that he uses two present active participles—"addressing" and "singing"—to describe the actions of the Christian believers. The idea of "addressing one another" or "speaking to one another" (NASB) in song

---

[9] Psalm 9:1; 28:7; 30:4, 12; 33:2; 44:8; 57:9; 118:1 are a sample among many others.

Hymns sung to the Son and Father

carries the notion of community and sharing; the image being presented here is likely that of corporate singing.[10] The phrase "addressing one another" should sound familiar as we have already come across something very similar when we looked at the Letter of Pliny the Younger to the emperor Trajan. There he described a Christian worship service where the Christians gathered "to recite a hymn among themselves to Christ, as though he were a god."[11] An alternate translation of this same text can be read as Christians gathered to "sing *responsively a hymn* to Christ as to a god."[12] What is singing "responsively"? It would have been the act of alternative singing, otherwise known as antiphony.[13] The Merriam-Webster Dictionary defines the word antiphony as a "responsive alternation between two groups especially of singers."[14] According to the Talmud, the Psalms and prayers were read responsively.[15] Is it conceivable that what Paul meant by "addressing one another" was a responsive address in psalms, hymns and spiritual songs, as Pliny described Christians engaged in around AD 112? It is. What is more important, however, is to whom these songs were addressed.

As noted above, hymns have both a vertical and horizontal dimension. We worship God through them (vertical dimension), but we also edify each other as we sing with one voice to God (horizontal dimension). A striking difference appears in Ephesians 5:19 when comparing it to Colossians 3:16. We saw in Colossians 3:16 that psalms, hymns, and spiritual songs were to be sung to God. In Ephesians 5:19, however, Paul states that these hymns and spiritual songs were to be sung *to the Lord*. Who is "the Lord" here referring to? We observed in 1 Corinthians 8:6 how, in Paul's letters, the word "God" is generally used of the Father whereas the word "Lord" is generally used of Jesus or the Son.[16] We also noted that the terms "God" and "Lord" are both divine

---

[10] Costa, *Worship and the Risen Jesus*, 213.

[11] Pliny the Younger, *Letters* 10:96.

[12] "Pliny the Younger," Early Christian Writings, Peter Kirby, accessed April 23, 2020, http://www.earlychristianwritings.com/text/pliny.html. (italics mine)

[13] This seems to be supported by the Latin of Pliny's letter *secum invicem* ("back and forth between themselves"). See Angela Kim Harkins and Brian P. Dunkle, SJ, "Hymns and Psalmody," in *The Oxford Handbook of Early Christian Ritual*, eds. Risto Uro, Juliette J. Day, Richard E. Demaris, and Rikard Roitto, eds. (Oxford: Oxford University Press, 2019), 615. This may also "have been a liturgical recitation." John S. Andrews, "Hymns," in *New International Dictionary*, 494. A liturgical setting for this hymn would imply a worship context, in this case to Christ.

[14] *Merriam-Webster*, s.v. "antiphony," accessed April 24, 2020, https://www.merriam-webster.com/dictionary/antiphony.

[15] *b.Taanit*. 16b.

[16] There are clearly exceptions to this rule; Paul sometimes does refer to Jesus as "God" as seen in Titus 2:13 and likely in Romans 9:5. Paul also refers to him as "deity" in Colossians 2:9.

titles used in Deuteronomy 6:4, especially in the LXX, and that Paul appropriates these titles respectively to the Father and the Son. In other words, when Paul refers to "the Lord," he is referring to the Lord Jesus Christ and once against suggests that the Lord Jesus was worshipped by the earliest Christians by means of psalms, hymns, and spiritual songs. Notice that this is the *same* worship that Paul calls for in Colossians 3:16 to be ascribed to God. And in Ephesians 5:19 he directs that the *same* worship be given to the Lord Jesus Christ, thereby showing the equality between the Father and the Son. If Jesus were a mere man or prophet, such worship would have amounted to idolatry; the fact that they had no hesitation in worshipping the risen Christ reveals again that from the earliest times he was seen as the divine Son who shared in the divine identity of God himself.

It is from such early-Christian thinking that phrases like this one from the Nicene Creed were so readily confessed of the Son in the fourth century AD: "God of God, Light of Light, true God of true God; begotten, not made, of one substance with the Father." This again demonstrates how the deity of Christ was held to by the earliest Christians. Gerhard Delling comments that "in Eph. 5:19 praise is directed primarily to the [Lord] so that we have a hymn to Christ."[17] We should recall, as stated earlier, that there are no hymns to Moses, Elijah or any of the prophets, or even to the angels and heavenly beings.[18] Larry Hurtado has noted that there is no precedence in Judaism for the worship of any other god, as all hymns in Judaism had God as their object.[19] And yet Hurtado also admits that the "singing/chanting (the singing was probably unaccompanied) in honor of Jesus was a very characteristic feature of early Christian worship."[20]

We have seen, both in Colossians 3:16 and Ephesians 5:19, that the earliest Christians kept the Word of Christ in their hearts, that they encouraged one another, and that they sang psalms, hymns, and spiritual songs both to God the Father, and the Son. Having seen how hymns played such an important role in the early Christian movement, we are now ready to examine

---

[17] Gerhard Delling, "ὕμνος, ὑμνέω, ψάλλω, ψαλμός," in *The Theological Dictionary of the New Testament*, eds., G. Kittel, G. W. Bromiley, and G. Friedrich (Grand Rapids: Eerdmans, 1964–1976), 8:498. See also Fee, *Pauline Christology*, 493.

[18] On the question of the worship of angels mentioned in Colossians 2:18 see Costa, *Worship and the Risen Jesus*, 116–127, 265.

[19] Larry W. Hurtado, *One God, One Lord: Early Christian Devotion and Ancient Jewish Monotheism* (Philadelphia: Fortress Press, 1988), 102.

[20] Hurtado, *Lord Jesus Christ*, 148.

some of these early hymns that Christians would have sung in the first century AD.

12
THE *CARMEN CHRISTI*
PHILIPPIANS 2:6-11

The phrase *Carmen Christi* is Latin for "hymn of Christ" or "hymn to Christ." It refers to the passage in Philippians 2:6-11, which speaks of Christ in the following words:

> Who, though he was in the form of God, did not count equality with God a thing to be grasped, but made himself nothing, taking the form of a servant, being born in the likeness of men. And being found in human form, he humbled himself by becoming obedient to the point of death, even death on a cross. Therefore God has highly exalted him and bestowed on him the name that is above every name, so that at the name of Jesus every knee should bow, in heaven and on earth and under the earth, and every tongue confess that Jesus Christ is Lord, to the glory of God the Father.

This passage is believed to be an ancient Christian hymn, held by many scholars to be pre-Pauline. As such, it was not written by Paul but, like the creed in 1 Corinthians 15:3-4, would have been received and passed on by him. In terms of dating, the *Carmen Christi* is believed to have been written sometime between the mid AD 50s to early 60s.[1] However, that is just the dating of the letter to the Philippians; if the *Carmen Christi* is pre-Pauline, then it could be even earlier. This would not only place the *Carmen Christi* at an earlier date but would also establish it as the earliest Christological material we possess. If this is indeed the case, there is no better place to start than the *Carmen Christi* if one wants to discover what the earliest Christians believed about Jesus.

One of the reasons the *Carmen Christi* is believed to be pre-Pauline is because of "its uncharacteristically rhythmical, poetically elevated style, and the balancing of verses 6-8 and 9-11 suggest an earlier hymn incorporated by

---

[1] Carson and Moo, *Introduction to the New Testament*, 506-507.

EARLY CHRISTIAN CREEDS AND HYMNS

Paul."[2] The church historian J.N.D. Kelly notes regarding Philippians 2:6-11 that "so far from being Pauline, it is almost certainly an ancient Christian hymn, probably of Palestinian derivation, which was already arranged in rhythmic strophes by the time it fell into St. Paul's hands."[3] I. Howard Marshall also notes that "the Gentile origin of the hymn in Philippians 2:6-11 is certainly to be rejected ... its ideas are certainly Jewish rather than Gentile."[4] There is some debate among scholars as to whether or not this hymn is actually pre-Pauline or whether Paul actually did write it.[5] But even those scholars who are not fully convinced that this hymn pre-dates Paul nevertheless grant that its origins are Semitic and early.[6] If the origins of the *Carmen Christi* are Jewish then, like the creed in 1 Corinthians 15:3-4, this brings us back to the Jerusalem church and to the apostles themselves. Given its Jewish origins, it has also been postulated that this hymn may have originally been written in Aramaic and finds its source in the Syrian or Aramaic speaking church.[7]

How do we know how to identify a hymn in the New Testament? The answer is grammar. Ralph Martin has provided five criteria for detecting hymns in the New Testament text, particularly in epistles or letters.[8]

1. Context dislocation. This occurs where the flow of the letter is interrupted, thus indicating the insertion of other material.
2. Terminology and style occur that are different from the rest of the letter, e.g., where words are used that appear different than the writer's style.
3. Introductory phrases are brought into the text such as "thus it says" (Eph. 5:14), "confessedly" (1 Tim. 3:16), and the initial relative

---

[2] Levine and Brettler, eds., *Jewish Annotated New Testament*, 402.

[3] J.N.D. Kelly, *Early Christian Creeds*, 2nd ed. (London: Longmans, 1960), 18.

[4] Marshall, *Origins of New Testament Christology*, 106.

[5] Carson and Moo are initially willing to say that this hymn may be an "early Christian hymn that Paul has quoted" but then make the caveat that "it is just possible that Paul himself is its author." However, they still maintain that many scholars think that this hymn represents "pre-Pauline thought." Carson and Moo, *Introduction to the New Testament*, 372, 499-500, 608. There is no unanimous agreement on this point. See further comments in Costa, *Worship and the Risen Jesus*, 424 n.3 and on studies and bibliography on the *Carmen Christi* see 424-425 n.5.

[6] Carson and Moo admit that "this hymn is early-at least as early as Philippians, and maybe earlier." Carson and Moo, *Introduction to the New Testament*, 512

[7] Cullmann, *The Earliest Christian Confessions*, 22 n.4.

[8] In what follows I will be borrowing and paraphrasing from Ralph P. Marin, "Hymns, Hymn Fragments, Songs, Spiritual Songs" in *Dictionary of Paul and His Letters*, eds., Gerald F. Hawthorne, Ralph P. Martin and Daniel G. Reid (Downers Grove/Leicester: InterVarsity Press, 1993), 420-421; See also Reymond, *Jesus*, 245 n.11.

pronoun "who" (Phil. 2:6; Col. 1:15), which can indicate a "performed composition."
4. A contrast is set up in an antithetic style on grand scale (Phil. 2:6-11) usually using couplets. Rhyme is usually seen in these couplets.
5. The vocabulary is rare, ceremonial, highly stylized and full of instances of *hapax legomena* (words only appearing once).

D.A. Carson and Douglas Moo also comment that we are able to extract hymnic material from Paul's letters by examining "various early Christian creedal formulations, hymns, and traditional catechetical material. Unusual vocabulary, rhythmic and poetic patterns, and un-Pauline theological emphases are the criteria used to identify early Christian traditions that Paul may have quoted."[9] The *Carmen Christi* also contains a number of creedal features. The point has already been made that hymns and creeds often overlap with one another. Ralph Martin notes that the *Carmen Christi* represents a type of literature that has "cultic or confessional" features.[10]

The *Carmen Christi* can be divided into two parts: Philippians 2:6-8, and Philippians 2:9-11. It seems to have been prompted by Paul's concern for "encouraging Christian unity by urging reciprocal respect and consideration for one another."[11] This is seen in Philippians 2:4-5, "Let each of you look not only to his own interests, but also to the interests of others. Have this mind among yourselves, which is yours in Christ Jesus." From here he moves into the *Carmen Christi* in verse 6. The call to Christians is a call to consider others and their interests before their own, the way Christ did. This is a theme that Paul had enunciated elsewhere, "Let no one seek his own good, but the good of his neighbor" (1 Cor. 10:24).

The *Carmen Christi* is best understood as a descent to the lowest point (2:6-8), followed by an ascent to the highest point (2:9-11), resembling something like a "V" shaped paradigm. The *Carmen Christi* is also a Christologically-saturated hymn; it is full of Christ. We are led from the incarnation of the pre-existent Son to his ignominious suffering and death (though nothing is said directly about his atonement, it is implied), finally followed by his exaltation

---

[9] Carson and Moo, *Introduction to the New Testament*, 371.
[10] Ralph P. Martin, *An Early Christian Confession* (London: The Tyndale Press, 1960), 7.
[11] Costa, *Worship and the Risen Jesus*, 235.

Early Christian Creeds and Hymns

to the heights. The *Carmen Christi* may have also been sung responsively,[12] a point I discussed above in light of Ephesians 5:19.

We begin with the pre-existent Son "who was in the form of God" and had "equality with God" (Phil. 2:6). The hymn uses the present active participle *huparchon*, which is literally translated as "being," or "existing," and is reflected in translations such as the AV, NKJV and NJB, which read, "Who, *being* in the form of God" (italics mine), while others have "*existing* in the form of God" (ASV, HCSB; italics mine). Fee argues that the reason the present active participle *huparchon* is used in the hymn is because of the belief that Christ is always "being" or "existing," and "presupposes [his] prior existence as God."[13] Barclay notes that the use of this present active participle in 2:6 was used to show that "Jesus was essentially, unalterably, and unchangeable [*sic*] God."[14] This is a direct statement of the deity of Christ. The NIV brings the sense out even more clearly by translating "the form of God" as "being in very nature God." The phrase "form of God" is only used here and so accords with point five in the criteria for hymnic material. The grammatical indicator that this is the beginning of a hymn, is the nominative masculine singular relative pronoun ὅς (*hos*), or "who," at the beginning of verse 6, which in verse 5 refers to Christ Jesus; this agrees with point three in the hymn criteria list above.[15]

The first part of this section (2:6-8) begins with the incarnation (Christ's descent). Here we are told that pre-existent Son "emptied himself" (Phil. 2:7, NASB), or "made himself nothing" (ESV) or, as the AV reads, "made himself of no reputation." A number of scholars have noted that this language of the Son emptying himself is the dynamic equivalent of the passage in Isaiah 53:12, which speaks of the Servant of the Lord "pouring out his soul to death," which is another way of saying that he "voluntarily died."[16] Note that in the incarnation, the Son takes on the form of a "servant," (2:7), which is yet another echo

---

[12] Levine and Brettler, eds., *Jewish Annotated New Testament*, 402.

[13] Fee, *Pauline Christology*, 376-377.

[14] William Barclay, *The Letters to Philippians, Colossians, Thessalonians* (Edinburgh: The Saint Andrew Press, 1963), 43-44. Barclay also notes that this word can refer to "that which a man is in his very essence, that which cannot be changed, that which he possesses inalienably and in such a way that it cannot be taken from him" (43).

[15] See also Wallace, *Greek Grammar Beyond the Basics*, 341; Wallace, *Basics of New Testament Syntax*, 151-152.

[16] Reymond, *Jesus*, 263.

of Isaiah 53, in which the Servant of Yahweh is mentioned.[17] It is important to stress here that Christ's act of making himself nothing was a volitional act *which the Son himself accomplished*. Neither the Father or the Holy Spirit could empty the Son, nor force the action upon him; the Son willingly made himself nothing, as indicated by the reflexive pronoun "himself.[18] In this case, God the Father is passive, and the Son is active in his condescension. He also took on the "form of a servant," or "the form of a slave" (HCSB, NET, NJB, NRSV), which contrasts with the "form of God" found in verse 6, an aspect which agrees with point four of our hymn criteria.

The Son, in the incarnation, was "born in the likeness of men," or better, was "made in the likeness of men" (NASB), and found "in human form." In verse 8, the descent of the incarnate Son is now further extended by his willingness to humble himself in becoming obedient even to the point of such a debased and humiliating death as the "death on a cross." One who must endure such a death has hit rock bottom—the very dregs of the barrel as it were—as crucifixion was usually reserved for violent criminals, slaves,[19] and those at the very bottom of the social ladder.[20] It should also not be lost on us that Jesus took on "the form of a slave" or "bond-servant" (NASB). His death on a cross is the extremity of the descent of Christ in his incarnation. It should be noted here that while the death of the cross is mentioned, nothing is directly or explicitly said about its atoning significance, unlike the earliest creed in 1 Corinthians 15:3 which states that "Christ died for our sins."

After Christ's humiliating death, part two of the hymn (2:9-11) begins with a change in direction, from descent to ascent; the exact reversal of part one. The humiliation of Jesus in 2:8 now sets the stage for the sharp contrast of his exaltation in 2:9.[21] This exaltation would have included both the

---

[17] Reymond, *Jesus*, 263-264.

[18] Fee, *Pauline Christology*, 394; Moisés Silva, *Philippians*, 2nd ed. (Grand Rapids: Baker Academic, 2005), 99; Hurtado, *Lord Jesus Christ*, 121. Hutardo comments that "most scholars take these verses [Philippians 2:6-8] to reflect a belief in the personal pre-existence and incarnation of Christ."

[19] J. Schneider, *TDNT*, 572-584.

[20] Joel B. Green, *1 Peter*, The Two Horizons New Testament Commentary (Grand Rapids/Cambridge: Eerdmans, 2007), 87 n.61.

[21] Costa, *Worship and the Risen Jesus*, 235. The contrasting theme between humiliation and exaltation is echoed in the gospels where Jesus states that whoever humbles themselves will be exalted and conversely whoever exalts themselves will be humbled (Matthew 23:12; Luke 14:11; 18:14). There are similar statements made throughout the general epistles. For example, "Humble yourselves before the Lord, and he will exalt you" (James 4:10), and "Humble yourselves,

resurrection and ascension aspects of Jesus. The apostles could speak both about God raising Jesus from the dead (Acts 2:32), and also how "God exalted him at his right hand as Leader and Savior" (Acts 5:31).[22] This is the second couplet, and agrees with point four of the hymn criteria above. Whereas in 2:6-8, we saw that the Son was the active agent in his condescension, we see now in 2:9-11 that God the Father becomes the active agent in the exaltation of his Son.[23] The connecting conjunction "therefore" links verse 8 to verse 9 by explaining why God highly exalted Jesus; it was because of his willingness to make himself nothing, to take on the form of a servant, and to humble himself to even the denigrating death of the cross. When it states that God highly exalted Jesus, the Greek word (another case of *hapax legomenon*) literally means that God "hyper-exalted" him.[24] This also meets point five of the criteria for hymns above.

Jesus was exalted to the pinnacle of the cosmos, a position which evokes a status of tremendous honour. Note the contrast: Jesus condescended to the very depths, and as a result, God has exalted him to the very heights. The idea of height being associated with honour should not be lost on us as God is often called "the Most High" (Deut. 32:8), or "God Most High," (Gen. 14:18-20, 22), or even "the Highest" (Matt. 21:9; Mark 11:10; Luke 2:14) in Scripture. In the Old Testament, Yahweh is said to be exalted over all the nations (Ps. 18:46; 21:13; 46:10; 57:5,11; 118:28). The exaltation of Jesus to the highest place also has Messianic significance as God has promised that he would make the Messiah "the highest of the kings of the earth" (Ps. 89:27), or "the most exalted of the kings of the earth" (NIV). The exaltation language of Jesus also has overtones that point to his deity. While Yahweh is "highly exalted" (Ps. 47:9), so is Jesus. When Isaiah saw the Lord in his vision, he saw him "high

---

therefore, under the mighty hand of God so that at the proper time he may exalt you" (1 Peter 5:6). In the Apocrypha (Sirach 7:11), it states that God is the one who humbles and exalts. See comments in Costa, *Worship and the Risen Jesus*, 426 n.16.

[22] Notice how the resurrected Jesus could also speak about his coming ascension, "Do not cling to me, for I have not yet ascended to the Father" (John 20:17). Luke is the only writer who informs us that the period between the resurrection of Jesus and his ascension was forty days (Acts 1:3; cf. Luke 24:51). The reading in Mark 16:19 is spurious and is part of the longer ending of Mark (16:9-20) not generally acknowledged to be original as it adds no new information to what we already know in the other gospels. The original text is believed to have ended at 16:8. See Metzger, *Textual Commentary*, 102-107; Reymond, *Jesus*, 216.

[23] Costa, *Worship and the Risen Jesus*, 235.

[24] I-Jin Loh and Eugene A. Nida, *A Translator's Handbook on Paul's Letter to the Philippians* (New York: United Bible Societies, 1977), 61.

and lifted up" on a throne (Isa. 6:1). The very same language is used by Yahweh to describe himself as "the One who is high and lifted up" (Isa. 57:15). That the One Isaiah saw seated on a throne in his vision was the pre-incarnate Christ is confirmed by the evangelist John who tells us that Isaiah "saw his glory and spoke of him" (John 12:41; see vv. 38–41).

As we saw with the creeds in Chapter 5, there is also an anti-imperialist theme in this hymn. Philippi was a very loyal and pro-imperial city with a long history of emperor devotion and prided themselves in being part of the Roman empire. It is no surprise, then, that Paul chooses two titles that the emperor was known by, "Lord," and "Saviour,"[25] and then applies them to the exalted Jesus. Some of the Roman emperors even claimed to have been exalted to heaven.[26] It is also not surprising that Paul refers to Jesus as "Saviour" in Philippians 3:20 and reminds the believers that "our citizenship is in heaven." It is interesting to note that only in Philippians 3:20 does Paul uses the word citizenship, which comes from the Greek word πολίτευμα (*politeuma*), and this in a letter written to a very pro-imperial city.

In highly exalting Jesus, God also "bestowed on him the name that is above every name." Though I commented on this briefly above, it bears repeating. Many Christians have mistakenly believed this "name" that is above every name to be the name of Jesus. We are all familiar with the contemporary song, "Jesus, Name Above All Names," which continues to promote this view. It is important to remember that the name Jesus was a common Jewish name in the first century AD. The name that is above every name, however, the name that God has bestowed on Jesus, is Yahweh, which comes into the LXX and Greek New Testament as "Lord." Such a title is also used at the end of the hymn in verse 11.[27] What should not be missed here is that God "bestowed on him *the name*" (italics mine). This is important for several reasons and here I need to pause for a necessary tangent.

When the Jews referred to God, they would sometimes use what is called a circumlocution or periphrasis, which means to use words in a round-about way in order to avoid referring to God directly. Words used as substitutes for God would include "heaven" (Luke 15:18, 21)—as in "kingdom of heaven"

---

[25] Costa, *Worship and the Risen Jesus*, 236, 427 n.29. The title "Saviour" is used of both the Lord Jesus and God.

[26] Wright, *The Resurrection of the Son of God*, 228.

[27] That the name above every name is the name of God himself, Yahweh, is held by the vast majority of scholars. See comments in Costa, *Worship and the Risen Jesus*, 236–237, 427–428 n.39.

(used throughout Matthew), rather than "kingdom of God" (used throughout Mark)—also, "the Blessed" (Mark 14:61), "Power" (Mark 14:62), and "the Name" (Lev. 24:16). In the Old Testament, the name of God is said to be exalted above everything (Ps. 18:1; 138:2; 148:13) and is always associated with honor (Mal. 1:6; 2:2) throughout Scripture. In rabbinic literature, God is usually referred to as "the Holy One, Blessed be He." One of the ways Jews refer to God is by referring to him as *ha Shem* ("the Name"); we see such a term bestowed on Jesus himself in Philippians 2:9. The New Testament elsewhere speaks of Jesus in terms of "the name," as we will see in the following passages.

After the apostles were beaten and told not to preach in the name of Jesus, we read in Acts 5:41 that they went out, "rejoicing that they were counted worthy to suffer dishonor for *the name*" (italics mine). Similarly, James 2:7 warns believers about the rich who seek to abuse them: "Are they not the ones who blaspheme *the honorable name* by which you were called?" (italics mine). John, in speaking about showing hospitality to Christian evangelists and preachers says, "For they have gone out for the sake of *the name*, accepting nothing from the Gentiles" (3 John 7; italics mine).[28] The idea of "the name" in the Bible also communicates, among other things, notions of person and reputation. When someone gives another person "a bad name," it means they have sullied their reputation. When someone is said to have "dragged someone's name through the mud" it communicates the idea of slander and libel against their character. Similarly, to bless the name of God is to bless God himself, as his name is representative of who he is. The same applies to the Lord Jesus. When someone prays in the name of Christ, they are praying that God would respond for the sake of his Son.

Let us now return to the hymn in Philippians 2:10, which states "that at the name of Jesus every knee should bow, in heaven and on earth and under the earth." Here, the name of Jesus is a name that both belongs to him and is bestowed on him in verse 9. The phrase "so that" at the beginning of verse 10 signals the action that follows, a structure that is also known as a "purpose-result."[29] Jesus is bestowed with the name Lord, or Yahweh, so that every knee in the entire cosmos—heaven, earth, and under the earth—will bow in submission to him. As we shall see, the exaltation of Christ is intended by God to

---

[28] Note the NASB reading which capitalizes the word "name": "For they went out for the sake of *the Name*, accepting nothing from the Gentiles" (italics mine).

[29] Wallace, *Basics of New Testament Syntax*, 206.

purposely bring about an intended result. The act of bowing is an action of submission to a monarch who has been enthroned. As the extent of his reign is universal, this posture of submission would not only include believers but unbelievers as well.[30] The Roman emperor was used to having his subjects bow the knee to him, but this emperor Jesus requires the entire universe bow to him.[31] The act of bowing here is obviously an expression of worship; bowing to anyone other than God in a religious context was strictly forbidden and deemed idolatrous.[32] Surely, "the drift of this passage makes it clear that Jesus is the direct object of worship."[33]

In Philippians 2:11, Paul brings the hymn to its crescendo, "And every tongue confess that Jesus Christ is Lord, to the glory of God the Father." In addition to the cosmic bowing in 2:10, all those who bow, represented by "every tongue," will also make a confession: "Jesus Christ is Lord." As we have seen in Chapter 5, this was the one-clause creed that Christians confessed. In this hymn, however, we see that *all* will confess this creed—both believer and unbeliever alike. It is also important to realize that the word "Lord" in the original Greek is in the emphatic position; all the cosmos will make the universal acclamation and confession that Jesus Christ is Lord.

That the name "Lord" is in view here is further supported as we recognize that the background to Philippians 2:10-11 is Isaiah 45:23, where Yahweh says, "By myself I have sworn; from my mouth has gone out in righteousness a word that shall not return: '*To me every knee shall bow, every tongue shall swear allegiance*'" (italics mine). In Isaiah 45:23, it is to Yahweh that every knee will bow and every tongue swear allegiance; in Philippians 2:10-11, it is to Jesus

---

[30] Costa, *Worship and the Risen Jesus*, 428 n.51. Notice how Paul also speaks of bowing as a sign of submission out of reverence to God in Ephesians 3:14.

[31] We see something similar in Revelation 5:11-14 where the myriad of heavenly beings, along with all of creation, praise and worship the Lord Jesus Christ (the Lamb). Note the reference to "every creature" that is in heaven, on earth, and under the earth—the same tri-partite division we see in Philippians 2:10. The text reads: "Then I looked, and I heard around the throne and the living creatures and the elders the voice of many angels, numbering myriads of myriads and thousands of thousands, saying with a loud voice, 'Worthy is the Lamb who was slain, to receive power and wealth and wisdom and might and honor and glory and blessing!' And I heard *every creature in heaven and on earth and under the earth and in the sea*, and all that is in them, saying, 'To him who sits on the throne and to the Lamb be blessing and honor and glory and might forever and ever!' And the four living creatures said, 'Amen!' and the elders fell down and worshiped" (italics mine).

[32] Costa, *Worship and the Risen Jesus*, 242. On the act of bowing in a non-religious context see comments in Costa, *Worship and the Risen Jesus*, 430 n.93.

[33] Loh and Nida, *Translator's Handbook*, 62.

Christ that every knee will bow and every tongue confess allegiance. Paul is here identifying the exalted Christ with Yahweh, who is the Lord, and clearly understands Isaiah 45:23 to be referring to Yahweh because he also quotes it in Romans 14:11. This connection between Philippians 2:10-11 and Isaiah 45:23 is well recognized among scholars.[34] The connection between Philippians 2:11 and Isaiah 45:23 can be further shown grammatically in that the same word Paul uses for "confess," ἐξομολογέω (*exomologeo*), in 2:11, is used in the LXX of Isaiah 45:23. I discussed the word ὁμολογέω (*homologeo*), "to confess," in Chapters 1 and 5. Here in Philippians 2:11 the word Paul uses (taken from Isa. 45:23), is a stronger word than confess, and means "to acknowledge a fact publicly."[35] Jesus will be openly, publicly acknowledged as Lord by the cosmos.

The background of Isaiah 45:23 is important because it emphasizes the uniqueness of God's ability (Isaiah 40-48 constitutes one of the most emphatic claims of monotheism in the Bible) to save to the ends of the earth (Isa. 45:22). Yahweh is acclaimed as the one true God who deserves the allegiance of the nations, all of whom will one day acknowledge his universal sovereignty by bowing and confessing him as Lord.[36]

The connection between Philippians 2:10-11 and Isaiah 45:23 not only identifies the exalted Christ with Yahweh, but also demonstrates that the exalted Christ receives the same worship and adoration that was rendered to Yahweh in the Old Testament.[37] Oscar Cullmann also recognizes that the name "Lord" is the name above all names and acknowledges that this passage "speaks of His [Jesus'] work as servant which culminates in His elevation to the rank of *Kyrios-Adonai*, a name which is above all names, since it formerly belonged to God alone."[38] The short, one-clause creed "Jesus Christ is Lord," is clearly a claim to the deity of Christ, as well as a means of affirming him as the Sovereign and Ruler of all. The Lordship of Christ is all encompassing. In this hymn Paul reveals that confessing Jesus as Lord does not only refer to "a

---

[34] On the connection between Isaiah 45:23 and Philippians 2:10-11 see Costa, *Worship and the Risen Jesus*, 240-245, 247-248, 276-277; 428 n.42. Origen, in the early third century AD, already saw a connection between Philippians 2:10-11 and Isaiah 45:23. Origen, *Or.* 31.3.

[35] Louw and Nida, *Greek-English Lexicon*, 33.275.

[36] Costa, *Worship and the Risen Jesus*, 244-245.

[37] Henn, *One Faith*, 49.

[38] Cullmann, *The Earliest Christian Confessions*, 55. See also Marshall, *Origins of New Testament Christology*, 106.

final *universal and eschatological affirmation*" but also refers to the present practice in the Christian community of confessing Jesus as Lord (Rom. 10:9-13; 1 Cor. 1:2; 12:3; 2 Cor. 4:5).[39] Here again is an example of the "now/not yet" tension we often see in Scripture. It is also seen in the Old Testament where Yahweh is said to be King *now* (Exod. 15:18; Ps. 95:3), while at the same time foreseeing the day when Yahweh *will be* King over all the earth (Zech. 14:9). Jesus Christ is Lord now, but not yet in the fullest manifestation of lordship, which will only be realized when he returns again.

The *Carmen Christi*, however, does not end with the mere existence of the creed "Jesus Christ is Lord"; rather it ends with the creed being confessed and acknowledged. For what purpose? For the purpose that all will confess Jesus' Lordship "to the glory of God the Father." The ultimate purpose and aim of all things is towards one specific end: the glory of God. But that final glorification of God will not be achieved without the cosmos' confession of Jesus as Lord. As Paul says elsewhere, it is this cosmic worship, expressed through the Lord Jesus Christ, that will finally render God as the "all in all" (1 Cor. 15:28). It should also be noted that there is no sense of rivalry here between the worship of the Lord Jesus and God. I have argued previously that,

> This worship of the exalted Jesus is not perceived by Paul as a rival worship of God, or a usurpation of God's glory; rather, Paul sees the worship of the exalted Christ as *divinely sanctioned* by God himself and willed by God as necessary to bring about the ultimate glory to God ... The worship given to the exalted Jesus does not threaten or challenge the worship of God; it is not an act of "Jesus-olatry," rather it complements the worship of God ... God is worshipped through the worship of the exalted Jesus. The worship which is given to the exalted Jesus does not usurp the worship of God, nor does it rival the worship of God; it rather *complements* the worship of God and facilitates it. ... God cannot be ultimately and maximally glorified according to Paul, without, or apart from the exalted Jesus.[40]

The *Carmen Christi*, as we noted at the beginning, is believed to pre-date Paul. Paul would likely have obtained it from the earliest followers of Jesus, the

---

[39] Costa, *Worship and the Risen Jesus*, 243-244 (italics in original).

[40] Costa, *Worship and the Risen Jesus*, 246, 249 (italics in original). The term "Jesus-olatry" is not my own but is used in James D.G. Dunn, *Did the First Christians Worship Jesus? The New Testament Evidence* (Louisville: Westminster John Knox Press, 2010), 147. See my brief critique of Dunn's use of this term in Costa, *Worship and the Risen Jesus*, 432 n.126.

EARLY CHRISTIAN CREEDS AND HYMNS

Jerusalem apostles. This indicates that this hymn may have originally been sung in Aramaic, the language of Jesus.

The *Carmen Christi* has been identified as a hymn because it contains features of the five criteria for hymns that I listed at the beginning of the chapter. When Christians sang this hymn, they were at the same time confessing what they believed; remember that the line between hymn and creed is thin. If you recall the Apostles' Creed and the Nicene Creed we referred to in the first chapter, many of the points made in the *Carmen Christi* are also found in these historic creeds. Its contents show us what the earliest Christians believed about Jesus. In 1 Corinthians 15:3-4 we saw what the earliest Christians believed about *what Jesus did*; in this hymn you will notice that the emphasis is not only what he did, but on *who Jesus is*. We saw from Philippians 2:6 that the earliest Christians sang about Jesus being in "the form of God" and that he had "equality with God." This shows us once again that the deity of Christ was held to by Christians from the earliest times, possibly even before Paul.[41] They also sang about the incarnation—that the Son willingly made himself nothing, taking on "the form of a servant," and became human (Phil. 2:7). We see this theme repeated in John 1:1,14. Is it any surprise that John later makes the denial of the incarnation the litmus test of whether someone is from God or not (1 John 4:1-3)?

And here, in the humbled state of a human being, we see that Jesus became obedient even to the point of death on a cross (Phil. 2:8). The death of Jesus was central to these earliest Christians. They would have sung about Jesus' humiliation in the incarnation, his ignominious death, and then there would have probably been a shift in their tone as they proceeded to sing about his ascension and exaltation, reaching a crescendo as they declare the one with the name above all names as Lord (Phil. 2:9). Their enthusiasm would reach its peak as they closed their hymn with the reminder that one day the entire cosmos would bend the knee to Jesus Christ and confess that he is Lord, to the glory of God the Father (Phil. 2:10-11). Thus, the *Carmen Christi* ends on a high note, and with the realization of the end of all things: the glory of God.

---

[41] A point even Carson and Moo, in *Introduction to the New Testament*, 512 agree with, "So it [*Carmen Christi*] constitutes powerful evidence for the confession of a high Christology at a very early date in the church's life." It is for this reason that the language of the Son being in the form of God is another way of saying he had equality with God (Philippians 2:6). R.H. Fuller comments, "To be in the 'form' of God, means to exist in a state of equality with God." R.H. Fuller, *The Foundations of New Testament Christology* (London/Glasgow: Collins, 1965), 208.

13
THE GREAT CONFESSION IN A HYMN
1 TIMOTHY 3:16

While the *Carmen Christi* is the most well-known of all the hymns in the New Testament, likely due to its length and its beautiful content, there are still others worth focusing on. Another one is found in 1 Timothy 3:16: "Great indeed, we confess, is the mystery of godliness: He was manifested in the flesh, vindicated by the Spirit, seen by angels, proclaimed among the nations, believed on in the world, taken up in glory."

1 Timothy, 2 Timothy, and Titus are known as the "pastoral epistles" or "pastoral letters." In these letters, believed to be among the last that Paul wrote, a number of things are laid down, including instructions on church order and leadership—hence the reference to these letters as "pastoral." After discussing the office of overseer in 1 Timothy 3:1-7, and then the office of deacon in 3:8-13, Paul moves on to tell Timothy that he hopes to come to him soon (1 Tim. 3:14), but that if he is delayed, instructions are included that "[he] may know how one ought to behave in the household of God, which is the church of the living God, a pillar and buttress of truth" (1 Tim. 3:15). Here, Paul is implying that "in the household of God," one ought to behave in an orderly manner. Paul also wrote elsewhere that when it concerned the worship service, "all things should be done decently and in order" (1 Cor. 14:40) and that God is not a God of confusion but of peace (1 Cor. 14:33).

Paul goes on to further define this household of God as "the church of the living God, a pillar and buttress of the truth." God's family is his church; it is "the church of the living God" because all in Christ have been made alive to him (Matt. 22:32; Mark 12:27; Luke 20:38). Whenever we see the phrase "the living God" in Scripture, it is usually used in contrast to idolatry, which is nothing more than the worship of lifeless idols (Ps. 115:4-8; Jer. 10:1-15; Rev.

9:20).[1] Christian believers worship the one true God because they have turned from dead idols to serve the living God (1 Thess. 1:9).

Paul then also mentions that the church is "a pillar and buttress of truth." This is an important statement in that it demonstrates how important the church of God is. The church is two things: a pillar, and a buttress of truth. A pillar is something that holds a building up, while a buttress can either be a support, a foundation, a ground, or a basis.[2] Every pillar is built on some kind of foundation. What is the church's ultimate foundation? Paul tells us elsewhere that it is "built on the foundation of the apostles and prophets, Christ Jesus himself being the cornerstone" (Eph. 2:20). Paul also refers to the church, as "the household of God," as it is described in Ephesians 2:19. The most important part of the foundation, the cornerstone, is Jesus Christ (1 Cor. 3:11) himself. Without him, the whole building of the church collapses. Built on him, the church can then be the pillar that upholds the truth of God. This is why Paul mentions the church in relation to the "truth" in this passage. Christians who make up the church are to collectively hold up the truth so that it's light can shine out for all to see (Matt. 5:15-16). It is no surprise that truth is mentioned so frequently in the pastoral letters (1 Tim. 4:3; 6:5; 2 Tim. 2:15, 18; 3:8; 4:4; Titus 1:14). If Christians claim to follow him who came as "the truth" (John 14:6), then truth should also be paramount for us. Because the church is the repository of truth, the saints are to contend for, safeguard, and proclaim the faith that has once for all been entrusted to us (Jude 3). In this way, the church is called to be a kind of custodian of truth. The pastoral letters' emphasis on truth, in addition to 2 Peter and Jude, is also to be understood in light of the many false teachings and teachers that were rampant throughout the early church.[3]

---

[1] When Peter acknowledges that Jesus is "the Christ, the Son of the living God" (Matthew 16:16), it is important to note that this confession was made in the district of Caesarea Philippi (Matthew 16:13). This was a predominantly Gentile and pagan area, and at one time was a sacred pagan site of Canaanite fertility gods. A sanctuary was later erected there to the Greek god Pan (god of forests, flocks, and fields) and statues of various gods were also placed in that region. It was no accident that Jesus chose this area, among the dead gods of the Gentiles, to have himself disclosed as the Messiah and the Son of the living God. See *The ESV Archaeology Study Bible* (Wheaton: Crossway, 2017), 1399.

[2] A survey of various Bible translations of 1 Timothy 3:15 will show that these various words are used.

[3] Carson and Moo, *Introduction to the New Testament*, 563-564.

1 Timothy 3:16

Now, when Paul speaks of the church here as a buttress and pillar of truth, is he speaking about the church universal or local churches? Some groups will latch on to 1 Timothy 3:15 to argue that their specific church is the ground and pillar of the truth. C.K. Barrett comments that "neither 'household' nor 'pillar and bulwark [buttress]' has an article [the word *the*] in Greek; it may be that the author is thinking of *each local congregation* as severally a pillar and bulwark [buttress]."[4] Donald Guthrie agrees, "It is important to notice that no articles are used with either *pillar* or *foundation* in the Greek. And this must be considered intentional. A building needs more than one pillar. The pillar in fact stands for each Christian community."[5] This is important as it demonstrates that each local church is to be a buttress and pillar of truth, and throughout the world also united together as one building. Paul is not thinking of some centralized church in a capital city. He is speaking of each and every local church working together; this should underscore the importance of the local church for us.

After having established the importance of the local church, Paul then moves to 1 Timothy 3:16, a verse that is also widely believed to be a hymn.[6] How can we tell? Again, as with the *Carmen Christi*, the grammar alerts us. Notice Paul prefaces the hymn with the words, "Great indeed, we confess, is the mystery of godliness." He states that this confession is "great indeed," and also something that all Christians hold to by common consent; it is something that "we confess."[7] Here again we see that close association between a creed and a hymn. Moving on, we see that the content of their confession is "the mystery of godliness." In the New Testament, the word "mystery" should not be confused with our current English usage, i.e., as something that cannot be understood. Rather, it is used more to mean "the content of that which has not been known before but which has been revealed to an in-group or restricted constituency."[8] It generally refers to something in the past that

---

[4] C.K. Barrett, *The Pastoral Epistles* (Oxford: Clarendon Press, 1963), 63 (italics mine).

[5] Donald Guthrie, *The Pastoral Epistles*, TNTC (Downers Grove: InterVarsity Press, 1990), 103 (italics in original). In the Dead Sea Scroll collection called the "Community Rule," Jews who withdrew into the wilderness and joined the community of Qumran were described as those "that they may lay a foundation of truth for Israel, for the Community of the everlasting Covenant" (1QS 5:5). Some of this language resonates with Paul's words in 1 Timothy 3:15.

[6] Fuller, *The Foundations of New Testament Christology*, 216; Wallace, *Basics of New Testament Syntax*, 152.

[7] Guthrie, *The Pastoral Epistles*, 103.

[8] Louw and Nida, *Greek-English Lexicon*, 28.77.

was once unknown but that now has been revealed to the church under the New Covenant (Col. 1:26-27). Jesus used the word "mystery" in this same way (Mark 4:11, NASB, AV, NKJV).[9] So what is the mystery of godliness? It is Jesus Christ himself (Col. 2:2). Here again we see the Christocentric emphasis of this hymn. Here it is again without the preface: "He was manifested in the flesh, vindicated by the Spirit, seen by angels, proclaimed among the nations, believed on in the world, taken up in glory."

The hymn is made up of six phrases. It begins with the statement that "He was manifested in the flesh." The "he" here is Christ. The word "manifested" comes from the Greek root word *phanero* and means, "to cause to become visible—'to make appear, to make visible, to cause to be seen.'"[10] The idea here is that the pre-existent Son, by means of his incarnation, became visible. The invisible one became visible. In this sense, he truly is the image of the invisible God (Col. 1:15). If you have an AV or NKJV you may notice that it says, "God was manifest in the flesh" whereas many modern translations have "He was manifested in the flesh." The reason for this seeming discrepancy is that later manuscripts of 1 Timothy 3:16 had "God," but the earliest and most ancient manuscripts have "He." We will opt for the latter.[11]

Just as we saw with the hymn in Philippians 2:6-8, and in other texts like John 1:14 (which is considered by some to be part of a hymn which will be addressed later) and 1 John 1:1-2, the deity of Christ is already presupposed

---

[9] Some Bible versions like the ESV, NIV, RSV and NRSV translate the word *mysterion* as "secret."

[10] Louw and Nida, *Greek-English Lexicon*, 24.19. It also means "to cause something to be fully known by revealing clearly and in some detail." Louw and Nida, *Greek-English Lexicon*, 28.36.

[11] Translating this word as "God" instead of "He" has been explained in several ways. The relative pronoun "who" looked like this in ancient Greek: OC. The word for "God" in ancient Greek looked like this, ΘC and would have a line over it. The practice of placing lines over words deemed sacred was called *nomina sacra*, meaning "sacred names." There is not much difference between these two words other than the bar inside the word for God. There may have been some confusion as to which word was represented here, but the evidence that it was the relative pronoun is very early and explains the variant "God" coming into the text in the transmission of the manuscripts. See Metzger, *Textual Commentary*, 573-574; Wallace, *Greek Grammar Beyond the Basics*, 341-342; Barrett, *The Pastoral Epistles*, 65. In the title page of Barrett's book, there is a photograph of Codex Sinaiticus from the fourth century which shows 1 Timothy 3:16 with the reading "who." Above it, a scribe has manually tried to correct it to "God." Metzger in the citation already mentioned claims that the corrector's emendation dates to the twelfth century. If "God" was the original reading, no scribe would have changed it to "who," as the deity of Christ was central to Christianity. The relative pronoun "who" also agrees with other hymns like Philippians 2:6 and Colossians 1:15, which also begins with "who." As we have seen, this is often a grammatical indicator for the appearance of a hymn in the text.

1 TIMOTHY 3:16

in the Pastoral letters, and he is in several places identified both as God (Titus 2:13), and as pre-existent (1 Tim. 1:15; 2 Tim. 1:9). We see again how central the incarnation was for the earliest Christian believers and, as we saw in 1 John 4:1-3, this was the test of whether one was a false prophet.

The second line of the hymn states that Jesus was "vindicated by the Spirit." This is likely a reference to the resurrection as it was there that Jesus was declared to be the Son of God with power according to the Spirit of holiness (Rom. 1:3-4). We are also told that Jesus was raised by the Spirit of God (Rom. 8:11; 1 Pet. 3:18) and finally vindicated by him as Lord and Messiah (Acts 2:36).

The third line of the hymn states that Jesus was "seen by angels." There does not seem to be much to go on here. Are these evil or heavenly angels? Are they "messengers" in the same way that the apostles who witnessed the risen Christ were messengers?[12] This latter interpretation is highly unlikely as the word for "apostles" could easily have been used instead. It is possible that the reference to angels covers the general idea that Jesus both conquered the evil spiritual powers (1 Cor. 2:8; Col. 2:15), but was also witnessed and ministered to by angels throughout his life and ministry. Angels are described as keen observers of God's plan of salvation, "things into which angels long to look" (1 Pet. 1:12). The announcement of his coming and conception was revealed to Mary by the angel Gabriel (Luke 1:26-38; cf. Matt. 1:18-25), the same angel who also directed Joseph to protect the child Jesus (Matt. 2:13, 19-20). Jesus' birth was also announced to the shepherds by angels (Luke 2:8-15). After the temptation, angels also ministered to Jesus (Matt. 4:11; Mark 1:13), appeared in the garden of Gethsemane to strengthen Jesus in his hour of agony (Luke

---

[12] This has been suggested by Barrett, in *The Pastoral Epistles*, 65, but ultimately dismissed. Some have speculated that the reference to Jesus having been "seen by angels" might have been a reference to the descent of Jesus to Hades or hell following his death. This was based on the later addition to the Apostles' Creed, "he descended to the dead," also traditionally translated, "he descended into hell" after the Latin text of the Creed *descendit ad inferos*. This was believed to have been inserted after the fifth century AD, when the question of what happened to Jesus between his death and resurrection arose. Some Christians believed he went to Hades—the place of departed spirits—and freed the Old Testament saints and others who awaited his coming. Others took this reference to Jesus being seen by angels to refer to the fallen angels who would have seen him in his descent to Hades. They based this idea on certain New Testament texts like Ephesians 4:8-10 and 1 Peter 3:18-20; 4:4-6. For more on this issue see Erickson, *Christian Theology*, 706-709. This latter interpretation is highly unlikely in terms of 1 Timothy 3:16.

22:43-44),[13] were present at the empty tomb after Jesus' resurrection (Matt. 28:2-7; Mark 16:5-7; Luke 24:4-7; John 20:12), and nearby at the ascension of Jesus (Acts 1:10-11). Jesus was indeed "seen by angels." They served as both his witnesses and his servants, and even as "his angels" (Matt. 16:27; 2 Thess. 1:7), since he is superior to the angels and even worshipped by them (Heb. 1:6).

The fourth line of the hymn goes on to state that Jesus was "proclaimed among the nations." This indicates that by the time Paul wrote it, the Christian faith had already gone beyond the land of Israel to the Gentiles. The word "nations" in this hymn comes from the Greek word *ethnos*, where we get our English word ethnic and ethnicity. When used in the plural, it can refer to either nations or ethnicities, and can also be translated "Gentiles" (as we see in AV, NKJV, HCSB, NET, NRSV, and NJB). It is no surprise that Paul, who wrote the letter in which we find this hymn, is also called the "apostle to the Gentiles," or nations (Rom. 11:13). Paul wrote 1 Timothy somewhere in the mid AD 60s,[14] which, being at least thirty years after Paul's conversion and calling, means the gospel would have already gone out into the Greco-Roman world (cf. Acts 1:8).[15] The first century AD Jewish historian Josephus also wrote about the followers of Jesus, "He won over many Jews and many of the Greeks ... And the tribe of the Christians, so called after him, has still to this day not disappeared."[16]

---

[13] There is some debate as to whether Luke 22:43-44 was part of Luke's original gospel. While these verses are found in some significant manuscripts, they are nevertheless lacking in the best and earliest manuscripts. See Stein, *Luke*, 559; Carson and Moo, *Introduction to the New Testament*, 215. In one late manuscript they appear after Matthew 26:39. This story has ancient roots and it has been suggested that while it may not be part of Luke's original gospel, it may still be historically accurate. The editors of the NET on Luke 22:44 tc113 note that, "Floating texts typically suggest both spuriousness and early scribal impulses to regard the verses as *historically* authentic ... But even if the verses are not *literarily* authentic, they are probably *historically* authentic ... it is very likely that such verses recount a part of the actual suffering of our Lord" (italics in original).

[14] Carson and Moo, *Introduction to the New Testament*, 571-572.

[15] It is also possible that Paul had taken the gospel as far as Spain, but we are not sure on this point. Spain would have been understood as the farthest westerly point (the Iberian Peninsula), and the "uttermost ends of the earth" to those living in the first century AD. This kind of language is also used in Acts 1:8, and Paul did mention a desire to visit Spain in Romans 15:24, 28. On this question see Tony Costa, "Paul's Westward Mission in Acts and the Epistles: Incidental, Deliberate, or Prophetic?" *AJBT* 9, no. 28 (August 2008). Online access https://www.biblicaltheology.com/Research/CostaT02.pdf.

[16] Josephus, *Antiquities* 18.3.3 §63. This section in Josephus, known as the *Testimonium Flavianum*, has been a controversial text and some believe there may have been some interpolations

1 TIMOTHY 3:16

The fifth line of the hymn goes on to say that Jesus was "believed on in the world." This appears to be a triumphant statement that Christ has reclaimed the world to himself. God's love for the world in saving sinners and giving them eternal life is a confirmation of this truth (John 3:16-17). In his hymn, Paul uses the same word Greek word for world (*kosmos*) that John uses in his gospel. The promise of God to his Son is that he would make the nations his inheritance and "the ends of the earth" his possession, which Jesus would acquire through his suffering and resurrection (Ps. 2:8; 22:27; cf. Acts 1:8).

In the sixth and final line of the hymn, it concludes with the words, "taken up in glory." This appears to be a reference to the ascension of Jesus (Acts 1:9-11). The ascension marks the inauguration of the session of Christ and his enthronement in heaven at the right hand of the Father (Ps. 110:1). The ascension of Jesus, then, acts as a kind of coronation, marking the point at which the King of glory returns to his heavenly city (Ps. 24:7-10). In the *Carmen Christi*, Jesus is described as being "highly exalted" (Phil. 2:9), and it ends with the universe itself bowing to the enthroned Christ (Phil. 2:10-11).

As we look at the hymn in 1 Timothy 3:16 we see once again that the core element is Jesus himself. Early Christians, under the pastoral care of Timothy, would have together sung this hymn about the pre-existent Son who became flesh, was vindicated by the Spirit in his resurrection, was witnessed and seen by angels, was proclaimed among the nations through the gospel message, was believed on in the world, and finally taken up in glory. This is the hymn of a victorious Savior who entered our world from glory, accomplished his mission in the world, and then returned back to glory. Its trajectory is similar to the "V" paradigm we saw in the *Carmen Christi*, and clearly demonstrates a high doctrine of Christ. Robert Reymond correctly notes, "Here is, indeed, a high Christology, found in the confessional framework of an early Christian hymn, that is in accord with that high Christology found throughout the Pauline corpus, and it confesses a Messiah who is Deity incarnate!"[17] There are many similarities between the hymn found in 1 Timothy 3 and the *Carmen Christi*. In both cases, Jesus is stated as being the pre-existent true God who takes on human flesh, is vindicated, and then taken up into glory.

---

by Christian scribes. However, when these perceived interpolations are removed, the text appears to be genuinely that of Josephus. The citations I have quoted are considered sound. See John P. Meier, *A Marginal Jew: Rethinking the Historical Jesus*, vol. 1, *The Roots of the Problem and the Person* (New York: Doubleday, 1991), 63-65.

[17] Reymond, *Jesus*, 271-272.

The work of the gospel is also implied in this hymn as it speaks of Christ being proclaimed among the nations and believed on in the world. We see the descent of Christ into the world, and then his ascent back to glory, a theme which we also saw in the *Carmen Christi*. What is absent from this hymn, however, is any explicit reference to the suffering and death of Jesus. The reference to the resurrection is clear enough from Paul's claim that Jesus was "vindicated in the Spirit"; a statement which assumes the death of Jesus.[18] As we consider the grammar of 1 Timothy 3:16, we find further evidence that we are likely dealing with a hymn. The first indicator is that in the Greek text it begins with the relative pronoun ὅς (*hos*), which means "who," just as we find in Philippians 2:6. The NASB brings this pronoun out nicely by translating the beginning of 1 Timothy 3:16 as, "He *who* was revealed in the flesh" (italics mine). This agrees with point three of the criteria for hymns listed in Chapter 12, which indicates the frequent use of the relative pronoun in hymnic material.

We notice a number of other criteria evident in 1 Timothy 3:16. First, there is an "antithetic style" that uses "couplets" (point four), and a vocabulary that is also "highly stylized" (point five). The antithetic style is seen in the contrast between the heavenly and earthly spheres; Jesus is manifested in a body (earthly), vindicated by the Spirit (heavenly), seen by angels (heavenly), proclaimed to the nations (earthly), believed on in the world (earthly), and then taken up in glory (heavenly). When we look closely, we see the use of three such couplets, which can be represented in an "AB" pattern, where "A" represents the earthly sphere, and "B" represents the heavenly sphere. The structure looks something like this:[19]

1. A (manifested in the flesh) B (vindicated in Spirit)
2. B (seen by angels) A (proclaimed among nations)
3. A (believed on in the world) B (taken up in glory)

In this hymn there are also six dative nouns, some of which are preceded with the preposition "in" (*en*): flesh, Spirit, angels, nations, world, and glory.[20]

---

[18] Guthrie, *The Pastoral Epistles*, 105.
[19] I am following the example in Reymond, *Jesus*, 269. See also Fuller, *The Foundations of New Testament Christology*, 216–217.
[20] Reymond, *Jesus*, 269.

1 Timothy 3:16

One of the uses of the dative case is to communicate the idea of an action being done in an instrumental or local sense.[21] This would mean in the case of this hymn, that the emphasis is on the local spheres of the heavenly realm (Spirit, angels, glory) and the earthly realm (flesh, nations, world) This hymn thus seems to be using the local, or spatial, aspect of the dative, as seen in the reference to the heavenly and earthly sphere. It is Christ himself who is at the centre, and who unites both the heavenly and earthly spheres in himself.[22]

Why did Paul refer to this hymn in his letter? Likely to reconfigure the church towards what was most important: the identity and work of the Lord Jesus Christ. It was also to ground them in true doctrine. In the pastoral letters, a recurring phrase Paul uses is "sound doctrine," or "sound words" (1 Tim. 1:10; 6:3; Titus 1:9; 2:1). Notice that immediately after citing this hymn, Paul issues a stern warning (remember that there were no chapter and verse divisions in the original manuscripts of the New Testament), "Now the Spirit expressly says that in later times some will depart from the faith by devoting themselves to deceitful spirits and teachings of demons" (1 Tim. 4:1). Paul later expressed concern that "the time is coming when people will not endure sound teaching" (2 Tim. 4:3). One of the ways his readers could safeguard themselves against heresy is to know how to rightly handle God's breathed-out Word, and so be fully equipped (2 Tim. 3:15-17) to divide the word of truth (2 Tim. 2:15). Gordon Fee correctly notes that "the content of the hymn exists precisely to prepare the way for the indictment of false teachers in [1 Tim.] 4:1-5."[23] It is encouraging to know that the precious truths of sound doctrine are contained in God's Word, and were historically expressed and sung in a hymn the likes of which we find in 1 Timothy 3:16.

As we look at this ancient hymn, we also see sections which are referred to in the Apostles' Creed, such as the reference to the ascension of Jesus, "He ascended into heaven, and is seated at the right hand of the Father." This seems to coincide with the hymn's line that he was "taken up in glory." We see also parts which are referenced to in the Nicene Creed: "Who, for us men and our salvation, came down from heaven ... and was made man," which matches with the hymn's line, "He was manifested in the flesh." The Nicene

---

[21] Wallace, *Greek Grammar Beyond the Basics*, 138.
[22] Reymond, *Jesus*, 269. Fuller, *The Foundations of New Testament Christology*, 217 notes "the hymn does not follow a chronological order."
[23] Fee, *Pauline Christology*, 432.

Early Christian Creeds and Hymns

Creed also says, "And [he] ascended into heaven, and sits at the right hand of the Father, and he will come again with glory to judge the living and the dead" which also matches the hymn's line that he was "taken up in glory." The Apostles' and Nicene creed, then, seem to function as an elaboration and expansion of this ancient hymn.

As with all the hymns we have examined up to this point, Jesus remains the focal point. This reminds us that there is no Christianity without Christ. While all other religions may continue to exist without their founders, Christianity cannot exist without Christ. Christianity rests on the claim that its Founder was not only raised from the dead, but is still alive today.

14
THE WAKE-UP HYMN
EPHESIANS 5:14

Another important hymn, and perhaps one of the shortest, is found in Ephesians 5:14. Before moving directly into this hymn, it might be profitable to first examine its underlying context. In Ephesians 5:1-2 Paul lays down a set of rules for the believers as they embark on the new life they have come into through Christ.

He calls them to be imitators of God, like children who should naturally want to emulate their heavenly Father (verse 1). He tells them to walk in love just as Jesus loved them and demonstrated it in offering himself up to God as a fragrant offering and sacrifice (verse 2). Notice how Paul defines the love of Jesus by pointing to his redemptive work on the cross and his total submission to God. In verses 3-19 Paul then challenges these believers to not only mature in their Christian walk (which he also mentions in Eph. 4:13-14), but to renounce the old ways in which they formerly lived—sexual immorality, greed, filthiness and coarse language, warning that those who indulge in such practices have no inheritance in God's kingdom. He calls on them to be children of light and not darkness; as they are a changed people, they are now to seek God's will for their lives. He also encourages them to avoid carousing and drunkenness, and instead to be filled with the Holy Spirit (Eph. 5:18). He then tells them to sing to the Lord in psalms, hymns, and spiritual songs, and to always give thanks to God in the name of Jesus (Eph. 5:19-20). It is here that Paul cites the hymn which is embedded in Ephesians 5:14: "For anything that becomes visible is light. Therefore it says, 'Awake, O sleeper, and arise from the dead, and Christ will shine on you.'"

Upon first inspection we note how short this hymn is. It is believed by some scholars to be "a fragment of an early Christian hymn ... one of the first hymns the Christian Church ever sang."[1] The hymn itself is comprised of the words,

---

[1] William Barclay, *The Letters to the Galatians and Ephesians*, rev. ed. (Burlington: G.R. Welch Co. Ltd., 1976), 165-166.

EARLY CHRISTIAN CREEDS AND HYMNS

"Awake, O sleeper, and arise from the dead, and Christ will shine on you."[2] How do we know this is a hymn? Once again we must turn to the grammatical structure for confirmation. The preface to the hymn contains the words, διὸ λέγει (*dio legei*), "therefore it says." In point three of the criteria for hymns noted in Chapter 12, we saw how hymns could be identified by introductory phrases such as "thus it says," or, as we have it, "therefore it says."[3] Here Paul is citing a well-known poetic saying which also happens to be a hymn.

Although foreign to us, this hymn was obviously known by Paul and his readers. We do not know the origin of this hymn other than a possible allusion to some Old Testament passages that we shall see below. It may also have been one of the "spiritual songs" that Paul mentions in Ephesians 5:19 and Colossians 3:16, which we examined in Chapter 11. Paul interjects this hymn into his letter as a gospel call to those who were still asleep: they were to wake up so that the light of Christ could shine on them.[4] Paul has just spoken at the beginning of verse 14 of what is visible being in the light, the implication being that those who still walk in darkness cannot see. He reminds them in Ephesians 2:1–6 that they were once dead in trespasses and sins but that God in his rich mercy and grace made them alive again and raised them up with Christ.

The backdrop to this hymn in Ephesians 5:14 may be two Old Testament passages from Isaiah. The first is Isaiah 60:1, "Arise, shine, for your light has come, and the glory of the LORD has risen upon you"; the second is from Isaiah 26:19, "You who dwell in the dust, awake and sing for joy!" Another potential source text is Jonah 1:6, "What do you mean, you sleeper?"[5] Isaiah

---

[2] The Church Father Jerome was of the conviction that these words were uttered to Adam by Christ while releasing him from Hades (known in the West as "the harrowing of hell"). Adam was believed by both Jerome and Epiphanius to have been buried and held prisoner underneath the place where Jesus was crucified at Golgotha and that the reason the place was called "Golgotha" was because it was also the place where Adam's skull was! See F.F. Bruce, *The Epistles to the Colossians, to Philemon, and to the Ephesians*, NICNT (Grand Rapids: Eerdmans, 1984), 376–377 n.43.

[3] Wallace, *Greek Grammar Beyond the Basics*, 533 notes that the third person singular *legei*, "it says," is usually used to introduce a quotation from the OT. In this case Wallace states that "it may well be a quotation of an early Christian creedal hymn."

[4] In the second century AD, the *Gospel of Peter*, an apocryphal gospel with gnostic leanings, states in 10: 41-42, "And they were hearing a voice from the heavens saying, 'Have you made proclamation to the fallen-asleep?'" The "fallen-asleep" here refers to the ones who have not awakened to spiritual enlightenment and illumination.

[5] Bruce, *Epistles to the Colossians*, 376. The context of Isaiah 26:19 clearly shows that the *bodily* resurrection is in view here and not just a spiritual one. In Jonah 1:6 the text is referring to Jonah, who is asleep on a boat during a storm and is woken up by the captain of the boat. Though the captain is a pagan, he encourages Jonah to call out to his God.

60:1 certainly seems to be a passage that resonates with the hymn found in Ephesians 5:14 as the call is to arise in light of the glory of Yahweh which has risen upon them. Isaiah 60:2 contrasts the light which Yahweh will shine with a gross darkness that covers the people, "For behold, darkness shall cover the earth, and thick darkness the peoples; but the LORD will arise upon you, and his glory will be seen upon you." We also see that the call of Isaiah is not reserved only for Israel, but to the surrounding nations as well, "And nations [the Gentiles] shall come to your light, and kings to the brightness of your rising" (Isa. 60:3). So in Ephesians, the gathering of Jews and Gentiles into the Messiah's one body is a major theme (Eph. 2:11-22; 3:1-11). Words like "arise," "darkness," and "light" in Isaiah 60:1-3 also suggest similarities with the hymn of Ephesians 5:14.

F.F. Bruce states that this hymn was "a primitive baptismal hymn, in which the congregation greets the new convert as he or she emerges sacramentally from the sleep of spiritual death and into the light of life."[6] William Barclay similarly states, "Perhaps these were the lines which were sung as they [baptized Christians] arose from the water, to symbolize the passage from the dark sleep of paganism to the awakened light of the Christian way."[7] Paul reminds them that, "for at one time you were darkness, but now you are light in the Lord. Walk as children of light" (Eph. 5:8), and further admonishes them to "take no part in the unfruitful works of darkness, but instead expose them" (Eph. 5:11). Note the reference to both "light" and "darkness," which have been set up antithetically to each other.[8] Paul further reminds his readers that their warfare is "against the rulers, against the authorities, against the cosmic powers over this present *darkness*, against the spiritual forces of evil in the heavenly places" (Eph. 6:12; italics mine). The "darkness" here is associated with the "spiritual forces of evil." The hymn here is speaking of the illumination which occurs at regeneration, and is repeated in the line from the beloved hymn "Amazing Grace": "I once was blind but now I see." This verse is clearly referring to spiritual illumination as it is only Christ who is able to give light, and coming to Christ is elsewhere described as being "enlightened" (Heb. 6:4; 10:32). Jesus said, "For judgment I have come into this world, so that those who do not see may gain their sight, and the ones who see may

---

[6] Bruce, *Epistles to the Colossians*, 376.
[7] Barclay, *Letters to the Galatians and Ephesians*, 165.
[8] We see the same contrast between light and darkness in the letters of John (1 John 1:5, 7; 2:8-10).

become blind" (John 9:39). This may sound confusing at first, but remember that the context here is Jesus' healing of the blind man (John 9:1-11), who can now see both physically and spiritually, while the Pharisees who claimed to be able to see are actually spiritually blind (John 9:40-41).

In the hymn of Ephesians 5:14, we first find an imperative—the command to "awake." When Jesus raised Lazarus from the sleep of death, he gave a similar command to "come out" (John 11:43).[9] The same thing happens in spiritual awakening; the spiritually dead hear the voice of the Son of God and come to life (John 5:25). The implication again being that those who are unregenerate are still "asleep," or spiritually dead (cf. Eph. 2:1), hence the reference in this hymn to "arise from the dead." This command to awake is addressed in the vocative case to "the sleeper." The vocative case is used as a form of address (thus we have, "Awake, O sleeper" where "sleeper" is a nominative present participle being used as a vocative).[10] The sleeper is called to awaken out of the slumber of spiritual darkness into the light of Christ (cf. Acts 26:18; Col. 1:13). The word "sleeper" is actually a participle in the original Greek and carries the idea of "the sleeping one." Jesus, of course, is that source of light (John 1:9), and even claimed to be "the light of the world" (John 8:12). As the risen Christ dwells in the believer and his light radiates within them, they too are called to be "the light of the world" (Matt. 5:14). I mentioned earlier that this hymn appears to be a gospel call and perhaps would have been sung in the context of an evangelistic service. This hymn also communicates what the earliest Christians believed about sinners; they needed to be awakened, raised from death, and receive the light of Christ.

Compared to the other two hymns we looked at in Philippians 2:6-11 and 1 Timothy 3:16, this hymn is quite different. Its primary motive is to inspire the kind of hope that would call lost sinners to salvation in Christ. Notice, however, that Jesus is still mentioned in this hymn as the light who will shine on the sleepers. Theologically speaking, this hymn does not promote a synergistic view that the sinner is able to achieve both the awakening and arising on their own. Paul has elsewhere made it abundantly clear that it is God alone who

---

[9] Notice how Jesus refers to Lazarus, who had died, "Our friend Lazarus has *fallen asleep*, but I go to *awaken him*" (John 11:11; italics mine). The disciples thought Jesus meant that Lazarus was having an afternoon nap, but "then Jesus told them plainly, 'Lazarus has died'" (John 11:14). See also Mark 5:39 and Luke 8:52.

[10] On the vocative case see Wallace, *Greek Grammar Beyond the Basics*, 65-71.

Ephesians 5:14

gives life and raises sinners from the state of spiritual death to life in Christ (Eph. 2:1-6). This is why I referred to this hymn as a gospel call. When we call people to the gospel, we do so indiscriminately; we implore and plead with sinners to wake up from their slumber in sin and come to Christ. We also pray that God, by his irresistible grace, would call to himself those whom he foreknew and predestined from before the foundation of the world (Eph. 1:3-9). We know that God not only ordains the end, but also the means to that end— and as so beautifully expressed in the short hymn of Ephesians 5:14, we see the means must involve the gospel call.

15
THE HYMN OF THE SUFFERING MESSIAH
1 PETER 2:22-24

We have so far examined three early Christian hymns: Philippians 2:6-11, 1 Timothy 3:16, and Ephesians 5:14. You will notice that all these hymns also come from Paul's letters. However, there also other hymns in the New Testament outside of Paul's letters that, although not so well-known, are equally worthy our attention.

We will next consider the hymn found in 1 Peter 2:22-24, which reads:

He [who] committed no sin, neither was deceit found in his mouth. [who]When he was reviled, he did not revile in return; when he suffered, he did not threaten, but continued entrusting himself to him who judges justly. He [who] himself bore our sins in his body on the tree, that we might die to sin and live to righteousness. By his wounds you have been healed.

We know that a hymn is embedded in this text because of the initial use of the nominative singular relative pronoun ὅς (*hos*), which as we have seen is characteristic of creedal and hymnic structures in the New Testament.[1] The relative pronoun appears right at the beginning of 1 Peter 2:22, 23, and 24—just as we saw with the *Carmen Christi* in Philippians 2:6. This hymn deals first with the sinlessness of Jesus and his purity. Regarding Jesus, the hymn mentions that "neither was deceit found in his mouth" (2:22), which is actually a citation from Isaiah 53:9, which states that "there was no deceit in his mouth." It should be noted that Isaiah 53 is one of several "servant songs" which refer to the Messiah's suffering, and which Peter and other early leaders were likely well aware of.[2] While Peter does likely have Isaiah 53 in the background, it is interesting that he orders the material in this hymn according to the pattern

---

[1] This is point three in the criteria for hymn structures. See Chapter 12.
[2] In Acts 8:26-35 the Ethiopian eunuch is reading from Isaiah 53 when Philip is divinely directed to him and explains that the text of Isaiah 53 is referring to Jesus.

found in the passion accounts of the gospels. He moves from Jesus' trials, in which he remained silent before his accusers and was mocked and beaten, to his death on the cross.[3] We see that the Servant of Isaiah 53 is not merely a servant, but the *suffering* Servant of the Lord. Peter later echoes this hymn when he says that there was no deceit found in Jesus' mouth, and exhorts his readers, "Let him keep his tongue from evil and his lips *from speaking deceit*" (1 Pet. 3:10; italics mine). Christians are to imitate their Lord and Master.

The fact that Jesus did not respond in kind to his enemies but submitted himself to God is also mentioned here. Jesus is once again referred to as a role model that Christian believers should follow. There is an allusion here to Isaiah 53:7 where the Servant of the Lord was oppressed and afflicted and yet he did not open his mouth in his own defense or revile those who oppressed him; rather he was like a lamb that is silent before its shearers.[4] The same verse goes on to describe the suffering Servant of the Lord as a lamb led to the slaughter. Earlier in the letter Peter had already mentioned that the believers he was writing to were redeemed by Christ's precious blood, who was like a lamb without blemish or spot (1 Pet. 1:19).

---

[3] Green, *1 Peter*, 85. Green makes the point on the same page that "Apparently, Peter found in Isaiah 53 a commentary on Jesus' passion which he then organized in relation to the events of Jesus' suffering and death." This is an important statement because it shows that Peter was not taking the events in Jesus' life and trying to woodenly match them with the order found in Isaiah 53. Rather, Peter interprets Isaiah 53 *after* the life, death, and resurrection of Jesus and seeing those events fulfilled in the text. This was, in fact, the way Jesus taught his disciples to interpret the OT (Luke 24:27,44). Green argues similarly that "in the first century [AD] ... scriptural texts were shaped in light of later events (rather than events being manufactured in order to "prove" ancient prophecies)." Green, *1 Peter*, 85-86 n.56. It is clear that Peter took the instructions of Jesus in Luke 24:27, 44 to heart. We can see this as we compare what Jesus said in Luke 24:26 to what he says in 1 Peter 1:10-11. In Luke 24:25-26, Jesus said, "O foolish ones, and slow of heart to believe all that *the prophets* have spoken! Was it not necessary that the *Christ should suffer* these things and *enter into his glory?*" (italics mine). Peter writes, "Concerning this salvation, *the prophets* who prophesied about the grace that was to be yours searched and inquired carefully, inquiring what person or time the Spirit of Christ in them was indicating when he predicted *the sufferings of Christ* and the *subsequent glories*" (italics mine). Note the order: suffering, and then entering into glory. There is no crown without the cross. Luke seems to have more affinity with Paul as he was his travelling companion, but here we see a close textual familiarity between Luke and Peter. See also comments in Green, *1 Peter*, 86.

[4] Critics raise the objection that Jesus did in fact speak during his trial when he spoke to Pilate and responded to the high priest's question. However, Isaiah 53 is not saying the suffering Servant would be a mute, but rather that he would not open his mouth *in his own defense*. Jesus could easily have saved himself from his trial as the witnesses contradicted each other. Amazingly, Jesus actually incriminates himself in responding to the high priest's question (Mark 14:61). He could have "pleaded the fifth" so to speak and walked away. Instead, his mission was to come and give his life as a ransom (Mark 10:45). He knew he would have to go to the cross and fulfill his mission.

1 Peter 2:22-24

Based on the truth of this hymn, Peter later encourages his readers to imitate the Lord Jesus, "For it is better to suffer for doing good, if that should be God's will, than for doing evil" (1 Pet. 3:17).[5] The theme of Jesus' sufferings becomes a model for the early Christians to follow because they too suffered for their beliefs. Peter, in fact, reminds them that just as Jesus suffered, so his followers would also suffer for his sake, "For to this you have been called, because Christ also suffered for you, leaving you an example, so that you might follow in his steps" (1 Pet. 2:21). The theme of 1 Peter is Christian suffering and persecution.

The hymn then continues to speak about Jesus bearing "our sins" in his body on the tree. Note that he "himself" bore our sins. Jesus is unique in that he alone could bear our sins, and did so voluntarily and once for all, as Peter later explains, "For Christ also suffered once for sins, the righteous for the unrighteous" (1 Pet. 3:18). Note the language of substitution here: the righteous [Christ] for the unrighteous. This is the great exchange. Christ takes the place of the unrighteous so they can in turn receive his righteousness. Yahweh said of the Suffering Servant, "By his knowledge shall the righteous one, my servant, make many to be accounted righteous" (Isa. 53:11). Here we find the great truth of justification in the Old Testament. Despite what some may think, the doctrine of justification by faith alone was not invented by Paul or the Reformers; rather, it is firmly rooted in the Old Testament and brought to fulfillment in the death of Christ in the New Testament. Justification must be by faith alone, as sinners are incapable of meeting God's righteous standards as "all our righteous acts are like a polluted garment" (Isa. 64:6).

The sufferings of Jesus are also unique in that they atone for sin. This means that while Christian believers share in Christ's sufferings by being in union with him, their sufferings are not redemptive and cannot atone for sin. Christ alone was without sin and only the righteous can suffer on behalf of the unrighteous. The atonement of Christ, then, is central to Christian faith. Paul makes a similar statement when he says, "Now I rejoice in my sufferings for your sake, and in my flesh I am filling up what is lacking in Christ's afflictions for the sake of his body, that is, the church" (Col. 1:24).[6] Paul wanted to be like his Lord and Saviour even in the sharing of his sufferings (Phil. 3:10), and

---

[5] The source for these ideas is found in the teachings of Jesus, which Peter would have heard in the earthly ministry of the Lord (Matthew 5:43-48; Luke 6:27-36). Paul also knew of this teaching of Jesus (Romans 12:14).

[6] See comments in Bruce, *Epistles to the Colossians*, 81-84.

understood that all Christian believers also share in this suffering as well (2 Cor. 1:5). Sharing in the afflictions and sufferings of Christ continue to the present day because the church is the body of Christ. When the body of Christ, the church, is afflicted and persecuted, the Head of the church is also to some degree afflicted and persecuted. When Saul of Tarsus met the risen Christ on the road to Damascus, the first words of Jesus to him were, "Saul, Saul, why are you persecuting me?" (Acts 9:4; cf. 22:7; 26:14). How was Saul persecuting Jesus? By persecuting his church. What we do the least of Christ's brethren, we also do to Christ himself (Matt. 25:40). That is how closely united Christ is to his church. Whoever hears the message of the apostles contained in Scripture hears Christ himself, "The one who hears you hears me, and the one who rejects you rejects me" (Luke 10:16). Christ is organically connected with his people.

The backdrop to this language of substitution in 1 Peter can also be seen in Isaiah 53:8. Here it says that the Servant of Yahweh was "cut off out of the land of the living," i.e., he died, and was "stricken *for the transgression of my people*" (italics mine). The word meaning "cut off" in Hebrew comes from the root word *gazar* and is used elsewhere in the Hebrew Bible to denote cutting or hacking off (1 Kgs. 3:24). It is a violent verb.[7] Note the language of substitution again: he was stricken *for* the transgression of God's people.

The reference to the body of Jesus also underscores both the reality of the incarnation and the reality of his death. Jesus was a real human being and really died—a point that later heretics like the Docetic Gnostics would deny.[8] The word "bore," from the Greek root word *anaphero*, refers to Jesus taking our sins on himself. This is the same Greek word used in the LXX for bringing sacrifices to God (Gen. 8:20; Lev. 14:20; 17:5), and the language of the Messiah bearing and carrying the sins of his people (Isa. 53:4, 11–12) and serves as

---

[7] J. Alec Motyer, *Isaiah: An Introduction and Commentary* (ed. Donald J. Wiseman; Vol. 20. TOTC; Downers Grove: IVP Academic, 1999), 380; Daniel 9:26 speaks of the anointed one or Messiah being "cut off" but a different Hebrew word, *karath*, is used.

[8] Already in the early second century AD (about AD 110), Ignatius, bishop of Antioch had to oppose the Docetic Gnostics. Notice Ignatius' emphasis on the word "truly" when speaking about the suffering, death, and resurrection of Jesus in his *Letter to the Trallians* 9:4 (italics mine): "Be deaf when anyone speaks to you apart from Jesus Christ, Who was of the stock of David, Who was born of Mary, Who was *truly* born, ate and drank, was *truly* persecuted under Pontius Pilate, was *truly* crucified and died in the sight of beings heavenly, earthly and under the earth, Who was *truly* raised from the dead, His Father raising Him."

1 PETER 2:22-24

the background for this hymn.⁹ The Servant of the Lord "shall bear their iniquities" (Isa. 53:11). The same word is also used by James when he describes Abraham offering up Isaac (Jas. 2:21).¹⁰ The Greek root word *anaphero* is a word used for sacrifice. This word communicates the notion of offering something or someone up to God.¹¹ This language of carrying the sins of others is similar to the creed we saw in 1 Corinthians 15:3, "Christ died for *our sins* in accordance with the Scriptures" (italics mine). Notice how Paul connects the death of Jesus for our sins with the Scriptures, which no doubt would have included Isaiah 53 and which Peter alludes to in this hymn. This is clearly a reference to the atoning death of Jesus on the cross.

Notice also that Peter refers to Jesus bearing our sins "on the tree" (1 Pet. 2:24) and does not use the word "cross" here. This reference points back to Deuteronomy 21:22-23 where it speaks about the curse of God being placed upon anyone who hangs on a tree. As we have seen, Paul deals with this same issue in Galatians 3:13 where he tells us that Christ became a curse *for us*. Repeatedly we see the atoning work of Christ taking centre stage in several of these hymns. In 1 Peter 2:22-24, this would indicate that the death of Jesus was understood as the death of one who was cursed by God; but since Jesus was without sin (1 Pet. 2:22), this means he bore the curse for us. This is why the hymn goes on to mention that Jesus died so "that we might die to sin and live to righteousness." In union with Christ (the meaning of being "in Christ"), we died to sin and now live to righteousness in sanctification. That this spiritual healing has taken place in the atoning work of Christ is made clear at the end of the hymn, "By his wounds you have been healed." That Peter had Isaiah 53 in his mind when citing this hymn is seen in 1 Peter 2:24 where he writes concerning Jesus, "By his wounds you have been healed"—a reference to Isaiah 53:5, "And with his stripes we are healed." What should not be missed here is that Peter cites the text of Isaiah 53:5 by turning it into a

---

⁹ Arnold G. Fruchtenbaum, *The Messianic Jewish Epistles*, Ariel's Bible Commentary (Tustin: Ariel Ministries, 2005), 350-351.

¹⁰ Fruchtenbaum, *Messianic Jewish Epistles*, 350-351.

¹¹ Louw and Nida, *Greek-English Lexicon*, 53.17 define the Greek root word *anaphero* as "to offer up someone or something as a sacrifice (a technical term in the sacrificial system)— 'to offer, to offer up, to make an offering.'" The preposition "ana" in *anaphero* carries the idea of upward movement and thus is also used to express other actions like "lead up" and "carry up." Louw and Nida, *Greek-English Lexicon*, 15.176, 206. The sacrificial victim was led up and carried up to the altar to be sacrificed and we can see how Jesus similarly was also led up and carried up to Calvary to become the perfect sacrifice.

EARLY CHRISTIAN CREEDS AND HYMNS

fulfillment, "By his wounds *you have been* healed" (italics mine). This text is speaking about *spiritual* healing, not physical healing, as some circles have supposed. In this hymn, Peter has been speaking about Jesus bearing our *sins* in his body, and how he has made atonement so that we might live in righteousness. This is soteriological language, and refers to the salvation Jesus accomplished in his death for believers.

The reference in 1 Peter 2:24 to Jesus bearing our sins in "his body on the tree," and the curse that follows would not have been lost on the Jews in Peter's day.[12] Since Peter was an apostle to the Jews (Gal. 2:7-8), he likely would have had to deal with this objection.[13] In fact it is likely for this reason that Paul states that the preaching of Christ crucified was a "stumbling block" to the Jews (1 Cor. 1:23). Peter, like Paul, shows that the death of Jesus on the tree was his taking our sins upon himself and bearing the curse that we deserved.

What were these earliest Christians singing about in the hymn of 1 Peter 2:22-24? They were singing about Jesus: who he was and what he did. Notice, as stated earlier, that the hymns we have examined are all Christocentric. In this hymn, they sing about Jesus being sinless, that he did not take revenge on his enemies, and that he did not return evil for evil. Peter will later tell believers to act in the same way, "Do not repay evil for evil or reviling for reviling" (1 Pet. 3:9; cf. Rom. 12:17; 1 Thess. 5:15). Rather, they were called to entrust themselves to the justice of God, as he is the one who will judge justly (cf. 1 Pet. 1:17). The hymn then speaks about the sacrifice of Jesus; he bore our sins on the accursed tree in his own body. As we said in our previous hymn, the incarnate Son truly became a human being (Phil. 2:6-8; 1 Tim. 3:16). This was absolutely necessary so that a sacrifice could be made on our behalf (cf. Heb. 10:5-10).[14] The importance of this truth is reflected in the Christian ordinance of the Lord's Supper, where we remember his *body* and *blood*, the reason being that the body of Jesus was the vehicle of his sacrifice for us. Jesus died, and in him we too have died to sin; through his resurrection, we also rise "to live to

---

[12] Other references that speak of the crucifixion of Jesus as hanging on a tree can be found in Acts 5:30, 10:39, and 13:29.

[13] If Christian tradition is correct, it is somewhat ironic that Peter was also crucified upside down in Rome in about AD 68. The words in the hymn that speak of Jesus bearing our sins on the tree would no doubt have resonated with Peter. Jesus predicted Peter would die as a martyr and describes the stretching out of the hands—an idiom for crucifixion (John 21:18-19). On Peter's martyrdom see Eusebius, *Hist. Eccl.* 3.1, 30; Carson and Moo, *Introduction to the New Testament*, 663; Donald Guthrie, "Peter the Apostle," in *New International Dictionary*, 770.

[14] Note Hebrews 10:10, "And by that will we have been sanctified through *the offering of the body of Jesus Christ once for all*" (italics mine).

1 PETER 2:22-24

righteousness." By his wounds (or "stripes," AV), we have been healed. Our salvation is an accomplished work.

After this hymn, Peter states, "For you were straying like sheep, but have now returned to the Shepherd and Overseer of your souls" (1 Pet. 2:25). The idea that believers formerly were "straying like sheep" is another allusion to Isaiah 53:6, "All we like sheep have gone astray; we have turned every one to his own way." We were all lost, turning to our own selfish and sinful ways, but Isaiah 53:6 goes on to say that "the LORD has laid on him [the Servant/Messiah] the iniquity of us all." Peter sees believers as those who were formerly lost and astray, but that now have returned to "the Shepherd and Overseer" of their souls. The image of a shepherd is one which runs throughout Scripture (Ps. 23), and Jesus also applies such imagery to himself as he appropriates the title of Shepherd over his sheep (John 10:11-18, 26-30). An overseer (or "bishop"; AV) was also a keeper and guardian.[15] These images show us that Jesus is not only a Shepherd, but the Guardian and Keeper of his sheep; for that reason, he says his sheep will never perish (John 10:28-29).

Echoes of this hymn can be also be seen in the Apostles' Creed where it states concerning Jesus, "He suffered under Pontius Pilate, was crucified, died." Notice that Jesus' suffering, his crucifixion, and his death are all mentioned in this hymn. In the Nicene Creed it also states that "he was crucified for us under Pontius Pilate; he suffered." This topic of the suffering of Jesus, and Christian believers by extension, is a major theme in 1 Peter and especially in the hymn of 2:22-24. As Christians sang it together, they were no doubt encouraged and blessed to know that they were secure in the hands of Jesus.

---

[15] The idea of a shepherd, or guardian, would resonate with Peter as he was also appointed by Jesus to be a shepherd over his sheep (John 21:15-17). The word translated as "pastor" in the New Testament is the word "shepherd" in the original Greek (Ephesians 4:11). Pastors are also "overseers" (1 Timothy 3:1-7; Titus 1:7) and "elders" (1 Timothy 4:14; 5:17-19; Titus 1:5) as these terms are used interchangeably. Peter also calls himself a "fellow elder" (1 Peter 5:1).

16
A JEWISH HYMN
HEBREWS 1:2B-4

We find another passage containing a hymn in Hebrews 1:1-4. I have placed the words believed to make up the hymnic portion of this text in bold lettering:

> Long ago, at many times and in many ways, God spoke to our fathers by the prophets, but in these last days he has spoken to us by his Son, **whom [who] he appointed the heir of all things, through whom [who] also he created the world. He [who] is the radiance of the glory of God and the exact imprint of his nature, and he upholds the universe by the word of his power. After making purification for sins, he sat down at the right hand of the Majesty on high, having become as much superior to angels as the name he has inherited is more excellent than theirs.**

The opening to the letter of Hebrews is interesting as there is no author mentioned, though there have been many theories as to who the author might be. The King James Version has as a superscript to the letter to the Hebrews, "The Epistle of Paul the Apostle to the Hebrews." This, of course, is not part of the inspired text. I personally doubt Paul was the author of this letter due to several internal textual factors.[1]

Apart from the author being unknown, we are also not explicitly told who the readers of the letter are, or to what church in which city the letter is being addressed to. What we *can* discern from the letter is that its readers are likely Jewish due to the fact that the letter covers mainly Jewish themes right from the first verse. The danger this letter addresses is that some Jewish believers were feeling tempted to go back to the Jewish sacrificial system, the temple, and the authority of the unbelieving Jewish leaders. The readers also appear to be well acquainted with all things Jewish (prophets, angels, Moses, Sabbath,

---

[1] On the question of the authorship of Hebrews see Carson and Moo, *Introduction to the New Testament*, 600-604; Fruchtenbaum, *Messianic Jewish Epistles*, 3.

Melchizedek, Aaron, the priesthood, sacrificial system, the tabernacle and its furniture, etc.).[2]

What is striking about Hebrews is that its Christology is very similar to Paul's and what we find in the Gospel of John. The fact that this letter was written to Hebrew believers and contains such a high Christology indicates that belief in the deity of Christ was *not* a later development in Gentile Christianity which occurred apart from its Jewish counterparts. Some scholars in the beginning of the twentieth century (and still today) argue that belief in the deity of Christ was a later doctrinal development, but this is certainly not the case as the deity of Christ was held to equally by Gentile and Jewish believers in the first century AD.[3] The dating of Hebrews can safely be placed before AD 70 as it still speaks of the sacrifices taking place in the temple, which implies that it had not yet been destroyed.[4]

The theology of Hebrews has been largely recognized by scholars as non-Pauline, thus attesting to its independent textual witness apart from Paul.[5] Donald Guthrie has argued that Hebrews "represents a position midway between Pauline and Johannine theology."[6] Carson and Moo acknowledge as well that there "are clear links with John and Paul ... in the high Christology

---

[2] Fruchtenbaum, *Messianic Jewish Epistles*, 3-4.

[3] A major contributor to this view was Wilhelm Bousset, *Kyrios Christos: Geschichte des Christusglaubens von den Anfängen des Christentums bis Irenaeus* (Göttingen: Vandenhoeck and Ruprecht, 1913). This book was translated into English by John E. Steely as *Kyrios Christos: A Brief History of the Belief in Christ from the Beginnings of Christianity to Irenaeus* (Nashville: Abingdon Press, 1970). Bousset was also the co-founder of the Religionsgeschichtliche Schule (German for "history of religions school") which held to the view that the structure of religion has evolved and developed over time. Rudolph Bultmann, *Theology of the New Testament*, trans. K. Grobel, vol. 1 (London: SCM Press, 1952), 124-125 argued with Bousset that the title "Lord" for Jesus only came into usage *later* among the Hellenistic churches. See Costa, *Worship and the Risen Jesus*, 400-401 n.368. I have noted that this view is incompatible with the evidence in Costa, *Worship and the Risen Jesus*, 383 n.186: "Bousset saw any notion of worship or devotion to Jesus as a product of Hellenistic influences which entered the Gentile churches and which were distinctly separate from the first-century Judean Christian church from where such devotion to Jesus was absent. Bousset's thesis cannot be sustained in light of Romans 10:12 and particularly 1 Corinthians 16:22, which shows Jewish origins." Also see Marshall's response against Boussett and Bultmann in Marshall, *Origins of New Testament Christology*, 24-29, 32-39.

[4] A.M. Stibbs, "Hebrews," *The New Bible Commentary Revised*, Donald Guthrie, J.A. Motyer, A.M. Stibbs and D.J. Wiseman, eds., 3rd ed. (Grand Rapids: Eerdmans, 1984), 1192; Fruchtenbaum, *Messianic Jewish Epistles*, 5-6.

[5] Werner Georg Kümmel, *Introduction to the New Testament*, trans. Howard Clark Kee (Nashville: Abingdon Press, 1975), 395.

[6] Guthrie, *New Testament Introduction*, 723.

[of Hebrews]."⁷ What this shows is that the witness to high Christology was not shared by one particular "school" of early Christianity, as some critics have claimed, but rather seemed to have been assumed by the *collective witness* of the early Christian movement. It is, therefore, not surprising to see points of agreement between these various texts and others we have examined on the person and work of Jesus. Martin Hengel acknowledges that "christological thinking between [AD] 50 and 100 CE *was much more unified in its basic structure* than New Testament research, in part at least, has maintained."⁸ As an example of this thinking, Werner Kümmel notes that there are theological points in Hebrews that are held in concord with Paul, such as Christ being the pre-existent Son who is the agent of creation.⁹

Hebrews 1:1-3 begins with a contrasting statement. It says that while in the *past* God spoke to the fathers through the prophets in various times and ways (1:1), *now* "in these last days" he has spoken to us by his Son (Heb.1:2). The contrast is significant. While God spoke through prophets in the Old Testament period, he is speaking now through his Son, who is better (a recurring theme in Hebrews) than the prophets by virtue of the fact that he is God's Son, and the one of whom the prophets spoke of (Luke 24:44).¹⁰ The Son is "the final and supreme speech of God to man."¹¹

The author then begins the citation of a hymn in 1:2b. How do we know this is a hymn? Again, because of the grammar. Hebrews 1:2b begins with the

---

[7] Carson and Moo, *Introduction to the New Testament*, 613.

[8] Hengel, *Studies in Early Christology*, 383 (italics in original).

[9] The points of agreement are so close between Hebrews and Paul that Kümmel, *Introduction to the New Testament*, 395 comments, "At some points the thought world of [Hebrews] must have been touched by the spirit of Paul."

[10] That the Messiah was the focal point of the prophets is admitted in the Talmud, which states, "All the prophets spoke only of the days of the Messiah." *b. Berakot* 34b. Throughout Hebrews Jesus is described as superior and better than the angels (1:4-2:9), Moses (3:1-6), the Levitical priesthood, and the high priest himself (4:14-5:10; 7). The idea that the Messiah would have this exalted status is also acknowledged in rabbinic literature, "The great mountain spoken of by the prophet Zechariah (4:7) is no other than Messiah, Son of David, and he is called 'the Great Mountain,' because he towers above the Patriarchs, is greater than Moses, and is above the ministering angels. As Isaiah says (52.10) [*sic*], 'Behold, my servant shall deal prudently, he shall be exalted and extolled and be very high.'" Midrash, *Tanchuma Toldos*. The citation from Isaiah in this quote is incorrect. It should be Isaiah 52:13.

[11] Reymond, *Jesus*, 298.

relative pronoun "who,"[12] and states, "whom [who] he appointed the heir of all things, through whom [who] also he created the world." God has appointed his Son as the heir of everything.[13] This is why Jesus is called "the firstborn of all creation" in Colossians 1:15, a passage we will examine below. The language of "firstborn" also communicates the idea of heirship and preeminence. The author of Hebrews also uses the term "firstborn" in reference to Jesus so that "heir" and "firstborn" are organically connected (Heb. 1:6).

The hymn then continues, "Through whom [the Son] also he created the world." This is an important statement. The Son is not only the creator of all things but also the divine agent *through* whom God made everything. We saw this language in Chapter 8 when we dealt with the creed in 1 Corinthians 8:6 where it says concerning the Lord Jesus Christ, "Through whom are all things and through whom we exist." This is usually the language appropriated to the Son whenever creation is discussed by the biblical authors; everything comes *from* the Father and *through* the Son. Hebrews 1:2b is simply corroborating what 1 Corinthians 8:6 says. The Greek word used in Hebrews 1:2b for "world" is *aionas* ("ages" which is plural, as in AV, ASV, NRSV, "worlds"), from the root word *aion*. It can also be translated as "the universe" (NIV, HCSB). Some translations render it literally as "ages" (YLT, NJB). The sense here seems to indicate spatial time, and hence is likely referring to the world, or universe.[14] The idea being communicated here is that everything that exists—the totality of existence encompassed by the word universe—came

---

[12] Point three in the criteria for hymns, see Chapter 12. The grammatical features in Hebrews 1:1-4 are so indicative of a hymn that Fuller, *The Foundations of New Testament Christology*, 220, comments, "This passage has never been treated as a hymn, although there are features which invite its reconstruction as such." See also F.F. Bruce, *The Epistle to the Hebrews*, NICNT, rev. ed. (Grand Rapids: Eerdmans, 1990), 47. On the various views of this text see Paul Ellingworth, *The Epistle to the Hebrews: A Commentary on the Greek Text*, NIGTC (Grand Rapids: Eerdmans, 1993), 96-98, 101.

[13] The Dutch Reformed theologian Abraham Kuyper put it succinctly when he said, "There is not a square inch in the whole domain of our human existence over which Christ, who is Sovereign over all, does not cry: 'Mine!'" James D. Bratt, ed., *Abraham Kuyper: A Centennial Reader* (Grand Rapids: Eerdmans, 1998), 461.

[14] The other place where this word is used in the context of creation in Hebrews is at 11:3, "By faith we understand that the universe was created by the word of God, so that what is seen was not made out of things that are visible." It is important to note the reference to the universe being created "by the word of God." The Word of God is Christ, the one through whom God made all things (John 1:1-3, 1 John 1:1; Revelation 19:13).

into being through the Son.[15] So if God created the universe through his Son, it logically follows that the Son is pre-existent, a theme which we have seen in other creeds (1 Cor. 8:6), as well as hymns such as those found in Philippians 2:6-11 and 1 Timothy 3:16. In other words, the Son pre-existed *as the Son*.

Some modalist (modalism denies the Trinity and instead believes that God is one person who takes on three different modes) groups today claim that God only became the Son in the incarnation and that the title "Son" only applies from the incarnation onwards. However, as we have seen in 1:1-2, it is the Son, a distinct person from the Father, who has been appointed heir of all things, and the same Son who is the divine agent through whom God created the universe. Here again in Hebrews 1:2b we see a testimony to the deity of Christ. As we have repeatedly seen in the creeds and hymns up to this point, this demonstrates that the earliest Christians believed in the deity of Christ; it was not an evolutionary development in Christian history or some doctrine invented at the Council of Nicaea in AD 325. The Lord Jesus Christ is presented as God, the Creator—a theme that is also mentioned in Hebrews 1:8-12.[16]

The hymn now begins to move towards a climax as the first three lines of two stanzas will focus on the "*who*" of the Son in Hebrews 1:3-4.[17] It also emphasizes the deity of the Son by stating, "He [who] is the radiance of the glory of God and the exact imprint of his nature, and he upholds the universe by the word of his power. After making purification for sins, he sat down at the right hand of the Majesty on high" (Heb. 1:3). As we have already seen above, a feature that is typical of hymns is the appearance of *hapax legomena* which are words only appearing once. These appear in Hebrews 1:3, where the identity

---

[15] Louw and Nida, *Greek-English Lexicon*, 1.2 admits that the reference here is to the creation of all things and further notes here that "in [Hebrews] 1:2 it may be essential in a number of languages to translate 'he [the Son] is the one through whom God created everything,' though in some instances a more idiomatic and satisfactory way of rendering the meaning would involve a phrase such as '... created both the earth and the sky' or 'the heavens and the earth.'" The idea here again is that the Son is the divine agent of creation, and echoes Genesis 1:1.

[16] In Hebrews 1:10 the Father addresses the Son and says to him, "You, Lord, laid the foundation of the earth in the beginning, and *the heavens are the work of your hands*" (italics mine). Note the Father addresses the Son as "Lord" (*kyrios*), which as we have seen is the Greek equivalent of Yahweh. In other words, the Father addresses the Son by the Divine Name! Remember that the background to Hebrews 1:10-12 is Psalm 102:25-27, in which Yahweh is the subject. I believe this is one of the strongest testimonies to the deity of Christ. The Father himself refers to the Son as "God" (Hebrews 1:8-9) and "Lord" (Hebrews 1:10-12). Anyone who denies the deity of the Son, then, must also defy the Father himself who has asserted his deity.

[17] Fuller, *The Foundations of New Testament Christology*, 220.

of the Son is central.[18] Notice how the language in this hymn grows increasingly richer and more emphatic. The Son is the radiance of the glory of God, and the outshining of God's glory.[19] That we are speaking about a person is seen in the use of the relative pronoun "who," translated here as "he." "It" was not the radiance of God, but rather "who," or "he," is the radiance of God. This outshining, or radiance, is not separable from the glory but connected to it, as the shining of a light is connected to the light source.

The only kind of light we experience is created light. The Son, however, was not created (which the Arian heresy would profess), but is himself the Creator, as we saw in 1:2b. Since we are speaking about an *eternal* person, and he is described as the radiance, or effulgence, of God's glory, this would imply that such radiance *eternally* shines out. This truth has ramifications for the later creeds, as will be discussed shortly below.[20] F.F. Bruce notes that this language "denotes the radiance shining forth from the source of light."[21] The idea of shining out is important as it communicates the function of the Son in bringing "out" God, an idea we will look at more closely in the next chapter. This idea of God's glory was usually associated with the *Shechinah* glory—a visible manifestation of the presence of God among his people.[22] This idea becomes more pronounced at the incarnation when the Word became flesh and "tabernacled" among us; the presence of God was made visible in Jesus Christ (John 1:14). The hymn goes on to say that the Son is "the exact imprint

---

[18] See point five of our criteria for hymns in Chapter 12. In Hebrews 1:3 these will be words such as "radiance" (*apaugasma*), "exact imprint" (*character*), and "uphold" (*pheron*). See Fuller, *The Foundations of New Testament Christology*, 220, 239 n.42.

[19] James 2:1 refers to Jesus as "the Lord of glory" or "glorious Lord" (NASB, NIV). James 2:1 literally reads "our Lord Jesus Christ the Glory" (author's translation). This is an allusion to Zechariah 2:5 where Yahweh is described as "the glory" within Jerusalem. See Reymond, *Jesus*, 282; B.B. Warfield, *The Lord of Glory* (Grand Rapids: Baker, 1974), 265. In the Apocrypha, the language of Wisdom 7:25-26 is similar to Hebrews 1:3 and even shares a common word with the passage, "For she [wisdom] is a breath of the power of God, and a *pure emanation of the glory of the Almighty*; therefore nothing defiled gains entrance into her. For she is *a reflection* [*apaugasma*; same Greek word used in Hebrews 1:3] *of eternal light*, a spotless mirror of the working of God, and an image of his goodness" (RSV; italics mine).

[20] H.P. Liddon brings this emphasis out when he states regarding the Son that, "He is One with God as having streamed forth *eternally* from the Father's Essence, like a ray of light from the parent fire with which it is *unbrokenly* joined." H.P. Liddon, *The Divinity of Our Lord and Saviour Jesus Christ* (London: Longmans, Green, and Co., 1908), 326 (italics mine).

[21] Bruce, *Epistle to the Hebrews*, 48.

[22] Fruchtenbaum, *Messianic Jewish Epistles*, 20. Paul points out that the light of God's glory is seen in the face of Jesus Christ, the Incarnate one. God has shone "the light of the knowledge of the glory of God in the face of Jesus Christ" (2 Cor. 4:6).

of his nature, and he upholds the universe by the word of his power." Notice again how the language of this hymn becomes more and more Christological as it goes on.

After speaking of the Son as the radiance of God's glory, he now addresses the nature or essence of the Son. The reference to "the exact imprint of his nature" is connected to the ancient practice of taking a signet ring with an image on it and impressing it on hot wax. What is left on the wax when it hardens is the image on the signet ring. It also brings to mind the image on a coin, which reflects the same image as the die that first imprinted it.[23] The Son is the exact imprint, or image, of God's nature; he is "the very stamp of his nature" (RSV), and "the very image of his substance" (ASV). He is, to use an old slang expression, the "spitting image" of his Father. Jesus taught in his earthly ministry that whoever saw him, saw the Father also (John 14:9). That is because he is the image of the invisible God (Col. 1:15). This is an ontological statement that deals with the nature, or the *what*, of God, i.e., what makes God, God. The Greek word *hypostasis* in Hebrews 1:3 means "the essential or basic nature of an entity—'substance, nature, essence, real being.'"[24] As such, all that is part of God's nature, including his attributes and properties, are necessarily shared by the Son, since he is the exact representation of the nature, substance, and being of God. This has rich implications for theology and the historic creeds of the church. The very nature and essence of God are impressed in the person of his Son, an impression especially realized in the incarnation.[25] This verse is one of the strongest affirmations of the deity of Christ.

---

[23] Bruce, *Epistle to the Hebrews*, 48; Fruchtenbaum, *Messianic Jewish Epistles*, 20.

[24] Louw and Nida, *Greek-English Lexicon*, 58.1. The reading in the AV and the NKJV, "The express image of his person," is an unfortunate translation in my opinion, as *hypostasis* refers to *being—what* something is—as opposed to person, that defines *who* someone is. It is a categorical fallacy to use "being" and "person" synonymously as this only lends to theological confusion. The meaning of words is crucial in theology in the same way that the meaning of words in medical science and law are crucial.

[25] Bruce, *Epistle to the Hebrews*, 48. Paul says the same thing in Colossians 2:9, "For in him the whole fullness of deity dwells bodily." The AV and NKJV render "deity" here as "Godhead." The word Paul uses for deity, *theotes*, is a word that only appears once in the New Testament and therefore is another instance of *hapax legomenon*. This word is another ontological term that deals with the *what* question of God and means "the nature or state of being God— 'deity, divine nature, divine being.'" Louw and Nida, *Greek-English Lexicon*, 12.13. Thayer also defines *theotes* as, "the state of being God, *Godhead*." Thayer also adds here an important comment between the word *theotes* used in Colossians 2:9, and the word *theiotes*, which means "divinity" or "divine nature" which appears in Romans 1:20. He notes that "[*theotes*] deity differs from [*theiotes*] divinity, as essence differs from quality or attribute." Joseph H. Thayer, *The New Thayer's Greek-English*

It is not surprising that during the Nicaean controversy in the first quarter of the fourth century AD, the Arians refused to acknowledge the authenticity of Hebrews because of the language used of Christ in Hebrews 1:3.[26]

The hymn goes on to state that "he upholds the universe by the word of his power."[27] Here we see the sustaining work of the Son. Since the Son possesses the being and nature of God, he necessarily has access to all of God's attributes, including omnipotence, which means he can sustain and uphold the universe he created in the first place. (Heb. 1:2b). Notice also that he sustains the universe by "the word of his power." This phrase has been recognized by scholars as an attempt to communicate a Semitism. A Semitism is a manner of writing a word or phrase with either a Hebrew or Aramaic manner of speech or expression.[28] The phrase "word of his power" is equivalent to "his mighty word."[29] The Greek word translated as "word" here is not the normal one we would expect to find, which would be the Greek word *logos* (John 1:1). Rather, it is the word *rhema*, which means "a minimal unit of discourse, often a single word—'word, saying,'"[30] and, "that which is said, *word, saying, expression, or statement of any kind.*"[31] What is being communicated here is the idea of utterance. God said "let there be light," and light, along with the entire universe, came into existence (Gen. 1:3). And yet it is God the Son who continues to sustain it. In the Greek myths Atlas, one of the Titans, was punished by Zeus with the task of bearing up the vault of sky upon his

---

Lexicon of the New Testament with Index (Peabody: Hendrickson, 1981), 288 (italics in original). It is noteworthy to consider that Thayer was a Unitarian who denied the deity of Christ, yet he was honest with his research and did not allow his religious presuppositions to interfere with his objectivity. In Jesus, then, the very nature and state of *being* God dwells in him bodily. Notice especially the reference to his body. In theology this is called the "hypostatic union," and embodies the truth that Jesus Christ is the God-man. He is the very being of God dwelling in a body, which is the reality of the incarnation.

[26] Wellum, *God the Son Incarnate*, 186.

[27] The background to this idea is also found in Sirach 43:26b, "and by his word all things hold together" (RSV).

[28] Carson and Moo, *Introduction to the New Testament*, 143-144 n.19.

[29] Maximilian Zerwick, *Biblical Greek* (Scripta Pontificii Instituti Biblica 114; Roma: Editrice Pontifico Instituto Biblico, 2001), 15.

[30] Louw and Nida, *Greek-English Lexicon*, 33.9.

[31] *BDAG*, 905.

shoulders.[32] The Son of God, however, powerfully upholds the universe by merely the *word* of his power.

Another word that communicates this sustaining power is providence—the idea that God is in absolute control. The act of upholding the universe means that he continually does so even to the present moment, but it also means that the universe is being carried towards a goal;[33] a goal that will be realized in the maximal glorification of God (cf. Phil. 2:11). Hopefully we can see now that the language of who the Son is, and his power to bear and uphold all things indicates a hymnic structure in the original text. This has to do with the presence of the relative pronoun "who," but also to do with the rhythmic structure of the words contained in the text.[34] The idea of the Son upholding the universe by the word of his power is a theme we will also encounter as we look at Colossians 1:15-20 below.

The hymn then continues at the end of Hebrews 1:3 with the second three lines in the second stanza which will focus on *what* Jesus has done for believers: "When he had made purification of sins, he sat down on the right hand of the Majesty on high." The hymn now moves from the identity of the Son and his creative work to his redemptive work. This, of course, implies the incarnation (Heb. 1:6a), as well as Jesus' death, resurrection, and ascension. Jesus is being depicted here in priestly language, which will become a central theme in this letter. We are told that he has made purification of sins. Note that this is something he did volitionally and that it was a unique work on his part. Bruce correctly notes that "the Son of God has accomplished something incapable of achievement by anyone else."[35] This is seen in the use of the third person singular pronoun *autou* ("himself") which appears at the beginning of this hymnic line and is the subject of the noun "purification" and, therefore, it is in the emphatic position. This is an example of the use of an intensive pronoun to focus on the person spoken of.[36] This sense is reflected in the AV rendering, "When he had *by himself* purged our sins" (italics mine). The purification for sin has been made and the finality of this action is seen in the fact that, after

---

[32] Atlas was punished, "To bear on his back forever [,] The cruel strength of the crushing world [,] And the vault of the sky ... A load not easy to be borne." Edith Hamilton, *Mythology: Timeless Tales of the Gods and Heroes* (New York: Mentor, 1969), 66.

[33] Fruchtenbaum, *Messianic Jewish Epistles*, 21.

[34] Bruce, *Epistle to the Hebrews*, 49.

[35] Bruce, *Epistle to the Hebrews*, 49.

[36] On the intensive pronoun, see Wallace, *Basics of New Testament Syntax*, 155.

accomplishing this action, he sat down at the right hand of God.[37] The priests were to continually stand in the temple as they offered sacrifices, implying that such a system was never meant to be final (Heb. 10:11–14). It is instructive to note that there were no chairs in the temple, or formerly the tabernacle, to sit on, because the work of sacrifice was ongoing. It would never be finished until the Messiah came and offered himself once for all (Heb. 7:27; 9:12, 26; 10:10). The purification for sin occurred and was completed on the cross when Jesus cried out, "It is finished" (John 19:30). The High Priest Jesus, having completed the one sacrifice, finally sat down.

At what point did Jesus sit down at the right hand of God? It would have been at his ascension, when the Father told him to sit at his right hand until he makes his enemies his footstool (Ps. 110:1). In the hymn found in 1 Timothy 3:16 we saw that the last line said that Jesus was "taken up in glory," which, as we saw, is also a reference to the ascension. The last line of Hebrews 1:3 says, "He sat down at the right hand of the *Majesty on high*" (italics mine). The reference to height here recalls the *Carmen Christi*, where Jesus was said to have been "highly exalted" by God (Phil. 2:9). Height is typically associated with honor and prestige. The reference to God as "the Majesty" refers to the fact that as Jesus sits at the right hand of the Father, he shares in his regal status. The author of Hebrews repeats this phrase in Hebrews 8:1. Jesus is also King (which, as we saw above, is implied in the title "Christ"). Here, then, we have a Priest-King.[38] Not only has he made purification for our sins as Priest, but he also reigns as King from the right hand of the Father, and intercedes there for the saints (Rom. 8:34).

When God established the Davidic covenant, it is interesting to read that "David went in and *sat before* the LORD" (2 Sam. 7:18; italics mine). David sat before Yahweh for a time, but the promised Son of David sits in the very presence of the Father for all time, thus fulfilling the promise made to David that he would have an eternal throne: "David shall never lack a man to sit on the throne of the house of Israel" (Jer. 33:17; cf. 1 Kgs. 8:25; 2 Chr. 6:16). No Davidic king has sat on the throne of the house of Israel since 586 BC, when the Davidic line came to an end with the Babylonian exile. This prophecy has

---

[37] Wallace, *Greek Grammar Beyond the Basics*, 624 n.30 comments, "To sit down at God's right hand meant that the work was finished, and this could not take place *until* the sin-cleansing was accomplished" (italics in original).

[38] This priest-king is already envisioned and prefigured in the person of the high priest Joshua (Zechariah 6:9-13). He was the high priest but also had a crown placed on his head, "He shall sit and rule on his throne. And there shall be a priest on his throne" (Zechariah 6:13).

HEBREWS 1:2B-4

been truly realized in Jesus as he is a man, a Son of David, who continues to sit on the throne even today and will do so forever. Hebrews 1:3 tells us that the promise that Gabriel spoke to Mary, "[He] will be called the Son of the Most High. And the Lord God will give to him the throne of his father David" (Luke 1:32), was fulfilled in Jesus. Note also how Luke mentions "the Son," "the Most High," and, "the throne"—the same themes reflected in the hymn of Hebrews 1:2b-3. Here Jesus is presented as "his Son" (1:2b), who sat down "on high" by virtue of him being seated by the Father's "throne." Sitting at the right hand of the Majesty is once again an example of a circumlocution, or periphrasis.[39] Jesus did this when he responded to the question of the high priest as to whether or not he was the Messiah, "the Son of the Blessed" (Mark 14:61; cf. Matt. 26:63), where "Blessed" here is being used as a surrogate word for "God." Jesus responds in the affirmative to the question and says that "you will see the Son of Man seated at *the right hand of Power*, and coming with the clouds of heaven" (Mark 14:62; italics mine). The "right hand of Power" equals the right hand of God (cf. Luke 22:69), or, as Hebrews 1:3 has it, "the right hand of the Majesty on high."

The fact that the Son sits at the right hand of the Father also emphasizes his equality with the Father, a point we already saw emphasized in the *Carmen Christi* (Phil. 2:6).[40] He sits at the right hand of the Father on the *same* throne (Rev. 22:1, 3; cf. 3:21).[41] According to Psalm 110:1, no Davidic king, with the exception of the Lord Jesus Christ, was ever told by God to sit at his right hand. This address was *only* made to Jesus because, as the Messiah, he is the only one who qualifies. In Psalm 110:1, David refers to the one whom he calls "my Lord," and to whom Yahweh says to sit at his right hand. Even Jesus drove this point home to the religious leaders of his day in telling them that the Messiah is not only David's Son, but is also the Lord of David (Matt. 22:41-46; Mark 12:35-37; Luke 20:41-44; cf. Rev. 5:5; 22:16). This too is an allusion to the hypostatic union; Christ is both God (Lord of David), and man (Son of David). It should also be recalled that it was the statement of Jesus sitting at the right hand of God that brought the railing accusation of blasphemy against

---

[39] Bruce, *Epistle to the Hebrews*, 49.
[40] Fruchtenbaum, *Messianic Jewish Epistles*, 21.
[41] Revelation 22:1,3 speaks of "the throne of God and of the Lamb." The word "throne" here in the Greek text, *thronos*, is a singular noun, meaning that it is the throne shared by both God and the Lamb. For further discussion on these verses see Costa, *Worship and the Risen Jesus*, 316-317 n.18.

EARLY CHRISTIAN CREEDS AND HYMNS

him by the high priest (Mark 14:61-64). In saying such a statement, Jesus was clearly alluding to Psalm 110:1, the most cited Old Testament text in the New Testament.

The ascension of Jesus is an important, and unfortunately often neglected, event in many evangelical circles today.[42] How high has Jesus gone in terms of his regal authority? Paul states that Jesus is the "one who also ascended far above all the heavens, that he might fill all things" (Eph. 4:10; cf. Eph. 1:20-22; 1 Pet. 3:22). How can Jesus "fill all things"? He can do so because he shares in the very nature and attributes of God, including his omnipresence. Recall that the background to Ephesians 4:10 is Jeremiah 23:23-24, which speaks of Yahweh filling "all things."[43] As we have seen in other passages, here again Jesus is being referred to in language that typically only refers to Yahweh: this is because Jesus is Yahweh. In Hebrews 1:3, we also see Jesus presented in his three-fold office. He is *the* ultimate Prophet who speaks God's final message to the world (1:1-2); he is *the* ultimate Priest who made purification for sins (1:3); and he is *the* ultimate King who has been exalted and sits on high at the right hand of the Majesty (1:3).[44]

The hymn then draws to a close in Hebrews 1:4, which states "Having become as much superior to angels as the name he has inherited is more excellent than theirs." The context of Hebrews 1 shows among other things the superiority of the Son over the angels (Heb. 1:5-7,13-14). There was a fascination in first century AD Judaism with angels, especially in joining in or imitating the worship angels offer to God.[45] This may have been because the law of Moses was believed to have been delivered by angels (Acts 7:53; Gal. 3:19; Heb. 2:2; cf. Deut. 33:2). However, the Son of God is much superior to the angels as he is their Creator (1:2b), and is himself the object of angelic worship (1:6).[46]

---

[42] Ascension Day is observed by several liturgical Protestant denominations along with Roman Catholicism and the Orthodox Church. It has been observed in the Christian church since the fourth century AD. Ascension Day comes forty days after Easter Sunday and always falls on a Thursday (the fifth Thursday after Easter), and ten days before Pentecost Sunday to match the time period in Acts 1 and 2. See R.E. Nixon, "Ascension" in *New International Dictionary*, 76; F. L. Cross and Elizabeth A. Livingstone, eds., *The Oxford Dictionary of the Christian Church* (London: Oxford University Press, 1957), 92.

[43] "Am I a God at hand, declares the LORD, and not a God afar off? Can a man hide himself in secret places so that I cannot see him? declares the LORD. *Do I not fill heaven and earth?* declares the LORD" (Jeremiah 23:23-24; italics mine).

[44] Bruce, *Epistle to the Hebrews*, 50.

[45] Costa, *Worship and the Risen Jesus*, 117-122; Vermes, *Dead Sea Scrolls*, 42.

[46] Costa, *Worship and the Risen Jesus*, 293 n.1.

HEBREWS 1:2B-4

It also mentions that the name he has inherited is more excellent than theirs. How is it that Jesus has *become* so much superior to the angels? Was he not *always* superior? The language here seems to be speaking more about what Jesus accomplished during his incarnation, in which he, for a little while, became lower than the angels (Heb. 2:9). After the resurrection and ascension, however, Jesus resumed his heavenly glory (cf. John 17:5), and as the glorified God-man, became even better than the angels. What is the name he has inherited? Some scholars believe it is "Son."[47] While other men are mere prophets (1:1), and angels are "minsters" (1:7) and "ministering spirits" (1:14), Jesus is the Son who is the exact representation of God's very nature (1:3). In this respect, the Son is greater than either prophets or angels. This point is made further by the author of Hebrews when he refers to Moses as being a servant in God's house, but Jesus as a Son over the house, and thus counted worthy of more glory than Moses (Heb. 3:1-6). Other scholars believe the name he inherited is the name "Yahweh," as we saw in Philippians 2:9. This may be the case, even though "Son" seems to be more of a title.

As stated earlier the hymn section in Hebrews 1:3-4 is composed of two stanzas with three lines each. They can be divided as follows:[48]

Stanza 1
He is the radiance of the glory of God
The exact imprint of his nature
Upholds the universe by word of his power

Stanza 2
After making purification for sins
He sat down at right hand of Majesty on high
Having become as much superior to angels

The hymn in Hebrews 1:2b-4 is a magnificent and rich piece. It reminds us that the Son is the heir of all things and the one through whom the universe was created. This is consistent with the creeds found in 1 Corinthians 8:6 and

---

[47] Bruce, *Epistle to the Hebrews*, 50. This does not mean that Jesus *became* God's Son after his exaltation, which would be the heresy of adoptionism. Jesus in his earthly ministry was *already* God's Son (Hebrews 5:7-8). On the heresy of adoptionism see Tony Costa, "Was Adoptionism the Earliest Christology: A Response to Bart Ehrman," *American Journal of Biblical Theology* 8, no. 28 (2015) (https://www.biblicaltheology.com/Research /CostaT01.pdf).

[48] I am adapting this material from Fuller, *The Foundations of New Testament Christology*, 221.

EARLY CHRISTIAN CREEDS AND HYMNS

John 1:3. We also see that the Son is the radiance of God's glory and the imprint of God's nature and saw this same idea present in the *Carmen Christi* (Phil. 2:6; John 1:1) He is also the one who made purification for sins, much like we saw in the hymn of 1 Peter 2:22-24. Finally, we see that the Son, after his redemptive work, sits down at the right hand of God on high; we saw a similar exaltation in the *Carmen Christi* (Phil. 2:9-11) and the hymn in 1 Timothy 3:16. It should be noted that while his excellence and superiority over the angels is implied in his exaltation, the hymn in 1 Timothy 3:16 also mentions that the incarnate Son was "seen of angels" and then "taken up in glory." We see once again that early Christians sang about their Saviour—who he was, what he did, and what he continues to do as their great High Priest.

Hebrews 1:2b-4 had a great impact on the Nicene Creed and the language found in this hymn fortified orthodox Christians against Arianism. The line in the Nicene Creed, which states regarding the Son, "through whom all things were made," accords with Hebrews 1:2b. When it states that the Son is "God of God, Light of Light, true God of true God," it is echoing the language of Hebrews 1:3, which states that the Son is the very imprint, radiance, and shining out of God's glory.

Perhaps the most important term that emerged from Nicaea was *homoousios*, a Greek word which means "of the same nature or substance."[49] The Son is the same nature and substance as the Father, hence the Nicaean Creed states, "of one substance with the Father." This is based on the language of Jesus being the exact imprint, stamp, and representation of the nature of God (Heb. 1:3). Other statements from the Nicene Creed, such as, "Who, for us men and our salvation, came down from heaven" and "that he suffered under Pontius Pilate by crucifixion and death," and, "was buried and raised," point to his purification of sin (Heb. 1:3). The statement in the Nicene Creed that says he "ascended into heaven, and sits at the right hand of the Father" is reflected as well in Hebrews 1:3.

It would have been wonderful to know and hear how this hymn was sung. It is a powerful Christological hymn that heightens and honours the Lord Jesus Christ as God the Son, Creator, Redeemer, and King, who is above all things and sustains all things—including the angelic beings.

---

[49] See Chapter 1.

17
THE LONGEST CHRISTIAN HYMN FOUND IN A GOSPEL
JOHN 1:1-18

We turn now to what is believed to be the longest hymn in the New Testament. Unlike what we have seen up to this point, this hymn does not appear in a letter but actually in the prologue to the Gospel of John. The passage is one of the most well-known and majestic pieces of Scripture and it is found in John 1:1-18:

> In the beginning was the Word, and the Word was with God, and the Word was God. He was in the beginning with God. All things were made through him, and without him was not anything made that was made. In him was life, and the life was the light of men. The light shines in the darkness, and the darkness has not overcome it. There was a man sent from God, whose name was John. He came as a witness, to bear witness about the light, that all might believe through him. He was not the light, but came to bear witness about the light. The true light, which enlightens everyone, was coming into the world. He was in the world, and the world was made through him, yet the world did not know him. He came to his own, and his own people did not receive him. But to all who did receive him, who believed in his name, he gave the right to become children of God, who were born, not of blood nor of the will of the flesh nor of the will of man, but of God. And the Word became flesh and dwelt among us, and we have seen his glory, glory as of the only Son from the Father, full of grace and truth. (John bore witness about him, and cried out, "This was he of whom I said, 'He who comes after me ranks before me, because he was before me.'") And from his fullness we have all received, grace upon grace. For the law was given through Moses; grace and truth came through Jesus Christ. No one has ever seen God; the only God, who is at the Father's side, he has made him known.

EARLY CHRISTIAN CREEDS AND HYMNS

This section of John's gospel is believed by most scholars to be hymnic material.[1] Their reasons for believing so include, among other things, the presence of the words "Logos" or "Word" in the prologue, which is marked off from the rest of the Gospel. It also appears to be balanced in a verse form.[2] This is seen in the contrast between couplets such as light/life and darkness, the eternal heavenly Word who is immaterial, coming down into time and taking on material flesh. We see it also in the opening verses (vv. 1-3) that while the Word *was/is*, everything else in creation *came to be*. Some, like Fuller, have even suggested that the "Logos hymn" as he calls John 1:1-18, is "a pre-Johannine hymn."[3] This means that the material is not John's but has been taken from another source and added to his Gospel. We discussed this theory as we looked at the creeds and hymns found in Paul's letters, which are believed by some to be pre-Pauline. Whether or not it is original Johannine material we cannot be sure, but that John has written it in his Gospel is plain.

The Gospel of John may have been written sometime between AD 80–AD 85.[4] It has been acknowledged that the New Testament passages closest in theology to John 1:1-18 are the hymns in Philippians 2:6-11, which we surveyed already, and Colossians 1:15-20, which we will examine next. The hymns in Paul's letters are believed to have started circulating in the mid 50's AD.[5] I would also add Hebrews 1:2b-3, which also shares common elements with John's prologue. This prologue not only functions as an early Christian hymn, but also affirms a strong Christology, and primarily seeks to answer the question, who is Jesus? It also is the lens through which the rest of the Gospel must be interpreted.[6]

There can be no doubt that the one mentioned in this hymn is Jesus Christ; this is made clear in verses 17-18. It begins with the memorable phrase "In

---

[1] Brown, *Introduction to New Testament Christology*, 188; Hurtado, *Lord Jesus Christ*, 147; Fuller, *The Foundations of New Testament Christology*, 222.

[2] Fuller, *The Foundations of New Testament Christology*, 222. Fuller notes here that some scholars, including Bultmann, believe John's prologue may have originally been written in Aramaic.

[3] Fuller, The *Foundations of New Testament Christology*, 224.

[4] Carson and Moo, *Introduction to the New Testament*, 267. It seems rather odd to me that if John was written in early AD 80, nothing at all is said about the destruction of the temple in Jerusalem in AD 70. John A.T. Robinson, a liberal scholar, is famous for arguing that this reason means that all the books of the New Testament were written well before AD 70. Robinson, *Redating the New Testament*, 3, 342-348. W.F. Albright took the position that no book of the New Testament was written beyond AD 80. Albright, *Recent Discoveries in Bible Lands*, 136.

[5] Carson and Moo, *Introduction to the New Testament*, 267.

[6] See comments in Hurtado, *Lord Jesus Christ*, 364.

the beginning," which is an echo from Genesis 1:1. The grammar used to describe the Word in verses 1:1-2 is the imperfect verb "was." Notice in verse 3 that the Word who *was*, created everything that *came into being*. Westcott captures the full force of the imperfect verb "was" when he says, "The verb *was* does not express a completed past, but rather a continuous state. The imperfect tense of the original suggests ... the notion of absolute, supra-temporal, existence."[7] The Word is clearly distinguished from things that are created and have a beginning. In verse 14, the hymn informs us that this same Word who always was, became flesh. He became something he was not before. But though the *human nature* of Jesus had a beginning in time, the Word, who is the Son, is eternal; thus John's use of the imperfect verb "was" when referring to the pre-Incarnate Word. He becomes what he was not before, but still remains who he always was.[8] This is the distinction between deity and humanity. He is the pre-existent Logos/Word who was with God, or face to face with God (*pros ton theon*; literally, *towards* God; cf. 1 John 1:2; 2:1), and was God in his nature, "The Word was God" (1:1). What God is, the Word is. The NEB captures this idea in its translation of John 1:1, "What God was, the Word was," or as Dana and Mantey put it, "the [W]ord was deity."[9]

The language of the Word being *with* God is extremely important. Not only does it convey personal relationship, which means the Word is a *distinct person* from God the Father,[10] but it demonstrates that he shares the nature of God,

---

[7] Westcott, *The Gospel According to St. John*, 2; Also see Reymond, *Jesus*, 302-303.

[8] Augustine, *Sermon* 69 captures this idea beautifully when he writes, "He was before His own flesh; He created His own mother. He chose her in whom He should be conceived, He created her of whom He should be created. Why do you marvel? It is God of whom I am speaking to you: The Word was God."

[9] Dana and Mantey, *Manual Grammar of the Greek*, 148.

[10] The phrase *pros ton theon* ("with God") in John 1:1b emphasizes that the Word is not only distinct from the Father, but also personal alongside him. The Word was "turned 'towards God' in a relationship to him." Fuller, *The Foundations of New Testament Christology*, 225. The phrase can also mean that the Word was "face to face" with God, thus communicating intimate and direct relationship. In Exodus 33:11 it states that God spoke to Moses "face to face, as a man speaks to his friend" (cf. Numbers 12:8; Deuteronomy 34:10). This language denotes direct, personal communication. In the LXX of Exodus 33:11 it states that God spoke face to face with Moses as if a friend would speak *pros ton heautou philon* ("towards his own friend"; author's translation). The grammatical construction here is parallel with John 1:1b. Westcott states that this phrasing of the Word being with God is "remarkable," and further notes, "The personal being of the Word was [realized] in active intercourse with and in perfect communion with God." Westcott, *The Gospel According to St. John*, 3. Dana and Mantey concur that the language of 1:1b, "points to Christ's fellowship with the person of the Father." Dana and Mantey, *Manual Grammar of the Greek*, 140.

and so "the Word was God." Distinction of persons in one essence or nature is what we see here, and this becomes the ground upon which trinitarian theology is built. This agrees with the *Carmen Christi* when it says that the Son was "in the form of God" and had "equality with God" (Phil. 2:6), as well as Hebrews 1:3 where it says that the Son is the exact representation and imprint of the nature of God. This Word, or Logos, derives its meaning from the Old Testament concept of the Word of God, or the Lord. John was not dependent on Greek philosophy for this word and Hurtado notes that there "is no evidence that the author of [John] had direct acquaintance with Greek philosophy."[11] In Greek philosophy, the Logos was more of an intermediary between the divine and the world—it could never enter into the world, nor was it ever specifically identified as a distinct person from God.[12]

---

[11] Hurtado, *Lord Jesus Christ*, 366.

[12] Even in Philo of Alexandria's thinking, which is heavily influenced by Plato, the Logos was not really a distinct person from God, but rather an *aspect* of God, even though Philo strangely referred to the Logos as a *deuteron theon* ("second deity/god"). It is important to remember that Philo takes the "image of God" in the Bible to refer to the Logos, so that Logos equals the image of God. Note in the quote below how Philo tries to safeguard the transcendence of God. Humans may bear the image of God as found in the Logos, but not of the supreme Being himself. Philo, *QG*. 2.62 (italics mine) comments, "Why is it that he speaks as if of some other god, saying that he made man after the image of God, and not that he made him after his own image? [Gen. 9:6]. Very appropriately and without any falsehood was this oracular sentence uttered by God, *for no mortal thing could have been formed on the similitude of the supreme Father of the universe*, but only *after the pattern of the second deity [deuteron theon], who is the Word [Logos] of the supreme Being*; since it is fitting that the rational soul of man should bear before it the type of the divine Word [Logos]; since in his first Word [Logos] *God is superior to the most rational possible nature*. But he who is superior to the Word [Logos] holds his rank in a better and most singular preeminence, and *how could the creature possibly exhibit a likeness of him in himself?*"

Philo also speaks of the Logos as *protogonos*, translated as "firstborn," but which also carries the meaning of "first created." See Murray J. Harris, *Colossians and Philemon*, Exegetical Guide to the Greek New Testament (Nashville: B&H Publishing, 2010), 40. This demonstrates that the Logos of Philo is very different from the eternal Logos of John. On the Logos as intermediary and mediator Philo states, "And the father who created the universe has given to his archangel and most ancient Logos a preeminent gift, to stand on the confines of both, and separate that which had been created from the Creator. And this same Word is continually a suppliant to the immortal God on behalf of the mortal race." Philo, *Her*. 1.205. Philo does refer to the Logos as "God," but with qualification. Philo, *Somn*. 1.229-230 again comments, "There is one true God only ... it is the true God that is meant by the use of the article, the expression being, 'I am the God (*ho theos*);' but when the word is used incorrectly, *it is put without the article*, the expression being, 'He who was seen by thee in the place,' *not of the God (tou theou), but simply 'of God' (theou)*; and what he here calls God is his most ancient [Logos]."

Philo is actually commenting on Genesis 31:13, but from the LXX version where it says, "I am God that appeared to thee in the place of God where thou anointedst a pillar to me, and vowedst to me there a vow." The Hebrew text says, "I am the God of Bethel, where you anointed a pillar and made a vow to me." What the LXX means by "the place of God" is "Bethel" in the

JOHN 1:1-18

Another grammatical feature that indicates that the prologue is likely a hymn is the fact that John 1:1 and 1:18 appear as bookends at the beginning and end of the chapter. Raymond Brown refers to this as an "inclusion [which] 'packages' a section by repeating at the end of a section an idea or phrase from the beginning."[13] John 1:1 has "the Word was God," and 1:18 has "the only God."[14] These two bookends also complement each other. In other words, 1:18 says exactly what 1:1 says: the Word is God. The climax in John's Gospel also appears to be connected to the prologue, when the risen Jesus appears to Thomas, he confesses him as "my Lord and my God" (John 20:28). Here John's Gospel comes full circle. The eternal Word who is God and who became flesh, is recognized as such by the doubter Thomas himself.

As we have seen with the creeds and some hymns, there is usually a polemic theme behind them, often with anti-imperialist undertones. We already noted above how the Roman emperor Domitian (AD 51-AD 96) demanded to be addressed as "dominus et deus noster", i.e., "our lord and god." In John 20:28, however, the risen Jesus is addressed as "my Lord and my God." He is the true Lord and true God—not Domitian or any of the Caesars.

Here we have a hymn where, in verses 1 and 18, and then again at John's climax in 20:28, Jesus is called God. This raises another interesting question. I discussed earlier the letter of Pliny the Younger to the Roman emperor Trajan where he described Christians singing a hymn "to Christ as to a god." Is it possible that they were singing the hymn of John 1:1-18, where Jesus is

---

Hebrew text. What Philo means here is that when the true God is referred to, which for Philo is "the supreme Father of the universe," he is usually referred to using the definite article "the" (*ho* in Greek) before "God" so that it reads *ho theos*. When the definite article (*ho*) is not used, it does not refer to the true God, the Father, but to the Logos, or Word. It is in this sense that Philo refers to the Logos as a "second deity." This of course, is *not* what John has in view in his use of the term. Philo's Platonic philosophical thinking precluded him from ever imagining the Logos becoming flesh, much less being a distinct person and God himself.

[13] Brown, *Introduction to New Testament Christology*, 188 n.273.

[14] There is a textual variant in John 1:18. Did John originally write "the only begotten God" (NASB), "God the One and Only" (NIV), "the only begotten Son" (AV, NKJV, ASV), or "the only Son" (RSV, NJB)? The reading "the only God," or, "the only begotten God," is considered the original based on its attestation in the oldest manuscripts and because it is the more difficult reading. The reading "the only begotten Son" is the easier reading and was probably influenced by scribal assimilation to John 3:16, 18 and 1 John 4:9. The tendency in scribal practice was to smooth out the reading to make it easier to follow. See Metzger, *Textual Commentary*, 169-170; Brown, *Introduction to New Testament Christology*, 178-179; Reymond, *Jesus*, 304-306. Some translations try to bring both these variant readings together, "God the only Son" (NRSV), "the one and only Son is himself God" (NLT).

referred to as "God" twice?[15] It is interesting to note that the group of Christians Pliny was describing would have been from Asia Minor (modern day Turkey) and that the Gospel of John is also believed to have been written in Ephesus, which is in Asia Minor.[16]

The hymn states that through him (the Word), all things were made, and without him nothing came into being (John 1:1-3,10). Note again the language of divine agency—all things were made *through* him, and *by* him (Ps. 33:6).[17] This is a point that is unanimously affirmed elsewhere in the New Testament in such creeds as 1 Corinthians 8:6 and in the hymn of Hebrews 1:2b which we examined above. We will encounter it again as we look at Colossians 1:15-20 below. The high Christology in John is already building up to the high Christology found in Paul's letters, some of which, as already noted, may even pre-date Paul.[18]

We also read that the Word became flesh (John 1:14), a truth we also saw affirmed in Philippians 2:6-8 and 1 Timothy 3:16. The doctrine of the incarnation differentiates Christianity from all other religious systems. While these all emphasize man's attempt to build a bridge to the divine, it is only in Christianity that God builds the bridge to man. He does not send an angel, or a mere prophet, but comes himself in the person of his Son.

The unique feature in this hymn is a statement that has forever changed the world, "And the Word became flesh and dwelt among us, and we have seen his glory, ... [he was] full of grace and truth (John 1:14)." The glory of the Word was most clearly seen in his incarnation. This one statement demonstrates that John was not relying on Greek philosophy when he wrote it for the simple fact that in Greek thinking, the Logos, or Word, *never became flesh*. In Platonic thought, the world was divided between ideas and forms; the spiritual realm could never enter into or become part of the physical realm. The incarnation of the Word, however, dashed this concept to pieces. God is inseparably tied to creation because he chose to be; through the incarnation, God was reclaiming the created order for himself.

---

[15] Brown, *Introduction to New Testament Christology*, 188 shares this conviction.

[16] Carson and Moo, *Introduction to the New Testament*, 254.

[17] The Apocrypha is filled with this theme as well. Consider Wisdom 9:1 (NRSV), "O God of my ancestors and Lord of mercy, who have made all things by your word."

[18] The claim that a high Christology is only introduced into the New Testament in the Gospel of John is false. Carson and Moo, *Introduction to the New Testament*, 267 rightly comment, "Attempts to date the fourth gospel [John] by charting Christological trajectories do not appear very convincing."

JOHN 1:1-18

In declaring that the Word became flesh and dwelled among us, John may be engaging in a polemical and apologetic discussion. There may have been some false teachers who were threatening John's faith community by attempting to introduce ideas that denied the incarnation. In his letters, John does seem to show special concern for confessing Jesus as coming in the flesh; those who would deny this reality are antichrists and false prophets (1 John 4:1-3; 2 John 7).

This hymn also speaks of the Word having life in himself, which is the light of men (1:4), and then speaks in terms of contrast between this light and the darkness which can never overcome or comprehend it (1:9). John 1:10 also beautifully shows how the Creator came into the world incognito, "He was in the world, and the world was made through him, yet the world did not know him." The Creator walked among us in the flesh and the irony is that the world did not know or recognize him. We also see a glimpse of the earthly ministry of Jesus in John 1:11, which tells us about his rejection from his own people, likely referring to the Jews: "He came to his own, and his own people did not receive him." Though in 1:10 we are told that the world did not *know* him, in reference to Jesus' own people, it says they did not *receive* him. This is also supported by the other Gospels. This, of course, does not mean that *none* of his own people accepted him—all the first Christians were Jewish believers— but they were the "little flock" (Luke 12:32) of the faithful remnant, which has always been a minority.

The gospel message is also proclaimed in John 1:12, which promises that, "to all who did receive him, who believed in his name, he gave the right to become children of God." Only those who believe and receive the Son of God have the right to become God's children, and it is the Son who makes this happen. This is nothing less than spiritual re-birth; these believers "were born, not of blood nor of the will of the flesh nor of the will of man, but of God" (John 1:13). Salvation, then, comes through receiving Jesus Christ and being born again through him, as would be said later on, "You must be born again" (John 3:7).

This hymn also uniquely refers to the ministry of John the Baptist. However, it should be noted that John is presented only as a witness to testify about the Light; the Light, Jesus Christ, is greater than John as he existed before him (John 1:6-8,15). It also makes mention of the categorical distinction between the Old and New Testament; in John 1:17 we are told that the Law came through Moses, but grace and truth came through Jesus Christ.

EARLY CHRISTIAN CREEDS AND HYMNS

The hymn then ends with John 1:18, the thrust of which points to the fact that no one has ever seen God. It is important to note here that this refers to God the Father and not God the Son. The Father is always described as never having been seen, a point Jesus himself makes (John 5:37; cf. Deut. 4:12; Exod. 33:23). Notice how John then mentions that "the only God, who is at the Father's side, he has made him known." This one who is at the Father's side is the Word/Son, who is also truly God and has made the Father known. The last word in the hymn is the Greek word *exegesato*, which is variously translated into English as "made him known" (ESV, NIV, RSV, NRSV), "declared him" (AV, ASV), "explained him" (NASB), and "has revealed him" (HCSB). The word literally means "to make something fully known by careful explanation or by clear revelation—'to make fully and clearly known.'"[19] It also carries the idea of translation or interpretation.[20] It is from this Greek word that we derive the English word "exegesis," which is the process of explaining what is in the biblical text. When this verb *exegesato* is applied to Jesus, it means that he has truly exegeted the Father to us; in other words, he has uniquely explained, made him known, and declared him. The Word made flesh is the perfect, most complete, and fullest expression of God.[21]

When Christians sang the hymn of John 1:1-18, they were singing about the Savior who had existed eternally. Because the Son existed eternally with the Father, and shared in the same essence, or being, as the Father, he was also God. As "the Word," or "Logos," he shares in the logic, mind, and reason of God. He was also the Creator and it was through him that all things were made. He was the life giver, the light, and came into this world full of grace and truth. The hymn beautifully draws to a close in 1:18 by coming full circle to the words of 1:1, where the incarnate Word is recognized as God—the true interpreter, translator and exegete of the Father. We have seen many similarities in this hymn with the hymns we have so far examined, including the identity of the Son as God (John 1:1,18 with Philippians 2:6), Jesus as the Creator (John 1:3 with Heb. 1:2b; cf. 1 Cor. 8:6), the incarnation (John 1:10,14 with Phil. 2:7-8;

---

[19] Louw and Nida, *Greek-English Lexicon*, 28.41.
[20] *BDAG*, 349.
[21] The idea of the Logos/Word perfectly revealing God was not possible in Greek thinking. Even the Hellenistic Jew, Philo of Alexandria said that "the living God is not of a nature to be described, but only to be." Philo, *Somn.* 1.230. The Greek philosopher Plotinus (AD 204–AD 270) would later make similar statements about God being utterly indescribable. The irony here is that if God is utterly indescribable, than describing him as indescribable would necessarily have to be false!

1 Tim. 3:16), and glory and light (John 1:4-5,9,14 with Heb. 1:3; 1 Tim. 3:16; Eph. 5:14). It is also in this hymn that we find the raw components for many of the well-known historic Christian creeds. The line in the Nicene Creed which describes Jesus as the "only-begotten Son of God" is language that could only have come from John 1:14,18 and John 3:16, 18. We find the statement that the Son is "God of God" in John 1:1,18 and the language of the Son being "begotten of the Father" is from John 1:14. When the Nicene Creed goes on to say that "through [the Son] all things were made," we see that this reflects the divine agency language ("through") that we saw in John 1:3, and also in Hebrews 1:2b and 1 Corinthians 8:6. Finally, where the Nicene Creed states, "Who, for us men and our salvation, [he] came down from heaven ... and was made man," we find a parallel in John 1:14 (cf. Phil. 2:7-8; 1 Tim. 3:16).

In all this we once again observe that what the earliest Christians sang in their hymns had to do with who Jesus was and what he came to do in providing redemption for his people. Is it any surprise that the focus of our historic Christian hymns has been on Christ, his identity, and his redemptive work? It may sound like I am belabouring the point but the consistent thread we have seen repeatedly is how Christocentric all these hymns are. Again, this was a significant turning point from Old Testament worship, in which hymns as expressions of worship would only have been directed to Yahweh. With the event of the incarnation, however, hymns began to be written and sung to the Eternal One who entered time and space to redeem humanity; from the beginning of John's prologue (v.1) to the end (v.18), we find Christ. To the early Christians who sung this hymn, Christ was all in all.[22]

---

[22] The famous prayer attributed to St. Patrick (c. AD 390-AD 461), sometimes called "St. Patrick's Breastplate" captures the complete supremacy and totality of Christ in the Christian's life: "Christ with me, Christ before me, Christ behind me, Christ in me, Christ beneath me, Christ above me, Christ on my right, Christ on my left, Christ when I lie down, Christ when I sit down."

18
THE GRAND FINALE HYMN
COLOSSIANS 1:15-20

We turn lastly to our final hymn, which is found in another letter of Paul.[1] In Colossians 1:15-20 we read,

> He is the image of the invisible God, the firstborn of all creation. For by him all things were created, in heaven and on earth, visible and invisible, whether thrones or dominions or rulers or authorities—all things were created through him and for him. And he is before all things, and in him all things hold together. And he is the head of the body, the church. He is the beginning, the firstborn from the dead, that in everything he might be preeminent. For in him all the fullness of God was pleased to dwell, and through him to reconcile to himself all things, whether on earth or in heaven, making peace by the blood of his cross.

Paul wrote this letter while he was in prison (Col. 4:3, 10, 18) and hence it is part of the "prison letters," along with Philippians, Ephesians, and Philemon. This passage has been called "the summit" of Pauline Christology.[2] This is because of the high view of Jesus found in this hymn, including his work of redemption, his place in the church as its head, and his preeminence over all things. The reason this section is considered a hymn is, once again, due to grammatical indicators. The hymn begins with the relative pronoun "who" in the original Greek text (cf. Col. 1:15, AV), a key indicator of hymnic material.[3] Like the *Carmen Christi*, this hymn is also regarded by scholars as "pre-

---

[1] There is a debate in scholarship circles as to whether Paul wrote Colossians. Some scholars take the view that Paul only wrote seven letters (Romans, 1 and 2 Corinthians, Galatians, Philippians, 1 Thessalonians, and Philemon); the rest are deemed "deutero-Pauline." This is a view that emerged in the nineteenth century. I hold to the traditional view, with other scholars that Paul wrote all the letters that bear his name. See Carson and Moo, *Introduction to the New Testament*, 517-518.

[2] Feuillet, *Le Christ*, 271.

[3] See point three in the criteria for hymnic material listed in Chapter 12. See also Fee, *Pauline Christology*, 292 n.10, 493.

Pauline."[4] If this is true, it may have come either from the Jerusalem apostles or from some other apostle who later brought the gospel to Colossae. Paul mentions Epaphras as the one from whom the Colossians heard the gospel message (Col. 1:7) and also admits that he did not start the church in Colossae (Col. 2:1). Paul never took credit for planting a church in a city which had already heard the gospel; for instance, he admits that he did not bring the gospel to Rome or even begin the church in Rome,[5] "I make it my ambition to preach the gospel, not where Christ has already been named, lest I build on someone else's foundation" (Rom. 15:20).

Paul had just described the salvation experience of the Colossian Christians by telling them that God in his grace had qualified them to share in the inheritance of the saints in light, and then reminds them that God transferred them from the domain of darkness into kingdom of his beloved Son. It is in this Son that they have redemption and the forgiveness of sins (Col. 1:12-14). After writing this, Paul then moves into the hymn portion which deals directly with Christ. It is important to realize that the relative pronoun "who" is referring to "his beloved Son" (Col. 1:13). Scholars refer to this point of reference as the antecedent. In other words, it refers to the nearest subject that has just been mentioned, which is God's Son. Notice also that the language of Colossians 1:16-17 presupposes the pre-existence of the Son.

The hymn begins, "He [who] is the image of the invisible God, the firstborn of all creation" (Col. 1:15). The language of "image" here is significant as it recalls the image of God in Genesis 1:26-27 that rested on Adam and Eve, who were created his likeness. Unfortunately, Adam rebelled against God and even though he still possessed the image of God, it was marred by sin, like a mirror that has been cracked and then distorts the image reflected on it. Jesus, however, comes as the true and ideal image of God. He is *the* image of the invisible God, a point we saw in John 1:18; whoever sees him, also sees the Father (John 14:9; 2 Cor. 4:4). He is the true and ideal image of God and the one in whom the fullness of the Father dwells (Col. 1:19). He also restores the

---

[4] Reymond, *Jesus*, 245.

[5] Irenaeus, in AD 180, claims that both Peter and Paul founded the church in Rome. Irenaeus, *Adversus Haereses,* 3.1.2. This tradition is highly doubtful as Paul himself admits he was a stranger to the church of Rome (Romans 1:10,13; 15:22). It is also highly doubtful that Peter founded the church in Rome at such an early stage, as Paul most certainly would have made reference to him in Romans. See Carson and Moo, *Introduction to the New Testament*, 395. We know Aquila and Priscilla were in Rome before they met Paul (Acts 18:2), and it is possible that they or other Jews from Rome who heard the gospel at Pentecost in Jerusalem took the gospel message back with them and started the church there (Acts 2:10).

true image and likeness of God in believers (Eph. 4:24; Col. 3:10). The readers of this letter seem to be aware that in Christ the fullness of deity dwells in bodily form (Col. 2:9) as an invisible image of an invisible God would be meaningless.

It should also be noted that Jesus is "the last Adam" (1 Cor. 15:45), as Adam was only a "a type of the one who was to come" (Rom. 5:14). Jesus came as the true image bearer of God and, during his incarnate ministry, was in the fullest sense the perfect image of God and continues to be so. It is also true that the eternal Son has always carried the divine image. As we saw in Hebrews 1:3, he has the very imprint of God's nature. Thus, the image title applies to the Son in his divine nature, and also to his incarnate perfect humanity.[6] Luke, in his genealogy of Jesus, traces his genealogy all the way back to "Adam, the son of God" (Luke 3:38). Jesus is the true Son and image bearer of God. He comes as the last Adam to restore to his people what the first Adam lost as their federal representative.

The hymn then moves on to describes the Son as "the firstborn of all creation" (Col. 1:15b). The word Paul uses here for firstborn is *prototokos*, a title which is connected to the role of the Son in all creation. In this case, the term firstborn seems to refer to Christ's right to rule over all creation,[7] and presents Christ as the rightful heir to all of the created order; this is akin to what we already saw in Hebrews 1:2a, where the Son is referred to as the "heir of all things." Thus, the title firstborn seems to refer to heirship. Adam, who was made in the image of God, was also given the right of the firstborn in being given dominion over all the earth (Gen. 1:28). The idea of bearing the image of God and dominion are closely linked. In contrast to the first Adam, the last Adam, Jesus Christ, has dominion not only over the earth but the entire universe. Jesus is on an infinite scale what Adam was on a finite scale. This title of firstborn also has Messianic significance, as Yahweh declares regarding the future Davidic king, "And I will make him the firstborn, the highest of the kings of the earth" (Ps. 89:27).

The association of "firstborn" with "the highest of the kings of the earth" illustrates the exalted status of the Messiah and we have seen such language used in several of the hymns we have examined (Phil. 2:9-11; 1 Tim. 3:16;

---

[6] Fee, *Pauline Christology*, 325, 521, 551.
[7] Note the reading in the NIV, NET, and NKJV, "The firstborn over all creation." Note also the NLT, "Supreme over all creation."

Heb. 1:3). The term *prototokos* can refer "either to first in order of time, such as a first born child, or it could refer to one who is preeminent in rank."[8] The use of firstborn in the context of Colossians 1:15 seems to refer to preeminence and rank. Murray J. Harris likewise agrees that "the 'firstborn' was either the eldest child in a family or a person of preeminent rank.'"[9] In a similar vein, Micahelis argues that *prototokos* should be taken "hierarchically ... what is meant is the unique supremacy of Christ over all creatures as the Mediator of their creation."[10] That the term "firstborn" is used in this manner is seen in various passages in the Old Testament. God calls Israel his "firstborn son" (Exod. 4:22); this surely does not mean that Israel was the first nation created before all other nations. Rather, it means that God had placed them, by virtue of their being his covenant people, on a higher level of preeminence and rank. God also refers to Ephraim as "my firstborn" (Jer. 31:9); but biologically, Ephraim was not the firstborn, Manasseh was (Gen. 41:51-52). When Jacob blessed Manasseh and Ephraim, he even placed his right hand (which was supposed to be placed on Manasseh) on the head of Ephraim, the younger brother, and his left hand on Manasseh.[11] When Joseph tried to correct him, Jacob pointed out that Ephraim would, in fact, be greater than his brother, "Thus he placed Ephraim before Manasseh" (Gen. 48:20). In other words, Ephraim was treated as the firstborn because he would be greater in rank, or preeminent (Gen. 48:8-20).[12]

---

[8] Colossians 1:15, NET n.28.

[9] Harris, *Colossians and Philemon*, 39.

[10] Michaelis, *TDNT*, 6:879.

[11] It is interesting that in blessing Ephraim and Manasseh, Jacob had to cross his arms and hands, "And Israel stretched out his right hand and laid it on the head of Ephraim, who was the younger, and his left hand on the head of Manasseh, *crossing his hands* (for Manasseh was the firstborn)" (Genesis 48:14; italics mine). Is this where the idea of making the form of a cross, representing blessing, comes from? In paleo-Hebrew script, the last letter of the Hebrew alphabet ת("tav"), was written this way: "x." The letter "tav" means "mark." In Ezekiel 9 the ones who were marked on their foreheads with a "tav" were spared from the judgment that would come upon Jerusalem (Ezekiel 9:4-6). Hebrews 11:21 (citing Genesis 47:31) informs us that when Jacob blessed Ephraim and Manasseh, "he was bowing in worship over the head of his staff." The actual quote comes from Genesis 47:31 (LXX).

[12] A similar event occurs with Jacob's election over his firstborn brother Esau. Even though Jacob takes the birthright from Esau through deceptive means, God had already decreed the elder would serve the younger, and declared that he loved Jacob, but hated Esau (Genesis 25:23; Malachi 1:2-3; Romans 9:11-13). We see a similar pattern with Cain and Abel. Cain was the firstborn son of Adam and Eve and Abel was his younger brother. Abel's sacrifice was accepted by God, while Cain, the firstborn's sacrifice, is rejected (Genesis 4:1-16). In a fit of rage, Cain then slays his younger brother Abel.

Attempts by Arians to claim that Jesus was created because he is called "the firstborn of all creation" is demonstrably false on two points. First, the interpretation of firstborn as indicating preeminent rank appears to be supported by the verses following Colossians 1:16-18. The Son cannot be the first among created things because, as we shall see in 1:16-17, he is the Creator of "all things." The interpretation of preeminence in rank better suits the context here. Second, if Paul wanted to communicate the idea that the Son was a creature, or even the first creature, (as Arius of Alexandria and modern-day cults teach), there were other suitable words available that Paul could have used to communicate this idea. He could have used adjectives like *protoktistos* or *protogonos* (both meaning "first created"), or *protoplastos* ("first formed"). But he did not.[13] Rather, he used the adjective *prototokos* to designate the Son as the heir over all creation, a point which is also corroborated in Hebrews 1:2a.

The hymn continues in verse 16, "For by him all things were created, in heaven and on earth, visible and invisible, whether thrones or dominions or rulers or authorities—all things were created through him and for him." Here, Paul seems to attribute the creation of the cosmos to the Son; this is a stupendous claim. As we have seen, the idea that all creation was made *through* Christ already appears in a creed (1 Cor. 8:6), and in a hymn (Heb. 1:2b). However, Paul goes further at this point. While in 1 Corinthians 8:6 Paul wrote of all things being made *through* the Lord Jesus Christ, in Colossians 1:16, he now introduces two other prepositions in addition to *dia* ("through"), when addressing the creative action of the Son: namely *en* ("in") and *eis* ("to"). While the Son is described as the Creator of *ta panta* ("all things"), he qualifies "all things" by breaking it down into two sets of groups, or couplets: heaven and earth, and visible and invisible.

As we have already seen, the use of couplets is a grammatical indicator of a hymn in the text.[14] These couplets, and the phrase *ta panta* ("all things"), appear to refer to "the universe."[15] The combination of heaven and earth

---

[13] Harris, *Colossians and Philemon*, 40. Reymond, *Jesus*, 247 notes that the context of Colossians 1:16-17 shows that, contrary to Arian claims, the genitive ("of all creation") should not be construed as a partitive genitive, i.e., that the Son is part of creation. On the contrary, he is the one through whom all things came into existence and who is before all things, which exempts him from being of the category of *ta panta* ("all things"). Origen, *Contra Celsum*, 6.17 also calls the Son the "unborn first-born."

[14] See point four of the criteria for hymnic material in chapter 12.

[15] Reicke, *TDNT*, 5:888. See also Anthony C. Thiselton, *The First Epistle to the Corinthians: A Commentary on the Greek Text*, NIGTC (Grand Rapids/Cambridge: Eerdmans, 2000), 1239.

often appear as a couplet in the Old Testament (Gen. 1:1) as well as in ancient oriental descriptions of the world, which at times, see them together as that which "constitute the cosmos."[16] The reference to heaven and earth may also be an allusion to Genesis 1:1 where God is described as the Creator of heaven and earth. Here, however, the writer attributes the creative act to the Son. We should also note that the reference to "all things" being brought into existence through the Son attests again to the deity of Christ. God alone is credited as the Creator of "all things" in Scripture (Isa. 44:24; 66:1-2).[17] The reference to the visible and invisible seem to communicate the totality of all created existence, as we saw with heaven and earth. Things that exist are either visible or invisible, and yet all are attributed to the creative act of God's Son. The writer further qualifies that the universe which the Son created also includes the powers and rulers—a concept which pervades the Colossian letter (cf. Col. 2:15). These powers and rulers are described in negative terms, and as hostile powers which are opposed to the Lordship of Christ even though he is their Creator. These are the same rulers and powers Paul states that Christian believers are in spiritual warfare against (Eph. 6:12) and are also described as being responsible for having orchestrated the crucifixion of Jesus himself, not knowing that he would be victorious in resurrection.[18] The writer seems to be assuaging the fears and concerns of his readers in showing that Christ is not only the Creator, but also the Ruler of all creation, including the rebellious powers and rulers that have been subjected to him (cf. 1 Cor. 2:6, 8; Eph. 1:20-22). This seems to be further supported by the title of "firstborn" given to Christ in Colossians 1:15, communicating that he is the heir of all things.

When Paul speaks of all things being created "in him" [Christ], he introduces an important idea.[19] When Paul speaks of believers being "in Christ" (2

---

[16] Sasse, *TDNT*, 1:678.

[17] The LXX of Isaiah 44:24; 66:2 also uses the Greek word *panta* to refer to "all things" Yahweh has created.

[18] Note 1 Corinthians 2:8, "None of the rulers of this age understood this, for if they had, they would not have crucified the Lord of glory." On the thrones, dominions, rulers and authorities, see Louw and Nida, *Greek-English Lexicon*, 37.52.

[19] Colossians 1:16a can also be translated "for in him [*en auto*] were all things created" (ASV, NJB, RSV). Harris however comments, "The prep[osition] [*en auto*] may ... be inst[rumental] ... 'by him' ... comparable in sense with ... 'through him' ... or even causal ('because of') ... in the work of creation God did not act apart from Christ" (Harris, *Colossians and Philemon*, 40). Fee notes in respect to the prepositions used in Colossians 1:16, *en*, *dia*, and *eis*, about the Son, respectively, "who is expressly identified as the sphere, agent, and goal of the whole created order" (Fee, *Pauline Christology*, 538).

Cor. 5:17), this phrase is usually associated with their social identity with Christ their new federal head. He uses the preposition of agency, namely *dia* ("through"), with the genitive, as in 1 Corinthians 8:6, whenever he speaks of the role of Christ in creation.[20] Thus, the Son is always described as the agent through whom God created all things, which we have already seen confirmed in several passages (John 1:3; 1 Cor. 8:6; Heb. 1:2b). In other words, Paul presents the Son as co-Creator with the Father.

Paul goes on to cite the remainder of the hymn in Colossians 1:16, "All things have been created through [*dia*] him and for [*eis*] him." Here we have an interesting statement. We have already seen how divine agency is attributed to the Son with the preposition *dia* ("through"). We see it again here as Paul summarizes the creative work of the Son by stating that "all things have been created through [*dia*] him," but now he introduces another preposition, *eis*, which has a very wide semantic range, but in this context means "for." This is the only text in the New Testament where creation is said to have been created "for him."[21] Here we see that "all things," the universe, was not only created *through* the Son, but *for* the Son; in other words, the universe was specifically created *for* Jesus Christ. He is the goal, end, and focal point, of all creation. The universe was made by, or in him, through him, and for him, and

---

[20] Paul also uses the preposition of agency, *dia*, with the genitive when he speaks of God's role in creation. For example, he states in his doxology in Romans 11:36 regarding God, "For from [*ex*] him and through [*dia*] him and to [*eis*] him are all things. To him be glory forever. Amen." The use of these prepositions seek to identify God as the *source, agent* and *goal* of all creation. Paul does not refer to Christ as the source of creation in Colossians 1:16, but only as the agent and goal of creation. Philo of Alexandria, a contemporary of Paul, also used similar language of God when he spoke of created things, "the rest have their existence both by [*hupo*] him and through [*dia*] him." Philo, *Leg.* 1.41. When the Greek preposition *hupo* is used with the genitive it carries the meaning of "by" and functions in "indicating an agent or marker of agency or cause" (*BDAG*, 1035; Wallace, *Basics of New Testament Syntax*, 173). Philo also spoke of God as the first cause, or source, of creation, "Because God was the cause, not the instrument; and what was born was created indeed through the agency of some instrument, but was by all means called into existence by the great first cause ... Now he by whom a thing originates is the cause" (Philo, *Cher.* 1.125). Philo is using language similar to Aristotle who also wrote about the first cause.

[21] The idea that the Messiah was the goal, or aim, of creation finds parallels in rabbinic literature. In the third century AD, Rabbi Yohanan opined that the world was created with a view to the Messiah or for the sake of the Messiah. See Babylonian Talmud *Sanhedrin* 98b. Also see Paul Beasley-Murray, "Colossians 1:15-20: An Early Christian Hymn Celebrating the Lordship of Christ," in *Pauline Studies: Essays to Professor F.F. Bruce on his 70th* Birthday, Donald A. Hagner and Murray J Harris, eds. (Exeter/Grand Rapids: Paternoster Press/William B. Eerdmans, 1980), 173.

exist for his glory. It is for this reason that Christ is said to "fill all things" (Eph. 4:10).

In this hymn, creation, far from being anthropocentric, is clearly portrayed as made for, and centred on, Christ.[22] In Romans 11:36 Paul uses the same language of agency, *dia* ("through"), and goal, *eis* ("to"), for God.[23] The only exception in this passage is that he also speaks of God the Father as being the source from (*ex*) whom all things come (cf. 1 Cor. 8:6). The same language is used of God the Father in Hebrews 2:10, "For it was fitting that he, for whom and by whom all things exist ... should make the founder of their salvation [Jesus] perfect through suffering." Ellingworth notes that this is the language of doxology like we find in Romans 11:36 and "suggests a liturgical setting," meaning that it would have been used in the worship setting of the early Christians.[24] Ellingworth continues, "God is presented as the efficient and final cause of all things."[25] As we have seen, this language is also used of the Son in Colossians 1:16 and presupposes the oneness of Father and Son. The Son, then, in Colossians 1:16, is described as the agent and goal of creation; the very same language that is used of God.

In Colossians 1:17, the hymn continues, "And he is before all things, and in him all things hold together." The hymn now highlights the pre-existence of the Son, which is already implied in Colossians 1:15–16. If the Son created all things (1:16), then it logically follows that he would have to be pre-existent. This also demonstrates that the term "firstborn" in 1:15 cannot mean first created, as "all things" were created through the Son, and for him, which means he is not part of the category of "all things."[26] We have already seen

---

[22] In the rabbinic writings, it states that "the whole world was created for the sake of Israel ... it is only through, and because of, Israel that the Gentiles exist ... if it were not for Israel, the Gentiles would not exist." *Pes. R.* 45b. Paul would demur from this position and argue that the whole world was created for the sake of the Christ/Messiah, and that everything that exists is because of Christ.

[23] While the preposition *eis* has a wide semantic range, one of its meanings is also that of an "extension towards a special goal." Louw and Nida, *Greek-English Lexicon*, 84.16.

[24] Ellingworth, *Epistle to the Hebrews*, 159.

[25] Ellingworth, *Epistle to the Hebrews*, 159. The language of efficient and final causes echoes the language of Aristotle's Four Causes. For Aristotle, these included the material, formal, efficient, and final cause.

[26] If Paul wanted to claim that Jesus was the firstborn part of creation, as Arians assert, then instead of stating that the Son created "all things" (1:16), he could have written that the Son created "all other things." Erickson, *Christian Theology*, 637. In fact, this is what modern day Jehovah's Witnesses claim. In their 1950 publication, *The New World Translation of the Christian Greek Scriptures* (New York: Watchtower Bible and Tract Society, 1950), 589 they translate

COLOSSIANS 1:15-20

that the pre-existence of the Son is a recurring theme (John 1:1-2; 17:5; Rom. 8:3; 2 Cor. 8:9; Gal. 4:4; Phil. 2:6). The Son of God, therefore, is before everything—he is the First Cause, or the Uncaused Cause. The hymn goes even further in stating that not only is the Son the agent and goal of creation, but also that "in him all things hold together."[27] The Son is the "glue" that holds everything together and in order. In this respect, Christ is not only the Creator and goal of the universe (1:16), but he is also its Sustainer (1:17). We saw this idea already in our examination of Hebrews 1:3 where the Son is said to uphold the universe by the word of his power. Here again we see the deity of Christ is

---

Colossians 1:16-17 as follows, "Because by means of him all other things were created in the heavens and upon the earth, the things visible and the things invisible, no matter whether they are thrones or Lordships or governments or authorities. All other things have been created through him and for him. Also, he is before all other things and by means of him all other things were made to exist." What should be noted here is the appearance of the word "other" in verses 16-17. The word "other" is absent in the Greek text and was deliberately inserted as if it was part of the original text. Of course, the average reader, not knowing the original Greek, would be unaware of this. Compare this to their 1961 publication, *New World Translation of the Holy Scriptures* (New York: Watchtower Bible and Tract Society, 1961), 1274 and all other following editions (1981 and 1984) which translates Colossians 1:16-17 as follows: "Because by means of him all [other] things were created in the heavens and upon the earth, the things visible and the things invisible, no matter whether they are thrones or Lordships or governments or authorities. All [other] things have been created through him and for him. Also, he is before all [other] things and by means of him all [other] things were made to exist."

Up until 1984, the Watchtower inserted the word "other" between square brackets, which are used to indicate that the word within the brackets is not in the original text. They argued that the square brackets were inserted for clarification. But why the need for clarification? Is not the text clear enough when it says, "All things were created through him and for him" (Colossians 1:16)? The answer is obvious. The word "other" in square brackets was added not because of textual considerations, but rather because of Arian theological presuppositions. These are further highlighted when one consults *The Kingdom Interlinear Translation of the Greek Scriptures* (New York: Watchtower Bible and Tract Society, 1969), 896 where they have the (Westcott-Hort) Greek text on the left side of the page and the *New World Translation* reading on the right column. The interlinear has English subtitles under the Greek text and at Colossians 1:16 it states quite literally, "Because in him it was created the all (things) ... the all (things) through him and into him it has been created." It should be noted that the word "other" is nowhere to be found in the Greek text, which in fact states that "all" was created in, through, and for Christ. The right side of the column has the word "other" in square brackets, placed in their text of the *New World Translation*, contrary to what the Greek text says. This is nothing short of intentional deception. The text as it stands supports and upholds the full deity of Christ. The citations above are examples of eisegesis and not exegesis. The revised edition of *New World Translation of the Holy Scriptures*, rev. ed. (New York: Watchtower Bible and Tract Society, 2013), 1576 removed the square brackets in Colossians 1:16-17, and reverted to leaving the word "other" in the text as they did in the 1950 edition.

[27] The background to this idea is also found in the Apocrypha in Sirach 43:26b, "And by his word all things hold together" (RSV). As we saw, the reading in Hebrews 1:3 is similar to this thought, "He [the Son] upholds the universe by the word of his power." In this text, the immediate antecedent is "the Son" (Hebrews 1:2a).

presented in glowing majesty. As we can see from this hymn, early Christians sang about the deity of Christ from the earliest days.

The root verb *sunistemi* ("hold together"), here means "continue, endure, exist, hold together."[28] The Greek philosophers known as the Stoics used this word to describe the "binding together" of the universe.[29] Louw and Nida define *sunistemi* as, "To bring together or hold together something in its proper or appropriate place or relationship."[30] This seems to indicate that not only does Christ sustain the universe, but that he will someday also restore harmony back to the universe, including the personal relationships of those he redeems (Col. 1:20-23). As Sustainer of the universe, Christ maintains order by keeping everything in its proper and ordained place.

The hymn then continues with the words in Colossians 1:18, "And he is the head of the body, the church. He is the beginning, the firstborn from the dead, that in everything he might be preeminent." The relative pronoun "who," the grammatical indicator of hymnic material, also appears here, "Who is the beginning" (AV). Here we see a progression from the top down. Christ is the firstborn of all creation, the image of the invisible God (1:15), the Creator and goal of all things (1:16), pre-existent, and holding the universe together (1:17); now he comes down to the earthly level, so to speak, as the "head of the body, the church." The church here is compared to the body of Christ, of which he is the head. It stands to reason that without the head, the body is lifeless. The faculty of reasoning and thinking is the head where the brain is (cf. Col. 2:19). If there is brain damage, a variety of negative conditions will go on to affect the body. The point here is that as the head, Jesus is absolutely essential to the very life of the body, which is his church.[31] The headship of Christ over the church also speaks of his authority, supremacy, and preeminence; he is "head over all things to the church" (Eph. 1:22; 4:15). The headship of Jesus over the church is also a paradigm of the headship of the husband over his wife (Eph. 5:23). In fact, Jesus is "the head of all rule and authority" (Col. 2:10), and all authority in heaven and earth has been given to him (Matt. 28:18).

---

[28] *BDAG*, 973.
[29] Beasley-Murray, "Colossians 1:15-20," 174.
[30] Louw and Nida, *Greek-English Lexicon*, 63.6.
[31] On the church as the body of Christ see Romans 12:5; 1 Corinthians 12:12-13:27.

COLOSSIANS 1:15-20

The hymn also says of Christ, "He is the beginning." This seems to echo Genesis 1:1, as the "image of God" language in Colossians 1:15 also does (cf. Gen. 1:26-27).[32] Jesus is the Re-Creator, so to speak, of the new creation. As the true image-bearer of God, he recapitulates all things in himself and conforms his people into that same image. Here the Son is spoken of as the source of the church, as believers were chosen in him before the foundation of the world (Eph. 1:4). It also speaks of his preeminence, which again recalls the title of "firstborn" in 1:15, and highlight his royal heirship. God is also called "the beginning" (Rev. 21:6) in the sense that he is the "first and the last" (Isa. 41:4; 44:6; 48:12). Jesus is also the "first and the last" (Rev. 1:17; 22:13), and "the Alpha and the Omega" (Rev. 22:13; cf. Rev 1:8), and "the beginning and the end" (Rev. 22:13).[33]

This hymn introduces a new theme, that of recreation in Christ, in terms of his salvific work. Whereas the first part of the hymn dealt with the creation of the universe (1:15-17), in verse 18, the hymn will now continue with the theme of creation, but now cast in reference to the new creation. The idea of new creation in Christ is a Pauline theme, as he sees anyone who is "in Christ" as a "new creation" (2 Cor. 5:17). In this hymn, Christ is not only the *Creator*, but the Re-Creator in terms of salvation and his role as *Saviour* is emphasized.[34] Christ then becomes not only the central figure in the creation of the

---

[32] Fee, *Pauline Christology*, 521.
[33] In Revelation 3:14, Jesus is also called, "the beginning of God's creation." This does not mean that the Son had a beginning, as we have seen in other passages that he is eternal and uncreated (John 1:1-2; 1 Corinthians 8:6; Philippians 2:6; Hebrews 1:2b; 8-12). The word "beginning" in Revelation 3:14, when applied to a person, can carry the meaning of "ruler" and authority, as in "the ruler of God's creation" (NIV). See *BDAG*, 138 s.v. 6. This is also seen in "the chief of the creation of God" (YLT). It can also refer to the origin of something, as the Greek word used here for "beginning" is *arche* from which we get our English words "architect" (originator of a building) and "archaeology" (study of origins and sources). This is reflected in the following translations of Revelation 3:14: "the Originator of God's creation" (HCSB, NET), "the origin of God's creation" (NRSV). The NJB renders it, "the Principle of God's creation." The NEB renders it, "the prime source of all God's creation" and the AMP as, "Beginning *and* Origin of God's creation." See *BDAG*, 138 s.v. 1b, 3. Surprisingly in this third edition, *BDAG*, 138 s.v. 3 (italics in original), states, "*beginning* = 'first created' is linguistically probable." This meaning is highly unlikely since the words "beginning," "ruler," and "originator" are much more probable in light of passages which speak of the pre-existence of the Son and his role in the creation of "all things." We see this in the Colossian hymn in 1:16-17. This would be an example of Occam's razor, which states that the simplest and clearest explanation is to be preferred to tenuous and complicated explanations.
[34] The role of Saviour is one which in the OT is usually attributed to God (2 Samuel 22:3; Psalm 17:7; 106:21; Isaiah 43:3; 45:15, 21; 60:16; Hosea 13:4). It is a title which Yahweh takes for himself and asserts that apart from him "there is no saviour" (Isa. 43:11).

EARLY CHRISTIAN CREEDS AND HYMNS

universe but the central figure in the salvation of fallen humanity; hence he is presented in terms of both Creator and Saviour. This is a common theme and frequently applied to God in the Old Testament.[35] As the head, Christ is also the authority figure; in the same way in which he sustains and holds the universe together (Col. 1:17), he also sustains and holds the church together. Christ is the life source of the church (Eph. 4:15–16).

The reference to Christ as the "beginning," therefore, is connected to Christ's description as the firstborn from the dead, just as the beginning clause in Colossians 1:18a functions as a couplet when it states that Christ is the head of the church. In the same way, there is a couplet here between the beginning, and the firstborn from the dead. The beginning, in reference to Christ, points to his being the firstborn from the dead, which would indicate the resurrection is in view here. In this case *prototokos* ("firstborn") takes on a chronological dimension. The hymn literally says that Jesus is "the firstborn out of the dead ones," from the Greek word *nekron*. In other words, Jesus is the first to rise from the realm of the dead. This demonstrates again his priority in rank as the risen one. This is why context is so important in determining the meaning of words. Since the theme in Colossians 1:18 refers to Christ's salvific work, we would expect it to naturally refer to the resurrection of Jesus (cf. Rom. 10:9). This is now Paul's second use of *prototokos*, the first one being in Colossians 1:15 in reference to the creation of the universe. The second use in 1:18 speaks of Christ's supremacy in rank as well, but also in terms of chronology as the one who is the firstborn from the dead,[36] being "first in order of time."[37] Jesus was *the first* to rise from the dead.[38] This needs to be qualified. When the hymn says Jesus is the firstborn from the dead, this refers to him being the first to rise with an *immortal, glorified*, and *incorruptible* body. The risen Christ will never die again (Rom. 6:9). But were there not others who had risen from the

---

[35] The conjoining of both titles of Creator and Saviour/Redeemer for Yahweh is a common motif. These two titles are evident in Isaiah 44:24 (LXX), "Thus saith the Lord that redeems thee, and who formed thee from the womb, I am the Lord that performs all things: I stretched out the heaven alone, and established the earth." Also note Isaiah 44:24 (MT), "Thus says the LORD, your Redeemer, who formed you from the womb: 'I am the LORD, who made all things, who stretched out the heavens alone, who spread out the earth—Who was with me?'" (RSV).

[36] Micahelis *TDNT* 6:881. The double meaning of *prototokos* seems to be at work here. Fee notes, "As the 'first' to rise from the dead, he [Christ] thus also has the rights of the 'firstborn' with regard to his church." Fee, *Pauline Christology*, 307.

[37] Colossians 1:15, NET n.28.

[38] Colossians 1:18, NET n.32.

COLOSSIANS 1:15-20

dead before Jesus? It is true that Jesus raised Lazarus from the dead (John 11:38-44), and the widow's son from Nain (Luke 7:11-17), and the daughter of Jairus (Mark 5:22-23, 35-43; Luke 8:41-42,49-56). However, these were resurrected to a *mortal* and *perishable* life; they would all die again. These were not a resurrection to immortal life like that which Jesus entered into. As the words of the hymn "Crown Him with Many Crowns" so beautifully states, "Behold his hands and side, rich wounds yet visible above, in glory beautified."[39]

Christ, then, is the first to rise to immortality through resurrection and will be followed by his people upon his return. The description of Christ as the firstborn (*prototokos*) is also used by Paul in Romans 8:29 where he refers to Jesus as "the firstborn among many brothers." Believers are being conformed to the image of God's Son (Rom. 8:29), which will also one day include their resurrection. Paul clearly states this fact elsewhere, "Just as we have borne the image of the man of dust [Adam], we shall also bear the image of the man of heaven [Christ]" (1 Cor. 15:49). Two federal heads are mentioned here; Adam, and Christ. All who are in Christ, "the man of heaven" will be made like him in resurrection (Phil. 3:20-21; 1 John 3:2).

This points to the future glory believers will share upon Christ's return.[40] In this sense, Paul speaks of Christ as the first among many, that is, the first of a newly resurrected humanity. For Paul, this new humanity will only be realized at the resurrection, when believers will be conformed to the image of the risen Christ. Notice that the "image of his Son" in Romans 8:29 is also the image which Paul refers to in 1 Corinthians 15:49, "We shall also bear the image of the man of heaven [Christ]." In context, Paul is speaking about the future resurrection of believers in which their bodies will be transformed by the risen Christ and conformed to his glorious risen body (Phil. 3:20-21). Romans 8:29, like Colossians 1:18, is speaking of Jesus as firstborn in terms of chronological priority.[41]

---

[39] Is it any wonder that when John saw the Lord Jesus in heaven, he described him as "a Lamb standing, as though it had been slain" (Revelation 5:6), and yet he was alive? I take this to mean that the marks of crucifixion are still visible on the Lord's resurrected body, the same marks Thomas saw (John 20:24-29).

[40] "The reference is to an eschatological transfiguration." Michaelis, *TDNT*, 6:876.

[41] Paul also addresses the chronological priority of Jesus' resurrection in 1 Corinthians 15:20,23 where he speaks of the resurrection of Jesus as "the firstfruits." Here Paul clearly has chronological priority in mind, "But each *in his own order*: Christ the firstfruits, *then at his coming* those who belong to Christ" (1 Corinthians 15:23; italics mine).

Notice also that the phrase "the firstborn from the dead" only appears in Colossians 1:18 and thus we find another criterion of hymnic material.[42] The reference to the resurrection of Jesus in the context of salvation here is significant. As we have already seen, the resurrection of Jesus is central to the Christian concept of salvation. It appears in the earliest creed (1 Cor. 15:3-4) and was present during belief (Rom. 10:9-13) and confession at baptism.

The hymn then closes this with the line, "That in everything he might be preeminent." Christ is to have preeminence "in everything." He is preeminent as the image of the invisible God, as the firstborn of all creation (1:15), as the Creator of all things, as the goal of the whole universe (1:16), as the pre-existent one (1:17), as the head of the church which is his body, and as the first to rise gloriously from among the dead (1:18). The word Paul uses for "preeminent" is the Greek word *proteuo*, which means, "to be in the first position, with the implication of high rank and prominence."[43] It is fitting that this hymn would draw to a close on the note of Christ's supremacy and preeminence.

Some scholars believe that the hymn in Colossians ends at 1:18 and that Paul added his own commentary in 1:19-20. This seems convincing (this is my own conviction) as it ends on a high note of the preeminence of Christ.[44] Since many are of the conviction that the Colossian hymn is composed of 1:15-20, we will also consider verses 19 and 20. The hymn continues in verse 19, "For in him all the fullness of God was pleased to dwell." The word translated as "fullness" here is the Greek word *pleroma*. It also carries the idea of completeness, as in Psalm 24:1, where it states that the earth is Yahweh's and "the fullness thereof," meaning everything that is in it is his. We have already seen how God is referred to as "filling all things" (Jer. 23:23-24), as well as Christ being he "who fills all in all" (Eph. 1:22; cf. 4:10). Both God and his Son possesses the divine attribute of omnipresence. Though the original Greek of Colossians 1:19 does not have the word "God" in it, various translations

---

[42] See point five of hymn criteria in Chapter 12.
[43] Louw and Nida, *Greek-English Lexicon*, 87.46.
[44] Douglas J. Moo, *The Letters to the Colossians and to Philemon*, The Pillar New Testament Commentary (Grand Rapids/Cambridge: Eerdmans, 2008), 131.

have supplied it because, contextually, it refers to God as the subject, as I will point out next.[45]

The word "fullness" is another example of circumlocution. In this case, the word "fullness" is being used synonymously with God, which is why a number of translations insert God into Colossians 1:19. If the line in the hymn read, "For in him all the fullness was pleased to dwell" one might be left wondering how "fullness" was "pleased" to dwell in Christ. Is "fullness" something personal? The addition of "God," or, "the Father," as the AV has it (even though the word "Father" does not appear in the original Greek text), is an attempt to contribute a personal dimension. As we will see below, "the fullness" refers to all that God is in his nature. In 1:19, the hymn reinforces the truth of the full deity of Christ. All that God is dwells in Christ. Here again, as we saw with the creed of the Christian *Shema* in Chapter 8, there is no tension or threat against monotheism. Early Christians were able to affirm the divine plurality of persons within the Godhead while at the same time affirming strict monotheism. N.T. Wright observes, "The full divinity of the man Jesus is stated without any implication that there are two Gods. It is the one God, in all his fullness, who dwells in him."[46]

Paul will use this word again in Colossians 2:9 when he writes, "For in him the whole fullness [*pleroma*] of deity dwells bodily" in Christ. This means that the Lord Jesus Christ is fully God but at the same time fully man. This is what theologians refer to as the hypostatic union and was enunciated at the Council of Chalcedon in AD 451.[47] It is important to stress from the language here that

---

[45] The following translations show the variety of ways this verse in Colossians 1:19 has been rendered. In some cases, the translator has supplied words indicated by italics that are not in the original. Notice that the words "Father" and "Son" have been added to some of the translations below, neither of which are found in the original Greek but are added for clarity: "For it pleased the Father that in him should all fulness dwell" (AV); "For it was the good pleasure *of the Father* that in him should all the fulness dwell" (ASV); "For in him all the fullness of God was pleased to dwell" (RSV, NRSV); "For it was the *Father's* good pleasure for all the fullness to dwell in Him" (NASB); "For God was pleased to have all His fullness dwell in Him" (HCSB, NIV); "For God was pleased to have all his fullness dwell in the Son" (NET).

[46] N.T. Wright, *Colossians and Philemon*, TNTC (Downers Grove: InterVarsity Press, 1986), 80.

[47] The Council of Chalcedon (AD 451) was extremely important in outlining what Christians believed about the hypostatic union in Christ. I am placing in italics the relevant parts about the two natures in the one person of Christ. These truths are seen in passages like Colossians 1:19 and 2:9, "So, following the holy fathers, we all with one voice teach the confession of one and the same Son, our Lord Jesus Christ: the same *perfect in divinity and perfect in humanity, the same truly God and truly man*, of a rational soul and a body; *of one essence with the Father as regards his divinity, and*

what Paul is saying is that the fullness of deity dwells in Jesus in bodily form *even now*. In Colossians 2:9 the word "dwells" is the present active indicative verb *katoikei*, which denotes present ongoing action.[48] Since the incarnation and into eternity, Jesus remains forever the God-man (John 1:14; Phil. 2:6–8; 1 Tim. 3:16). This point is reiterated in 1:19. Notice that the words "fullness" and "dwell" appear in both passages. There is a co-relation, then, between the words of the hymn in 1:19, and the statement in 2:9. Whatever 1:19 means by the fullness of God dwelling in Jesus is reinforced by the use of the same language in 2:9.

As I stated earlier, hymns often take on a polemical or apologetic function. Although debated among scholars, it seems that the Colossian believers were being confronted with what appears to be proto-Gnostic influences and teachings. While Gnosticism bloomed in the mid-second century AD, the seeds of this heresy seemed to be at work in the church of Colossae, and Bruce argues that there may have been "incipient forms of Gnosticism in the mid-first century."[49] The word *pleroma* was also used by the Gnostics to refer to the totality of emanations and aeons which proceeded from the true god, who was himself ultimately unknowable.[50] Paul argued, on the other hand, that this "fullness" could only be found in the Lord Jesus Christ. Some of these Gnostic teachings would have been strongly averse to the idea that the divine could enter into his creation as a human being. We also saw this theme in

---

the same of one essence with us as regards his humanity; like us in all respects except for sin; begotten before the ages from the Father *as regards his divinity*, and in the last days, for us and for our salvation, the same born of Mary, the virgin God-bearer, as *regards his humanity. He is one and the same Christ*, Son, Lord, Only-Begotten, *acknowledged in two natures* which undergo no confusion, no change, no division, no separation. At no point was the difference between the natures taken away through the union, but *rather the property of both natures is preserved and comes together into a single person and a single subsistent being*. He is not parted or divided into two persons, but is one and the same only-begotten Son, God, Word, Lord Jesus Christ, just as the prophets taught from the beginning about Him, and as the Lord Jesus Christ Himself instructed us, and as the creed of the fathers handed it down to us."

In the *Epistle to Diognetus*, 7.1–4, written sometime between AD 130–AD 200, we find the doctrine of the hypostatic union already foreshadowed two centuries before the Council of Chalcedon: "God Himself, who is almighty, the Creator of all things, and invisible, has sent from heaven, and placed among men, [him who is] the truth, and the holy and incomprehensible Word ... He did not, as one might have imagined, send to men any servant, or angel, or ruler ... but the very Creator and Fashioner of all things—by whom he made the heavens ... by whom all things have been arranged, and placed within their proper limits, and to whom all are subject ... This [messenger] he sent to them ... As a king sends his son, who is also a king, so sent he him [the Son]; as God he sent him; as to men he sent him [as a man]."

[48] Wallace, *Greek Grammar Beyond the Basics*, 516.
[49] Bruce, *Epistles to the Colossians*, 73.
[50] Moo, *Letters to the Colossians*, 132.

John's prologue, where John made the earth-shattering claim that the Word, who is God, became flesh and dwelled among us (John 1:14). Is it possible that John was polemically refuting false notions that denied the reality of the incarnation? In his letters, the truth of the incarnation certainly seems to be central to orthodoxy (1 John 4:1-3; 2 John 7).

The hymn in Colossians maintains that in Jesus the fullness of deity dwells. The idea of "dwelling" echoes the language from the Old Testament of God dwelling with his people in the tabernacle, and later in the temple. This relationship is sometimes spoken of in very concrete terms, "And let them make me *a sanctuary*, that *I may dwell* in their midst" (Exod. 25:8; italics mine). This language is not surprising when we recall that it has always been God's intention to dwell among his people. Whenever God does come and descend on his people, it is always described as glorious—and sometimes fearful—such as when God descended on Mount Sinai (Exod. 19:1-20). When the tabernacle was constructed in the wilderness, God would occasionally descend in a cloud, and his glory would fill the entire place (Exod. 40:34-35). The same thing occurred when Solomon built the temple in Jerusalem (1 Kgs. 8:10-11). When we come to the incarnation, what does John say that they saw? John 1:14 (italics mine) states, "And the Word became flesh and dwelt [or tabernacled, pitched his tent] among us, and *we have seen his glory*, glory as of the only Son from the Father, full of grace and truth." When God became man, his glory was seen in the most complete manner to date. This "glory," communicated by words like light and clouds, is always associated with Jesus' earthly ministry. It is present at his birth (Luke 2:9), in his signs (John 2:11), at his transfiguration (Matt. 17:2), at his resurrection (Luke 24:4), and finally at his ascension (Acts 1:9-10). When Jesus returns, he will also come with glory, and sit on the throne of his glory (Matt. 25:31).

In Genesis it mentions that God dwelled and walked in Eden with Adam and Eve (Gen. 3:8). In the new heavens and earth, we are told that God will also dwell personally with his people (Rev. 21:3; 22:4). In fact in the vision of the eschatological temple in Jerusalem, Ezekiel's last words are, "And the name of the city from that day on will be: Yahweh Is There" (Ezek. 48:35, HCSB). Jeremiah also spoke of the coming of the future King from David's line, whose name is "Yahweh our righteousness" (Jer. 23:5-6, author's translation), and that the future city of Jerusalem will be called "Yahweh is our righteousness" (Jer. 33:16; author's translation). This will be because the Messiah, "Yahweh is our righteousness," will be in her.

John 1:14 borrows the language of God's dwelling with his people when he states that the Word became flesh and *dwelled* among us. The word "dwelled" in the original Greek here can also be translated "tabernacled" or "pitched his tent." When the word "fullness" is used in Colossians, it is referring to the *incarnate* Son. The language of "all the fullness" might seem almost redundant until we realize that it seeks to express totality.[51] God's nature, in all its totality, resides in Christ. It also says in 1:19 that the fullness of God "was pleased to dwell" in Christ. It is important to note that this relationship was well pleasing to God; it was not a usurping of power on the part of the Son because, as we saw in the *Carmen Christi*, the Son already possesses equality with God (Phil. 2:6). The Son is not a rival against the Father but works in tandem with him for the redemption of his people (John 5:19-27). This language is very similar to that of Psalm 68:16 which, in the LXX, is Psalm 67:17 (italics in original), "*This is* the mountain which God has delighted to dwell in; yea, the Lord will dwell *in it* for ever." In speaking of Mount Zion, the temple mount, the psalmist here says that God is delighted, or pleased, to dwell in it. Again, temple language is important here as it points to Jesus who also identified *his body* as the temple of God (John 2:18-22). The same words used in Psalm 68:16, ("pleased" and "to dwell"), are used in Colossians 1:19 and 2:9.[52]

The Gnostics also believed that the universe was controlled by powers, rulers, thrones, and dominions. In the Colossian hymn these same powers are created by and in subjection to Christ, as we have seen, and it is the Son of God who holds all things together (1:16; cf. Heb. 1:3). The fullness that dwells in Christ, then, is a reference to his true and full deity, albeit embodying true humanity.

The hymn concludes with verse 20 in what appears to be the grand finale, "And through him to reconcile to himself all things, whether on earth or in heaven, making peace by the blood of his cross." In 1:18, the hymn had referenced the resurrection of Jesus in stating that he was the firstborn from the dead. Now the hymn will refer to his death on the cross and what it achieved. What should be noticed here again is the language of divine agency,

---

[51] Moo, *Letters to the Colossians*, 132.
[52] It is interesting that Psalm 68:16 (67:17, LXX) shares grammatical similarities with Colossians 1:19, 2:9. The same psalm is quoted by Paul in Ephesians 4:8 where Yahweh is said to have ascended on high, taking his enemies captive and distributing gifts to men. In his usual fashion, Paul takes a passage referring to Yahweh and applies it to the exalted Christ.

dia ("through"), in relation to Christ. It is through the Son that God created all things (Col. 1:16; cf. John 1:3, 10; 1 Cor. 8:6; Heb. 1:2b), and it is through the Son that he is reconciling to himself *ta panta* ("all things"). The reference to "earth" and "heaven" recalls 1:16, which states that heaven and earth were created by and through the Son (cf. Gen. 1:1). Where Colossians 1:16 states the order of heaven and earth as a top-down arrangement, Colossians 1:20 arranges it as earth and heaven—a bottom up arrangement. The last line of the hymn mentions the salvific work of God in making peace with his people by the blood of the cross of Christ. In the verses that follow the hymn, it is clear that Paul goes on to apply the last line of the hymn to redeemed humanity (Col. 1:21-22). By itself, Colossians 1:20 can be taken to imply that God is going to redeem all people without qualification. This, of course, is the heresy of Universalism, which believes that God will let no one be eternally separated from him.[53]

The wording of the hymn in 1:20, however, is not speaking about Universalism. Rather, it is employing the language of summation in attempting to bring all things into order and subjection under Christ. Paul here is looking forward to the eschaton, the time when "all things are subjected to him [Christ]" (1 Cor. 15:28). Even now, as Peter points out, Christ "has gone into heaven and is at the right hand of God, with angels, authorities, and powers having been subjected to him" (1 Pet. 3:22). Here again is the now/not yet tension we see throughout the Bible. Though all is subject to Christ now, the subjection has not yet reached its fullest, visible expression, which will only be realized when Christ returns. Note the regal language used in reference to Christ. He is at the right hand of God, as King, with both good and evil made subject to him.

The work of Christ does have cosmic significance; in fact it is God's eternal purpose (cf. Eph. 1:10) "that all things should be summed up in him [Christ]."[54] Since the Fall, all of creation has been affected by sin. What Adam did in rebellion against God had cosmic consequences. Conversely, what the

---

[53] In the third century AD, Origen was already teaching Universalism and cited Colossians 1:20 as proof, as many Universalists do today. Moo, *Letters to the Colossians*, 135. Closely connected to Origen's universalism was his rejection of the doctrine of the eternal punishment of the wicked. He believed the wicked would suffer temporarily and, after being purified, that everything would revert back to its original state of perfection prior to the Fall. This view of Origen is called *apokatastasis*. See Erickson, *Christian Theology*, 940. Origen's views were later condemned by the church.

[54] Bruce, *Epistles to the Colossians*, 74. Bruce also notes that "everything was created with a view to Christ" (74 n.167).

last Adam (Christ) did in obedience to God also had cosmic consequences. All things have been estranged from their Creator due to the Fall, as we read in Romans 8:20-23,

> For the creation was subjected to futility, not willingly, but because of him who subjected it, in hope that the creation itself will be set free from its bondage to corruption and obtain the freedom of the glory of the children of God. For we know that the whole creation has been groaning together in the pains of childbirth until now. And not only the creation, but we ourselves, who have the firstfruits of the Spirit, groan inwardly as we wait eagerly for adoption as sons, the redemption of our bodies.

Note the words "subjected" and "set free." The created order is now subject to corruption, but it will one day be set free and obtain the freedom of the children of God. In the description of the new heaven and new earth, it is described as the removal of the things which were once part of the Fall, "He [God] will wipe away every tear from their eyes, and death shall be no more, neither shall there be mourning, nor crying, nor pain anymore, for the former things have passed away" (Rev. 21:4). The One who sits on the throne also declares, "Behold, I am making all things new" (Rev. 21:5). Notice Paul also says that believers "groan inwardly," being part of this fallen creation, and wait eagerly for the resurrection which is "the redemption of our bodies" (Rom. 8:23). Even our bodies will be redeemed—that is what the resurrection entails and why it is so necessary. God will save the whole person, not just part of the person. We have the down payment now, the "firstfruits of the Spirit" (cf. Eph. 1:13; 4:30), and will someday participate in the final harvest (the resurrection), when the remaining balance of the payment will be rendered to us.

Note that the created order awaits a freedom that can only be realized when "the children of God" are finally freed in glory. In other words, creation will only be restored when God's children are fully restored at the consummation of the age when Christ returns. If creation fell due to Adam's disobedience, then creation will also be restored with the obedience of the last Adam. Since Christ has redeemed his people, the reconciliation of heaven and earth is assured and will occur in due time. This conflict, as Colossians 1:20 points out, can only be resolved as peace is made with God—an achievement that was secured by the redemptive work of Christ. Christ's redemptive work has colossal ramifications not only for believers, but also for the establishment of order in the created cosmos. Part of the means of this establishment includes not only the salvation of some of Christ's enemies (Rom. 5:10), but also, as Moo notes, the others are "vanquished by him" (cf. Col. 2:15).[55] Order will be established by keeping the powers and forces of evil "in check," somewhat like the picture we see in Revelation, where the unregenerate will be placed "outside" the holy city of the New Jerusalem (Rev. 22:15; cf. 21:8). Both Universalism and Annihilationism struggle with comprehending what will happen to the wicked when God eventually restores all things. Universalism attempts to remove this problem by stating that all will be reconciled to God, whereas Annihilationism maintains the wicked will simply be snuffed out of existence. Neither of these views are biblical, however, but are rather strained interpretations operating from a humanist and emotive worldview.

Millard Erickson, commenting on Colossians 1:20, correctly notes that this passage does "not say that all will be saved and restored to fellowship with God" but rather speaks "of the setting right of the disrupted order of the universe, the bringing of all things into a proper relationship with God. But this could be achieved by a victory forcing the rebels into reluctant submission; it does not necessarily point to an actual return to fellowship."[56]

The background to Paul's thinking in Colossians 1:20 may be rooted in the notion of the *Pax Romana* ("Roman Peace") inaugurated by the Roman emperor Augustus (27 BC-AD 14). The *Pax Romana* was established partly by conquering and subjugating enemy forces who opposed Rome's imperial rule. Rome would then guarantee their peace as long as they continued to submit to the emperor, willingly or unwillingly.[57] In the famous quote by C.S. Lewis, "There are only two kinds of people in the end: those who say to God, 'Thy will be done,' and those to whom God says, in the end, 'Thy will be done.'"[58] It is thus no surprise that the Roman emperor Domitian (AD 51-AD 96) was given the title "Peacemaker,"[59] and that Augustus (27 BC-AD

---

[55] Moo, *Letters to the Colossians*, 135.

[56] Erickson, *Christian Theology*, 945.

[57] On the *Pax Romana* see Adrian Goldsworthy, *Pax Romana: War, Peace and Conquest in the Roman World* (New Haven: Yale University Press, 2016).

[58] C.S. Lewis, "The Great Divorce," in *The Best of C. S. Lewis* (Grand Rapids: Baker Book House, 1969), 156.

[59] On this title and other titles given to the Roman emperors see Wayne Baxter, *Israel's Only Shepherd: Matthew's Shepherd Motif and His Social Setting*, Library of New Testament Studies (New York: T&T Clark, 2012), 93-94. It is interesting that one of the Beatitudes was, "Blessed

14) was known in the empire for establishing and maintaining peace.[60] Even Philo of Alexandria spoke about God as the peacemaker, or "giver of peace," who abolishes sedition, "in all parts of the universe."[61]

This seems to coincide with what the hymn says about the rulers and powers in 1:16, which may represent malevolent forces as in Ephesians 6:12. In subduing these powers God maintains order over the universe. Contrary to the doctrine of Annihilationism, the Bible teaches that the wicked will be eternally separated and banished from the redemptive presence of God (Matt. 25:41, 46; 2 Thess. 1:8-9), while still being described as being tormented in the presence of the Lamb and the holy angels "forever and ever" (Rev. 14:10-11). The hymn ends with a reference to the blood of Jesus. Through the blood of Jesus, God has made peace both with his people (Col. 1:14; cf. Eph. 1:7), and creation. As we have seen, God will ultimately reconcile the fallen cosmos back to himself. Though the coming of Jesus has inaugurated the renewal and restoration process, it will only be finally realized at the return of Christ, "whom heaven must receive until the time for restoring all the things" (Acts 3:21).

Another reason that Colossians 1:20 cannot be referring to a universalistic salvation of all humanity is that the preaching of the gospel, which Paul also calls the "word of the cross" (1 Cor. 1:18), or the "preaching of the cross" (AV), does double duty. The word of the cross is to those who are being saved, "the power of God," but to those who are perishing, it is "foolishness." Paul also speaks of believers being the aroma of Christ both to those who are being saved and among those who are perishing. To some, believers are a fragrance of life, while to others they are a fragrance of death (2 Cor. 2:15-16).[62] The

---

are the peacemakers, for they shall be called sons of God" (Matthew 5:9). There may be an anti-imperial statement implied here in that the real peacemakers are not those who wage war like Rome did; rather, the true peacemakers are the sons of God who, through the gospel, bring the kingdom of God to bear in the lives of people. The word for "peacemaker" in the original Greek is a *hapax legomenon*, only appearing in Matthew 5:9.

[60] R.B. Edwards, "Rome," in Green, McKnight and Marshall, eds., *Dictionary of Jesus and the Gospels*, 710.

[61] Philo, *Spec. Leg.* 2.192, "God as the giver of peace, who has abolished all seditions in cities, and in all parts of the universe, and has produced plenty and prosperity, not allowing a single spark that could tend to the destruction of the crops to be kindled into flame." Here we see the absolute sovereignty of God over the created order in establishing peace by abolishing sedition in the entire universe.

[62] "For we are the aroma of Christ to God among those who are being saved and among those who are perishing, to one a fragrance from death to death, to the other a fragrance from life to life" (2 Corinthians 2:15-16).

gospel is not a melting pot, it is a dividing line; it separates the elect from the reprobate. The meaning of words in context is vitally important here. The language of Colossians 1:20, when it speaks of God reconciling all things in heaven and earth, is one of cosmic reconciliation, not individual redemptive reconciliation.[63]

The hymn in Colossians 1:15-20 shows us that the place of Jesus in the Colossian church was central. It always came back to the "who" and "what" of Jesus. Who was Jesus and what did he come to do? The Colossian hymn states plainly that Jesus must be number one in the lives of Christian believers; that everything begins and ends with the supremacy of Christ. The key theme in the Colossians hymn is that Christ should have the preeminence in all things (1:18). This preeminence is demonstrated in the fact that he is the perfect image of the invisible God, the firstborn of all creation and over creation, and the heir of all things (1:15). We also saw this in Hebrews 1:2. He is also the pre-existent Son who is the Creator of "all things." All things were made in him, by him, through him, and for him (1:16). He precedes all things as the pre-existent Son, and holds the universe together (1:17), a truth that we also encountered in Hebrews 1:3. He is also the beginning and the source, not just of creation, as we also in Hebrews 1:2b, but also the firstborn from among the dead. He is the risen one and the conqueror of the grave, sin, death, and Satan (cf. Phil. 2:9-11; Heb. 2:14; 1 John 3:8). He has preeminence in time, space, and the universe, as its Creator and Sustainer (1:18). The fullness of God was pleased to dwell in him as the Incarnate one (1:19; cf. 2:9), a truth we also saw in John 1:1,14, Philippians 2:6-11, and 1 Timothy 3:16. He is the divine agent not only of creation, but of reconciling the created order back to himself, and has done so also by enacting a peace bond through the blood of Christ on the cross. In legal language, and I am speaking in the context of Canadian law here, a peace bond does not necessarily mean that two opposing parties have been amicably reconciled. Rather, it legally imposes that the guilty party will be on

---

[63] An example of redemptive reconciliation is seen in 2 Corinthians 5:18-19, "All this is from God, who through Christ reconciled us to himself and gave us the ministry of reconciliation; that is, in Christ God was reconciling the world to himself, not counting their trespasses against them, and entrusting to us the message of reconciliation." It is clear from the language that Paul is referring to Christian believers when he uses pronouns such as "us" in reference to those who have benefited from Christ's redemptive work. The term "world" here has to be understood as the elect which have taken from out of the world. For Paul, humans are either "in Adam" or "in Christ" (Romans 5). If they are in the former, they will die; if the latter, they will live. Earlier in the same chapter Paul wrote that it is only those who are "in Christ" who are made a new creation (2 Corinthians 5:17). Paul was not a Universalist by any stretch of the imagination.

his or her best behaviour and agree to the terms laid out. It is intended to ensure the innocent party is protected. To violate a peace bond brings serious consequences.

The death of Jesus, then, procures the salvation of his people (Col 1:22-23; cf. 1:14; Matt. 1:21), but also sets things right between God and the universe. In Christ, God has begun the reconciliation process, and it will be fully realized one day at the return of Christ. When early Christians sang this hymn, they would no doubt have been enthralled at their glorious Representative, Creator, Redeemer, Sustainer, and Consummator. This Christ-glorifying hymn would have assured the early Christians that Christ is indeed all (cf. Col. 3:11), and that he is enough.

19
CONCLUSION

If we are going to learn anything about what Christianity looked like in its earliest setting, or who the historical Jesus really was, or what the earliest Christians believed about him, we need to go where all historians and scholars go: the New Testament texts. It is because of these earliest sources that even a liberal critical scholar like Bart Ehrman can confidently assert, "One of the most certain facts of history is that Jesus was crucified on orders of the Roman prefect of Judea, Pontius Pilate."[1] It stands to reason, then, that if we want to identify the earliest Christian creeds and hymns, we need to extrapolate them from these same texts. Unlike modern day texts, however, there is nothing in these historic texts which state, "And now here is a creed that we confess," or, "Here is a hymn that we sing in our worship services." It is only through textual analysis that scholars have been able to identify creeds and hymns in the text; as we have seen, there are also a number of grammatical indicators, that point out when a creed or a hymn is present.

In our examination of the creeds and hymns of the New Testament we have discovered that they are unashamedly Christocentric. They are centred on Jesus Christ. Based on our findings regarding early creeds and hymns, we can submit the following portrait of the Lord Jesus Christ:

1. He is Lord (Rom. 1:3-4; 10:9-13; 1 Cor. 8:6; 12:3; 2 Cor. 4:5)
2. He is the Christ/Messiah (Matt. 16:16; Mark 8:29; Luke 9:20; John 1:49; 11:27; 20:31; 1 John 5:1)
3. He is the Son of God (Matt. 16:16; John 20:31; Rom. 1:3-4; Heb. 1:2b; 1 John 5:5)
4. He is Yahweh (Rom. 10:13; cf. Joel 2:32/1 Cor. 8:6; cf. Deut. 6:4/Phil. 2:9-11; cf. Isa. 45:23)
5. He is Pre-Existent (John 1:1-2; 1 Cor. 8:6; Col. 1:17; 1 Tim. 3:16; Heb. 1:3)

---

[1] Bart D. Ehrman, *The Historical Jesus: Lecture Transcript and Course Guidebook*, Part 2 of 2 (Chantilly: The Teaching Company, 2000), 162.

EARLY CHRISTIAN CREEDS AND HYMNS

6. He is God (John 1:1; 1 Cor. 8:6; Phil. 2:6; Heb. 1:3)
7. He is the Creator (John 1:3; 1 Cor. 8:6; Col. 1:16; Heb. 1:2b)
8. He is the goal and ultimate reference point in all creation (Col 1:16)
9. He is the Sustainer of the universe (Col. 1:17; Heb. 1:3)
10. He became Incarnate as man (John 1:10, 14; Phil. 2:7-8; 1 Tim. 3:16)
11. He was sinless (1 Pet. 2:22)
12. He died (1 Cor 15:3; 1 Pet. 2:24)
13. He died as a sacrificial victim and made atonement for sin (1 Cor. 15:3; Phil. 2:8; 1 Pet. 2:24; Heb. 1:3)
14. He made peace through the blood of his cross (Col. 1:20)
15. He was buried (1 Cor. 15:4)
16. He was raised from the dead (Rom. 10:9; 1 Cor .15:4; Col. 1:18; implied in Phil. 2:9-11 and 1 Tim. 3:16)
17. He ascended to heaven, was exalted, and bestowed with the name above all names (Phil. 2:9-11; 1 Tim 3:16; Heb. 1:3-4)
18. He raises spiritually dead sinners to life and shines his light on them (Eph. 5:14)
19. He is worshipped and adored with God the Father in hymns/songs in the church community (Eph. 5:19; Col. 3:16)
20. He was proclaimed to and among the nations (1 Tim. 3:16)
21. He was believed on in the world (1 Tim. 3:16)
22. He will be worshipped and acknowledged as Lord/Yahweh by all in the cosmos to the glory of the God the Father (Phil. 2:9-11; cf. Isa. 45:23)
23. He will be the divine agent through whom God will reconcile the created order back to himself (Col. 1:20)

I began Chapter 1 by dealing with various creeds and their definitions. We saw that our English word "creed" comes from the Latin word *credo* which means "I believe." We saw that throughout church history, creeds were formulated to articulate what Christians believed and what they didn't believe. We saw examples of this in the great historic creeds of the church such the Apostles' Creed and the Nicene Creed. Though there were other church councils that also published creeds, these two are the most ancient outside of the New Testament. Through Christian history and into the Reformation, creeds played an integral part in the expression of Christian beliefs. We also saw that creeds and

CONCLUSION

hymns often overlap with each other. Many creeds are hymn-like, and many hymns are creed-like.

We began in Chapter 2 by examining creeds and hymns in the Old Testament. We saw that the most famous of all creeds is the *Shema* (Deut. 6:4-5), which calls Israel to listen and hear that Yahweh, their God, is the one, true Lord and that they are to love him with all their heart, soul, and strength. We also looked at other creeds such as Deuteronomy 26:5b-9, which was recited by the Israelites at the harvest festival. Here they recounted their ancestral history, starting from Jacob, and how their fathers went to Egypt and endured bondage and hardship until God sent Moses to deliver them. We saw that creeds are rooted in history; they are not myths or imaginary tales of the past, but confessions of how the covenant God Yahweh related to his people and redeemed them in history.

We saw that hymns often appear at significant points in Israel's history and are sung to thank God for their deliverance from their enemies. After the crossing of the Red Sea, Miriam led the Israelites in a hymn of praise to God for saving them from their enemies while also proclaiming that Yahweh will reign forever and ever. The song of Miriam also highlighted God's role as the Warrior and Saviour of his people. These hymns not only speak of "who" God is, and "what" he has done, but also what he will do. The "who" and "what" questions about God and, later, Christ, are usually answered in the creeds and hymns found throughout Scripture. Hymns were so important to God's people that they even composed and gathered these hymns into a Psalter—a collection of 150 Psalms which comprise the largest section of the Bible. It is no surprise, then, that the Psalms continually refer to the law of the Lord as perfect (Ps. 19:7), and that the theme of the longest psalm (Ps. 119) is the Word of God.

The creeds and hymns of the Old Testament are theocentric; they focus on God's identity as Creator, Redeemer, Provider, and Sustainer of his people, all of which are communicated in the concept of covenant. The two basic ideas of a covenant in the Bible are embodied in the statement, "I will be your God, and you will be my people." God is in relationship with his people and they declare their loyalty and submission to him by the use of creeds and hymns. As they enter into worship, hymns assist the believer by putting their convictions about God into song.

In Chapter 3, we began with an introduction to creeds in the New Testament by looking at their nature. We saw that while the Old Testament is mainly theocentric, the New Testament is Christocentric. This does not mean the New Testament is not theocentric—it is—but that its focus is specifically on the person and work of the Lord Jesus Christ. We also examined how creeds can be identified in the text, which is primarily by grammar. We noted that creeds tend to be preceded by conjunctions like *hoti* ("that"), that work in the same way as quotation marks in introducing a saying, either directly or indirectly. There are a number of creeds that can be detected in the New Testament, and they are almost without exception about Jesus. New Testament creeds seek to answer questions about Jesus such as: Who was he? Why did he come into the world? What did he accomplish? Where is he now? Is he returning? What is his relationship to God?

In Chapter 4 we examined the earliest recorded creed in the New Testament: 1 Corinthians 15:3-4. This creed is believed by some scholars to have circulated within *months* of the death and resurrection of Jesus. This means that if Jesus died and was raised from the dead in the spring of AD 33, this creed would already have been circulating that same year. The creed is pre-Pauline; Paul had "received" and then "delivered" it to the believers in Corinth. Paul would no doubt have received this creed from Peter and James when he first visited them in Jerusalem to obtain information about Jesus after his conversion. The creed is simple and straightforward: Jesus died for our sins, was buried, and then was raised the third day. This creed captures the heart and core of the gospel. We can deduce from this that whatever we can say about the earliest Christians, the one thing we know with absolute certainty was that they believed that Jesus truly died on a cross and that his death was a vicarious atonement for sin. They also believed he was buried and, most importantly, that he rose from the dead on the third day, just as Jesus predicted during his earthly ministry. This creed is unparalleled in the study of classical history and it is astounding to have a source of such early provenance.

In Chapter 5 we turned our attention to the shortest known creed: "Jesus is Lord." We saw how it affirms Jesus as the supreme Sovereign over both believer and unbeliever. In addition, when the title "Lord" was applied to Jesus, it also functioned as an anti-imperialist creed. Among the titles which the Roman emperors took themselves, the title "Lord" or *Dominus* was one of them. The early Christians refused to acclaim Caesar as Lord because they believed Jesus, and only Jesus, was Lord.

We saw that this creed also affirms the deity of Christ. We looked at the fact that the Greek word for "Lord" (*kyrios*), was the same word used in the

Conclusion

Septuagint (LXX), for Yahweh. In the New Testament, Old Testament passages that refer to Yahweh in the LXX are applied to Jesus with ease by the New Testament writers (Rom. 10:13; cf. Joel 2:32/Phil. 2:10–11; cf. Isa. 45:23/1 Pet. 3:15; cf. Isa. 8:13). In other words, the creed "Jesus is Lord" also came to mean "Jesus is Yahweh." This demonstrates that belief in the deity of Christ was already held and confessed by the earliest Christians.

In Chapter 6, we examined the creed, "Jesus is the Christ." This creed naturally arose from the Jewish soil in which Christianity originated and had a polemical purpose behind it; namely, that Jesus of Nazareth was the promised Messiah spoken of in the Hebrew Scriptures, the true Son of David, and that other failed Messianic pretenders were not. While this creed served the purpose of identifying Jewish followers of Jesus from other unbelieving Jews, it also had an anti-imperialist function. The term "Christ," or "Messiah," meaning anointed one, also carried with it regal connotations—meaning that Jesus, and not Caesar, was King of kings. As King, Jesus is also the true Sovereign over all the cosmos. This creed also carries within it an implicit proof of the deity of Christ in that the title "King of kings" (Rev. 17:14; 19:16; cf. 1:5), is also a title used of God himself (1 Tim. 6:15).

In Chapter 7 we looked at the creed, "Jesus is the Son of God." I discussed various ways in which the term "son of God" is used in the Old Testament and in Second Temple Jewish literature.[2] We saw that it can be used in various ways depending on the context, but the way in which it was used in relation to Jesus was unique: it communicated that he was the only begotten Son of God. While others could be sons of God by creation, election, or appointment, Jesus is the Son of God by nature. We saw this theme repeated in some of the New Testament hymns we investigated. The Sonship of Jesus is one that speaks of his divine nature and equality with God and it was this claim that incited the Jewish Sanhedrin to have Jesus condemned and crucified.

The Son of God became human so that humans can become sons of God. Like the titles "Lord," and "Christ," the title "Son of God" also had an anti-imperialistic function. The Roman emperor, at least from Julius Caesar forward, was believed to be divine, and Augustus Caesar was even given the Latin title *Filii Dei* ("son of God"). We also saw that this creed was sometimes coupled with another creed, "Jesus is the Christ" (John 20:31; cf. Matt. 16:16).

---

[2] See Appendix 1.

Early Christian Creeds and Hymns

In Chapter 8 we explored the Christian *Shema* in 1 Corinthians 8:6. Remarkably, it seems that Paul took the traditional *Shema*, found in Deuteronomy 6:4, and revamped it for a Christian context. The *Shema* was the heartbeat of Israel. It emphasized that Yahweh was one, and that he must be loved with all one's being (Deut. 6:5). We observed how Paul re-interpreted it in light of the New Covenant with the coming of Christ, and in the incarnation and the outpouring of the Holy Spirit at Pentecost. Paul took the words "Lord" and "God" and applied them respectively to the two of the three Persons of the Trinity; God being applied to the Father, and "Lord" being applied to the Son.

These days Christians confess the *Shema* through Christological lenses, and we saw that from the earliest days, the deity of Christ was central to the Christian faith. Even in 1 Corinthians, a letter written between AD 50-AD 55, about twenty years after the death and resurrection of Jesus, he is already identified as Yahweh. This is unprecedented. Yahweh was a name reserved for the God of Israel, and yet the earliest Christians came to equate Jesus Christ, the Son of God, with Yahweh himself. So we see that Christians integrated Jesus into the very heart of Israel's ancient and most sacred creed, all the while remaining completely devoted to monotheism.

In Chapter 9, part two of the book, we turned to deal with the subject of hymns. We saw that hymns in the New Testament functioned in a dual role: they communicated truths *about* Jesus (John 1:1-18; Phil. 2:6-11; Col. 1:15-20; Heb. 1:2b-4) while also being sung *to* Jesus (Eph. 5:19). In this way, hymns reflected the Psalms, which were sung *to* God, but were also sung *about* him and his great redemptive works.[3]

We also noticed that there are a number of grammatical indicators that alert us to the presence of a hymn in the text, such as the appearance of the relative pronoun "who," the presence of *hapax legomenon*, rhythmic language, and the use of ideas collected in couplets.[4] Unfortunately, first-century Christians did not leave any musical notes or scores telling us how they actually sang their hymns, though we still have access to the words of these hymns. That early Christians did employ hymns in their worship gatherings is clear, and this has been confirmed in several places in the New Testament.

In Chapters 10 and 11 we examined three passages in Paul's letters that refer to the practice of singing hymns: 1 Corinthians 14:26, Colossians 3:16,

---

[3] Fee, *Pauline Christology*, 493.
[4] See Chapter 12 under criteria for hymnic material.

CONCLUSION

and Ephesians 5:19. In the first passage, Paul deals with the subject of worship and spiritual gifts (1 Cor. 12-14) and assumes that early Christians would have a hymn or a psalm to share and presumably sing. The words "hymn" and "psalm" are interchangeable and both were usually associated with song. These hymns, or psalms, may have been reinterpreted for a Christological context from the Old Testament Psalter or perhaps even given by divine inspiration to some of the early Christians. We know that the context for expressing these hymns would have been in a worship context because Paul uses the phrase "when you come together," i.e., to assemble for worship.

As we looked at Colossians 3:16 and Ephesians 5:19, we noted that these two passages were strikingly similar in wording, the only difference being between the object to whom these psalms, hymns, and spiritual songs were addressed. In Colossians 3:16 the object of worship is God, but in Ephesians 5:19 it is the Lord. We learned from usual Pauline usage that "God" generally refers to the Father whereas "Lord" refers to Christ. As we further compared these two passages, we saw that early Christians sang hymns to *both* God the Father and the Lord Jesus Christ and concluded once again that the Lord Jesus Christ was worshipped by the earliest Christians in song. We noted that the first extra-biblical source from the Roman writer Pliny the Younger to the emperor Trajan describes early Christians singing to Christ "as to a god." Though in Judaism, hymns would never be sung to biblical figures or angels, we see in the New Testament that the risen Jesus now also becomes a recipient of this unique worship.

In Chapter 12 we explored the most famous and well-known hymn, the *Carmen Christi*, which is embedded in Philippians 2:6-11. This beautiful hymn is believed to have been pre-Pauline and we saw that it progresses in a "V" shaped (from heaven, to earth, to heaven) direction. It outlines the true deity of the Son, who is both pre-existent and equal with God. We noted his volitional decision to humble himself, become a human, and be obedient to the Father, even to the point of a gruesome death on the cross. We saw that as a result of his absolute obedience and humility, he has been exalted by the Father and conferred with the name above all names: Yahweh, indicated by the substitute word, "Lord." It is to this Lord that the whole cosmos will bow the knee and confess, to the glory of God the Father. It is through Christ that God has wrought salvation for his people and through him that he will receive maximum glory by all of creation. Though this hymn is a sobering one, it ends on a note of triumph. This hymn is also Christocentric, centred on Christ, but also Christotelic, meaning that the ultimate goal and end of the hymn is Christ himself. Christ is glorified which then redounds to the glory of God the Father. This is one confession that all will someday make, either willingly or unwillingly.

In Chapter 13 we examined the hymn found in 1 Timothy 3:16. As it appears in all of the pastoral letters, it is likely that both Paul and Timothy would have been familiar with it. It is structured in six lines of couplets that alternate between the earthly and heavenly spheres. Though this hymn is brief, it also outlines the core beliefs of the Christian faith and is unapologetically Christocentric. It contains reference to the Son's incarnation, his vindication in resurrection, his life and ministry being witnessed to by angels, his gospel being proclaimed among the nations and being believed in by the world, and his glorious ascension into heaven. We also noted that this hymn was more thematic than chronological; for example, while the hymns states that he was proclaimed among the nations, the book of Acts attests that he had already ascended before this occurred. Again, as in the former hymn, the Lord Jesus Christ is the subject.

In Chapter 14 we moved on to Ephesians 5:14. In this short hymn we encounter what was probably the first evangelistic hymn as it is directed to those who sleep in spiritual death, and calls them to awake so that the light of Christ can shine on them. It is also possible that such a hymn would have been sung during baptismal services as the baptized emerged from his "watery grave." This would have been very similar to modern Baptistic baptismal circles where the congregation sings a hymn after the baptism of each candidate. It should be noted again that this hymn it is centred on Christ, as he is credited with being the one who raises and sheds light on the spiritually dead.

In Chapter 15 we moved outside the letters of Paul to examine the hymn found in 1 Peter 2:22-24. We noted that it was written to Christians who were experiencing persecution and that it points to Jesus as the Sinless One who had no deceit in him. It shares material from the passion narratives of the gospels themselves and reminds us that Jesus did not return evil for evil. When he was reviled, he did not retaliate in kind, but endured suffering because he had entrusted himself to God, the righteous Judge. The hymn then highlights the vicarious atonement of Jesus in that he bore "our sins" in his body; the same body that had been beaten, scourged, and pummeled by his adversaries— much like Peter's persecuted readership. It then mentions Jesus bearing our sins on "the tree," to highlight the fact that he became a curse for us (cf. Gal.

3:13). Jesus died that we might die to sin and live to righteousness, and he spiritually heals us from our sins by his wounds, or "stripes."

We saw that this hymn has much in common with Isaiah 53 by what it says about the Suffering Servant. It speaks at first of a very human Jesus; one who knows what it is like to be opposed, persecuted, and put to death. He identifies with our sufferings as he did with the martyrs before us. Because he had no sin, he is also able to be a perfect Saviour for his people. This hymn sings about the glory of Christ's death to his people and his representation on their behalf to take away their sin. It is his death as the perfect sin bearer that heals us from our sins so that we can live in righteousness. Again, we see that this hymn is centred on Christ.

In Chapter 16 we looked at another hymn which was addressed to early Jewish Christian believers, found in Hebrews 1:2b-4. I referred to it as a Jewish hymn. The fact that the letter containing this hymn was addressed to Jewish believers in Jesus demonstrates that the deity of Christ was held to from the very beginning in Jewish circles; it was not a "Gentile invention," nor an evolutionary idea developed throughout the Gospels. This hymn identifies Jesus as the pre-existent Son and as the one whom God has appointed heir of all things and through whom he created the universe. The idea of the Son as the divine agent is a recurring theme attested to repeatedly both in creeds and various other hymns (1 Cor. 8:6; John 1:3, 10; Col. 1:15-20). The Son is magnified as the radiance of God's glory and the exact imprint of the nature of God himself. He is also said to uphold the universe by the word of his power. This language is lofty, and seeks to convey in no uncertain terms the full deity of Christ in all his majesty.

The hymn goes on to declare that Christ is the Creator and one with the Father in his nature, or essence. The hymn also focuses on the perfect redemptive work of Jesus as it mentions him purifying his people from their sins and sitting down at the right hand of God. The posture of sitting demonstrates that he has finished his work. The hymn in Hebrews ends by stating that Jesus is far superior to the angels because the name he has inherited is greater than theirs. Jesus is not a heavenly being like the angels, but is the divine, eternal Son of God and perfect Saviour of his people.

In Chapter 17 we examined the longest hymn, found in John 1:1-18, and noted that it appears not in a letter or epistle, but in a Gospel account. This hymn is also known as the prologue of John. It is a magnificent hymn that begins with the same words as Genesis 1:1, "In the beginning." This hymn marks the Gospel of John as unique in that, unlike the other gospels, John speaks about the Son as the eternal Word of God, who is personally distinct from the Father, and yet shares his nature and essence; thus, "the Word was God" (John 1:1c). This affirms his role as the divine agent *through* whom all things came into being. It speaks of this Word as the light and life, and of his incarnation, the most salient feature in the hymn. God entered our space-time universe, the Eternal entered the temporal, the Infinite entered the finite, the one who was God became a human being, while still remaining who he always was. The incarnation was the event in which the Son became, and remains forever, the God-man.

As we saw, the prologue reaches its conclusion in John 1:18, where once again Jesus is called "God" and which nicely connects back with John 1:1. In 1:18 he is shown to be the one who is at the Father's side, or, "in the bosom of the Father" (AV, NASB), and the one who perfectly exegetes, or explains, the Father to us. We see once again the Christocentricity of this hymn. The confession of Thomas in John 20:28, as he addresses Jesus as "my Lord and my God," is considered the climax of the Gospel of John, and also brings us back full circle to the opening lines of the hymn: "the Word was God."

In Chapter 18, we returned to Paul's letters to look at our final hymn in Colossians 1:15-20. This hymn is chock-full of Christ-related content. It begins by identifying Jesus as the image of the invisible God and states that he is the perfect and pure image of God. What Adam was on a finite scale as God's image bearer, Jesus was perfectly; this is why whoever sees him can be said to have also seen the Father. As the last Adam, Jesus fulfills perfectly what it means to portray the image of God. The hymn recalls Genesis 1:26-27, where "the image of God" first appears in Scripture, and points to the last Adam, who has brought about the new creation. Jesus is also called the firstborn of all creation as he is also the heir of all things (cf. Heb. 1:2b). As Adam was to be the heir and have dominion over all creation (Gen. 1:28), so the last Adam, as the greater heir, has dominion over the entire universe. As dominion is connected to image bearing, so, like Adam, the final Image-Bearer was also given dominion, albeit on a cosmic scale.

The hymn continues to point out that it was in, through, and for Jesus Christ that all things were created. This language parallels what we saw in John 1:3, 1 Corinthians 8:6, and Hebrews 1:2b. The Son is the Divine Agent through whom all things were made, and that all things were made ultimately for him. Everything that exists, exists for Jesus Christ. Jesus Christ permeates

CONCLUSION

the universe and is himself the goal of the universe. This is a stupendous thought. This is not the language used of a mere creature or prophet, but of God alone and we see that the deity of Christ shines forth in blazing light from the Colossian hymn. The Saviour of Christian believers, the Messiah of Israel, is truly God, a thought that also overwhelmed Paul (Rom. 9:5).[5] The hymn also highlights that as Creator, the Son is before all things and holds everything together as the Sustainer of the universe. It goes on to praise him as the head of the body, the church, and the Beginning of all things. Here the hymn also speaks of the Son in incarnational terms; though he is the Beginning of all things, he is also the *new* Beginning. How did he bring about this new beginning? By becoming the firstborn from among "the dead ones" (literal reading). He has conquered death, was the first to rise in a glorified, immortal body— the model for the resurrection bodies of believers. The purpose in all of creation is that Christ would have first place in all things.

This hymn reminds us that even in his Incarnate state, the Son had the fullness of God dwelling in him. As we saw in John 1:14, the incarnation was a unique event in which God the Son took on an additional nature which he volitionally joined to himself. From the incarnation onwards, the Son forever remains the God-man, and will never cease to be so. He remains "*vere deus, vere homo*" (truly God, truly man), so that for all eternity he can identify with his people. These same people will one day be resurrected as immortal and glorified humans, and their bodies will be changed and conformed to their Saviour (Phil. 3:20-21). In the incarnation, the fullness of deity dwells, and will forever dwell, bodily in Christ (cf. Col. 2:9).

The hymn ends on a triumphant note that brings it to a climatic close. Once again, we see that all things were created through the Son, and it is through the Son that God will reconcile the cosmos to himself. This is an important statement as it deals with cosmic reconciliation. Though the cosmos has been affected by the Fall, through Christ, God is reversing the effects, which will be finally completed upon Christ's return. The means whereby God makes reconciliation possible is through the blood of the cross of Christ; his blood has guaranteed a peace bond between God and creation. In the end, God and the cosmos will be reconciled through Christ, order will be established, and all chaos and sinful rebellion against God will be subdued.

---

[5] "To them [Israelites] belong the patriarchs, and from their race, according to the flesh, is the Christ [the Messiah], who is God over all, blessed forever. Amen."

EARLY CHRISTIAN CREEDS AND HYMNS

This hymn is a full-orbed statement of the supremacy of Jesus Christ. It would have been much like Handel's "Hallelujah Chorus" in proclaiming the glory of the Son of God who for us became incarnate, enacted redemption, and will in due time bring the entire universe into harmony with God. Then and only then will God be "all in all" (1 Cor. 15:28).

We have also seen how the Apostles' and Nicene Creed borrowed various elements from these Scriptural creeds and hymns in an attempt to formulate these great truths in creedal charters that could be confessed by Christian believers throughout the centuries. While the historic Creeds of the Church are not infallible as the creeds and hymns found in Scripture are, they do help enunciate and communicate the truths contained in Scripture.

You are what you believe; this is partly why creeds are so important. It comes down to worldview. The lens through which Christians understand reality is their belief in the Triune God. It is disconcerting, then, to see so many professing believers who don't really know *why* they believe *what* they believe. For this reason, we need to recapture the importance of the biblical creeds in our churches today. Jesus regarded the creed of the *Shema* in the Old Testament as the first and most important of all the commandments, "There is no other commandment greater than these" (Mark 12:28–31). He likely would have recited the *Shema* all his life—both in prayer and in worship. These creeds were important to the earliest Christians as seen by the apostles' employment of them in their theology and teaching. The Reformers also understood the importance of creeds, and thus the Protestant tradition has conveyed to us some of the recaptured biblical truths of justification by faith alone in Christ alone, and the doctrines of grace. We need to rediscover this precious legacy today.

Another way the earliest Christians expressed what they believed was in the use of hymns. From Old Testament days into the New Testament and beyond, singing has been and continues to remain an integral part of Christian worship. Even within modern hymns one can find many creedal statements. One modern example is the hymn, "The Church's One Foundation" by S.J. Stone written in 1866. This hymn is peppered with creedal statement about what it believes about God's triune nature, and what Jesus has done in and through his church. The singing of hymns unites the people of God, and together lifts their joyful voices up to God through Christ; sometimes we sing them to the Lord Jesus, other times to the Holy Spirit, while at still other times to the whole Triune God. The author of Hebrews captures this sense when he

CONCLUSION

writes, "Through him [Christ] then let us continually offer up a sacrifice of praise to God, that is, the fruit of lips that acknowledge his name" (Heb. 13:15). The singing of hymns also joins the voices of the church on earth with the voices of the church in heaven (Heb. 12:22-24; Rev. 7:13-17). Hymns bind the church together in both its heavenly and earthly spheres.

In our day there has been a debate about the kind of music that should be sung in churches. Should it be contemporary music or classical hymns? Some believe that the only hymns that should be sung are the Psalms. Though this is not a settled issue, the only caution that I would propose is that hymns need to be glorifying to the triune God. They should be Christ-centred and gospel oriented and should sparkle with biblical truths. Singing hymns that are merely repetitive with no scriptural content does not edify or build up the people of God. Jesus taught his followers that God is not impressed with "meaningless repetition" (Matt. 6:7, NASB) in prayer—do we think repetitive singing would be viewed any different? We do not want to change our hymns into mantras. As we observed the various hymns found in the New Testament, we noted that they focused on the primacy of Christ, his sovereignty in all things, and the centrality of the gospel. We also need to recapture this legacy.

In closing, it has been my intent throughout this book to demonstrate that what the earliest Christians believed in their creeds, they sang about in their hymns. We owe it to our first-century brothers and sisters in Christ to maintain, preserve, and confess the creeds they confessed, and continue to sing the content of their hymns in our own present-day worship settings. We are organically connected to the creeds they confessed and the hymns they sang. As the Old Testament saints were to the New Testament believers, so our early fathers in the Christian faith are to us, as we too are "surrounded by so great a cloud of witnesses" (Heb. 12:1). What is it that overcomes the world? It is our faith, expressed in creeds and hymns, that Jesus is the Christ, the Son of God (1 John 5:1, 5). Upon this confession, the church is built, and the gates of Hades will not prevail against her; she will continue to march on and demolish its gates in triumph with the message of the gospel (Matt. 16:16-18). The continuity and permanence of the Church of Jesus Christ has been promised by God. The church from its beginning, and through the centuries, and into eternity, will demonstrate that she exists ultimately for one purpose—the worship of the triune God. With our first-century brethren, we can recite in unison the doxology that they would have recited, "To him be glory in the church and in Christ Jesus throughout all generations, forever and ever. Amen" (Eph. 3:21).

APPENDIX 1
THE TERM SON OF GOD IN THE APOCRYPHA, PSEUDEPIGRAPHA, THE TARGUMS, AND RABBINIC LITERATURE

Apocrypha and Pseudepigrapha
The intertestamental literature are Jewish texts that were written between the Old and New Testaments and are sometimes referred to as Second Temple Jewish literature. This period covers a time span of about 400 years and contains a rich cache of theological thinking. Here we are able to discover what the Jews thought about various theological issues. These texts have come to be known as the Apocrypha,[1] and Pseudepigrapha.[2] Though they are considered to be non-canonical, they may have been read as devotional material, much like when Christians read books by Charles Spurgeon or Oswald Chambers. Some, not all, possess special historical significance, particularly 1 and 2 Maccabees, which recounts the rededication of the temple after it was defiled by Hellenists and the rise of the Hasmonean dynasty, which established the office of high priest as the ultimate religious position. Hence the reason why the figure of the high priest is so prominent in the New Testament period. They also record the events that led to the creation and observance of the Jewish feast of Hanukkah (Hebrew word for "dedication"), a feast Jesus, being a Jew, would also have celebrated (John 10:22).

It is interesting that when we examine these texts, we see that they reveal that "son of God language" was widely used much like it was in the Old Testament. Angels are called "sons of heaven" and "sons of the God of heaven"

---

[1] Jews and Protestants both refer to this collection of books as the Apocrypha and view them as non-canonical. Roman Catholics and the Orthodox Church, however, accept them as "deuteron-canonical," and part of Scripture. The Roman Catholic Church officially declared seven of these books to be canonical at the Council of Trent in 1546. On a general and helpful introduction to the Apocrypha see Bruce M. Metzger, *An Introduction to the Apocrypha* (New York: Oxford University Press, 1957). On the reasons why the Apocrypha is not accepted as canonical Scripture, see the important work by Roger T. Beckwith, *The Old Testament Canon of the New Testament Church and its Background in Early Judaism* (Eugene: Wipf & Stock, 1985).

[2] On the Pseudepigrapha James. H. Charlesworth, ed., *The Old Testament Pseudepigrapha* (2 vols.; Garden City: Doubleday, 1985).

(*1 Enoch* 13:8; 106:5). Abel is said to be a judge of souls and is "like to a son of God"—an allusion to the heavenly beings (*Testament of Abraham* 12).

As we saw in Exodus 4:22-23, Israel as a whole is referred to as the "son of God" (Wis 9:7; 18:13; *Psalms of Solomon* 17:30), with God vowing to be a Father to him (*Jubilees* 1:22). The Maccabean martyrs are also called the "children of heaven" (2 Macc. 7:34). A righteous person who suffers for the sake of righteousness is also called a child and son of God, and who can call God his Father (Wis 2:13, 16, 18; 5:5). A wise man is referred to as God's son (Sir. 4:10; 51:10; *Psalms of Solomon* 13:8).

It is also in this intertestamental literature that we begin to see individual Israelites other than the king being called son of God. In the text *Joseph and Asenath*, Joseph is called the "son of God" because of his great beauty (6:2-6; 13:10; 21:3) and Levi is called a "son of God" at his consecration (*Testament of Levi* 4:2). The text of *1 Enoch* 48:2-10 also speaks of a "son of man" whose description is taken from Daniel 7:13-14 and who is spoken of as pre-existent and also as God's Messiah.[3]

In the text known as *4 Ezra* (in the Latin and Syriac versions), God refers to the Messiah as "My Son" (17:28-29; also 13:32, 37, 52; 14:9). Some scholars dispute whether the original text had "son" or "servant." This is not problematic, however, as the idea of son and servant were viewed as synonymous. For example, Israel was God's son, and yet God commanded Pharaoh to let Israel go so that he might *serve* Yahweh (Exod. 4:23). The son faithfully obeys the father by serving him. Thus, the idea that the Messiah was Son of God is also supported in the intertestamental writings.

The Targums

The Targums were Aramaic paraphrases of the Old Testament. They cannot really be called translations as their purpose was to expand on the Hebrew text for theological and didactic purposes. As such, it is important to note that the Targums are *not* a replacement for the Hebrew Bible, which the Jews

---

[3] "And at that hour that Son of Man was named in the presence of the Lord of the spirits, and his name before the One to Whom belongs the time before time. Yes, before the sun and the signs were created, before the stars of the heaven were made, *his name was named* before the Lord of the spirits ... he shall be the light of the Gentiles and the hope of those who are troubled of heart. All who dwell on earth shall fall down and worship before him ... For this reason has he been chosen and hidden before Him, *before the creation of the world* and for ever more ... for in his name they are saved, and according to his good pleasure has it been in regard to their life" (*1 Enoch* 48:2-5, 7; italics mine).

APPENDIX 1

considered sacred. They function more like commentaries than anything. For instance, whenever the Bible spoke about God creating, the Targum would say, "The Word [*Memra* in Aramaic] of the Lord" created. The phrase "Word of the Lord" is usually used as a substitute or a circumlocution for "God." The writers of the Targums also tried to safeguard God's transcendence by using substitutes such as the "Word of the Lord" and the "Glory of the Lord," whenever describing any of his contact with the physical world. This has enormous ramifications when we consider that the phrase the "Word of the Lord" sets the backdrop for John's Gospel: "In the beginning was the Word, and the Word was with God, and the Word was God ... we have seen his glory" (John 1:1, 14; cf. 1 John 1:1; Rev. 19:13).[4]

In terms of the usage of son of God, the Targums were hesitant to use it as a literal term. They were not so much opposed to its usage as to putting too high a priority on the term in relation to its biological context. Christians, of course, also do not take the language of the sonship of Jesus to be biological. As Christianity began to expand, the Jewish religious leaders began to tone down their use of son of God language as it pertained to the Messiah for obvious reasons. Christians were using Old Testament texts which referred to the Messiah as the Son of God. The view of the Messiah in the first century AD was one of a divine, pre-existent Person who would usher in God's kingdom, as we saw in *1 Enoch* 48:2-10. After the second century AD, rabbinic Judaism (in reaction to the expansion of Christianity) stripped the Messiah of all his divinity and reduced him to a mere human son of David—a view which Judaism continues to hold to this day.[5]

An example of the Targum's use of son of God language is seen in its interpretation of 2 Samuel 7:14, 1 Chronicles 17:13, and Psalm 2:7. It avoids any literalistic interpretation by rendering 1 Chronicles 17:13 as, "I will love him *as a* father loves a son, and he will love me *as a* son loves his father" (italics mine). Also, in Psalm 2:7, the Targum renders the passage as, "Beloved *as a* son is to his father you are to Me" (italics mine). Notice here the attempt to avoid a literal reading of the term "son." Jews have always understood, as

---

[4] For an excellent treatment of the Targums and their relevance to the New Testament see Martin McNamara, *Targum and Testament: Aramaic Paraphrases of the Hebrew Bible: A Light on the New Testament* (Shanon: Irish University Press, 1972).

[5] See the important work of Alan Segal, *Two Powers in Heaven: Early Rabbinic Reports about Christianity and Gnosticism* (Waco: Baylor University Press, 2012). Segal addresses the rabbinic reaction to the high Christology of the early Jewish Christians and the rejection of Messianic views held in Second Temple Judaism.

Christian did later, that when the language of son is used towards God it is not to be taken in a biological sense. This was partly to avoid the way their Near Eastern neighbours used terms of sonship when speaking of their gods' sexually procreating children.

Rabbinic Literature

In rabbinic writings such as *b. Sukkah* 52a, Rabbi Nathan (ca. AD 160) refers to the Messiah in Psalm 89:27, where the king is spoken of as God's "firstborn." One rabbi "Honi the Circle-drawer," was known for his miracles (first century BC), and was reputed to possess an intimate sonship with God (*b.Tann.* 3:8). This would be one explanation for his reported miracles.[6] Another rabbi by the name of Hanina ben Dosa, who lived a generation after Jesus, claimed that a heavenly voice addressed him as "my son Hanina" (*b. Tann.* 24b). God is also said to have appeared to Eleazer ben Pedath in a dream and say, "Eleazer, my son" (*b.Tann* 25a). On a midrash of the death of Moses, it states, "The Holy One immediately began to soothe him and said to him, 'My son Moses'" (Jellinek, *Bet ha-Midrash*, I, 121). The High Priest Ishmael ben Elisha was also said to have had a vision of God in the Holy of Holies who said to him, "Ishmael my son, bless me" (*Ber.* 7a).

It is clear from these rabbinic texts that the use of the term "son of God" was used of someone who shared a close and intimate relationship with God. Notice, however, that there is no aversion to the actual use of the term.

---

[6] See Tony Costa, "Exorcisms and Healings of Jesus Within Classical Culture" in Stanley E. Porter and Andrew Pitts, eds., *Christian Origins and Greco-Roman Culture: Social and Literary Contexts for the New Testament* (TENT 9; Early Christianity in its Hellenistic Context. Vol. 1; Leiden/Boston: Brill, 2013), 129–136.

Appendix 2
Jesus is the Son of Man

A favorite title Jesus used of himself was the "Son of Man" (Matt. 16:13–15). Outside of the gospels, it appears only in Acts 7:56, Hebrews 2:6, Revelation 1:13, and Revelation 14:14. The title has Semitic roots, which probably explains why it was so prominent during the ministry of Jesus, as he ministered primarily in a Semitic context. It seems that as the gospel message went out to the Gentiles, this title fell into disuse, although it was retained in the Gospel records. This word can be used in two ways in the Bible. The first way in reference to a human being, as we find it in Ezekiel 2:1 (and used throughout Ezekiel), and Daniel 8:17. The second way is when referring to *a divine being*, as mentioned in Daniel 7:13–14. How did Jesus use this term when applying it to himself? He used it the way Daniel 7:13–14 used it, which reads,

> I saw in the night visions, and behold, with the clouds of heaven there came one like a son of man, and he came to the Ancient of Days and was presented before him. And to him was given dominion and glory and a kingdom, that all peoples, nations, and languages should serve him; his dominion is an everlasting dominion, which shall not pass away, and his kingdom one that shall not be destroyed.

Notice also Jesus' words at his trial in Mark 14:61–64 (italics mine):

> But he remained silent and made no answer. Again the high priest asked him, "Are you the Christ, the Son of the Blessed?" And Jesus said, "I am, and you will see the *Son of Man seated at the right hand of Power, and coming with the clouds of heaven.*" And the high priest tore his garments and said, "What further witnesses do we need?[64] You have heard his *blasphemy*. What is your decision?" And they all condemned him as *deserving death.*

Note the question to Jesus: "Are you the Son of the Blessed (a substitute term for God)"? Jesus answers "I am." This means that Jesus understood himself to be the Son of God. Instead, he is charged with "blasphemy," a claim that carried with it the death penalty (Lev. 24:16). The reference to "coming with the clouds" is also interesting as this term was used only of a divine being both in the Old Testament and in the surrounding Near Eastern cultures.

In the ancient Near East, the gods were said to come or ride with the clouds of heaven. For instance, Baal in the Ugaritic literature is frequently referred to as "the Rider of the Clouds."[1] In the Old Testament, Yahweh is also said to be the one who rides the clouds, as the following passages demonstrate:

There is none like God, O Jeshurun [an affectionate term used of Israel], *who rides through the heavens* to your help, through the skies in his majesty (Deut. 33:26; italics mine);

To him [God] *who rides in the heavens*, the ancient heavens; behold, he sends out his voice, his mighty voice (Ps. 68:33; italics mine);

He [God] lays the beams of his chambers on the waters; *he makes the clouds his chariot*; he rides on the wings of the wind (Ps. 104:3; italics mine);

An oracle concerning Egypt. Behold, *the LORD is riding on a swift cloud* and comes to Egypt; and the idols of Egypt will tremble at his presence, and the heart of the Egyptians will melt within them (Isa. 19:1; italics mine).

It is clear from these passages that the cloud rider in view is seen as a divine being. This phrase is used four times of God but it is also used of the Son of Man in Daniel 7:13-14, the very figure that Jesus identified himself with. We can now understand why the high priest accused Jesus of blasphemy; he was claiming to be the divine person of Daniel 7, the one who, in Second Temple Judaism, was also believed to be the second Yahweh (cf. Gen. 19:24).

The divine nature of the Son of Man in Daniel is further reinforced by the fact that in Daniel 7:14,27, he is actually worshipped by all the nations. The NIV actually uses the words "worshiped," and "worship," whereas other translations use the word "served," and "serve." However, in the religious context of Daniel 7, serving a divine being easily translates into worship. The Aramaic word used here for worship and/or serve is *pelach* (Dan. 2:4b-7:28 is

---

[1] The phrase "coming with the clouds of heaven" was used in Canaanite mythology of the young god Baal who rides on the clouds of heaven to the supreme elder god El, "the father of years" (Marshall, *Origins of New Testament Christology*, 67-68).

APPENDIX 2

all in Aramaic), and every time it appears in the book of Daniel it is always used in a religious context, either dealing with the service or worship of gods, or even to the one true God (Dan. 3:12, 14, 17-18, 28; 6:17, 21). The lexicon defines this word as "pay reverence to, serve (deity) ... worship."[2] This meaning is further reinforced by the LXX reading of Daniel 7:14, which uses a word that comes from the Greek root word *latreuo*, which always refers to worship or service to a deity in a religious context. It is also used in reference to the Son of Man, who will someday be worshipped by the nations.

When we turn to Jesus, we note that he is identified in the New Testament as the Son of Man. Is all this beginning to sound familiar? The fact that Jesus was worshipped in the church from the earliest times and that millions around the world continue to worship him shows how the prophecy in Daniel 7:14, 27 has been fulfilled. The divine Sonship of Jesus and the worship of the Son of Man was already deeply rooted in the Old Testament and came to fruition in the New Testament.

---

[2] Francis Brown, S. R. Driver, and Charles A. Briggs, *A Hebrew and English Lexicon of the Old Testament with an Appendix Containing the Biblical Aramaic* (Boston / New York: Houghton Mifflin Co., 1907), 1108. Gesenius also states that the Aramaic word פלח (pelach) means "specially, to worship God." Gesenius also cites Daniel 7:14, 27 where the word פלח (pelach) is used in reference to the Son of Man, thus reinforcing the fact that the Son of Man is a divine being worthy of worship that is usually reserved for God alone. Heinrich F. W. Gesenius, *Gesenius's Hebrew and Chaldee Lexicon* (trans. Samuel Prideaux Tragelles; London: Samuel Bagster and Sons, Paternoster Row, 1859), 675.

Subject Index

Adoptionism, 159
Angels, 46, 73, 78, 85, 99, 108, 119, 123, 126, 127, 128, 129, 130, 131, 147, 149, 158, 159, 160, 189, 192, 201, 202, 203
Annihilationism, 191, 192
Anti-imperialism, 46, 47, 60, 64, 82, 83, 117, 166, 198, 199
Aphrodite, 88
Apocrypha, 21, 23, 38, 65, 77, 80, 98, 103, 116, 134, 152, 166, 179, 209
Apologetics, 6, 28, 167, 186
Apostasy, 57
Apostles' Creed, 1, 4, 5, 6, 7, 10, 11, 12, 15, 60, 66, 90, 122, 127, 131, 145, 196, 206
Aramaic Christian community, 46
Arianism, 4, 71, 154, 160, 175, 178
Arius, 51, 71, 175
Ascension of Christ, 116, 128, 129, 131, 155, 158
Athanasius, 35
Atonement, 43, 113, 141, 144, 196, 198, 202
Augsburg Confession, 3
Augustine, 4, 54, 67, 97, 163
Augustus, 47, 83, 191, 199
Babylonian Talmud, 55, 177
Baptism, 8, 9, 10, 36, 50, 60, 78, 84, 91, 92, 135, 184, 202
Belgic Confession, 3
Caesar, 45, 46, 47, 51, 52, 53, 58, 60, 65, 83, 198, 199
Caligula, 84
Calvin, John, 102
Carmen Christi, 58, 100, 111, 112, 113, 121, 122, 123, 125, 129, 130, 139, 156, 157, 160, 164, 171, 188, 201
Celsus, 53, 55
Chambers, Oswald, 209
Christology, 5, 7, 11, 82, 91, 92, 114, 122, 129, 148, 162, 166, 171, 211
Church Fathers, 2, 26, 63, 85
Council of Chalcedon, 185, 186

Council of Constantinople, 9
Council of Nicaea, 71, 89, 151
Council of Toledo, 8
Council of Trent, 209
Crucifixion, 7, 37, 54, 80, 115, 144, 145, 160, 176, 183
Cyprian, 85
Dead Sea Scrolls, 22, 23, 45, 49, 73, 76, 125
Decalogue, 16
Deity of Christ, 49, 51, 56, 59, 64, 89, 90, 92, 104, 105, 108, 114, 116, 120, 122, 126, 148, 151, 153, 154, 176, 179, 180, 185, 198, 199, 200, 203, 205
Descent of Christ, 114, 115, 127, 130
Docetism, 6, 142
Domitian, 47, 166, 191
Donatists, 54
Easter, 32, 38, 68, 92, 158
Ecclesiology, 5, 7
Eighteen Benedictions, 25, 26
Emperor, 45, 46, 47, 58, 64, 65, 82, 83, 84, 99, 107, 117, 119, 166, 191, 199, 201
Eschatology, 5, 7
Essenes, 21
Eucharist, 106
Eusebius, 33
Exaltation of Christ, 116
False Teaching. *See* Heresy
Gamaliel, 88
Gnosticism, 4, 9, 186, 188, 211
Greek philosophy, 164, 167
Hades, 5, 127, 134, 207
Heber, Reginald, 11
Hell, 5, 127, 134
Heresy, 4, 7, 25, 26, 51, 56, 71, 92, 131, 142, 152, 159, 186, 189
Holy Spirit, xv, 5, 6, 7, 8, 9, 10, 39, 48, 50, 51, 60, 74, 75, 77, 79, 81, 82, 91, 92, 93, 102, 115, 123, 126, 127, 129, 130, 131, 133, 140, 190, 200, 206

219

Homoousios, 9, 160
Hypostatic union, 82, 154, 157, 185, 186
Idolatry, 88, 108, 123
Ignatius, 6, 89, 142
Incarnation, xv, 4, 7, 10, 93, 113, 114, 115, 122, 126, 127, 142, 151, 152, 153, 154, 155, 159, 166, 167, 169, 186, 187, 200, 202, 204, 205
Intertestamental literature, 20, 209, 210
Irenaeus, 6, 34, 85, 172
Islam, 3
Jehovah's Witness, 51, 178
Jerome, 26, 38, 134
Josephus, 12, 49, 128
Julius Caesar, 83, 199
Justification, 35, 57, 141, 206
Last Supper, 38, 106
Law of treason, 46
Logos, 162, 163, 164, 165, 167, 168, 169
Lord's Supper, 17, 39, 106, 144
Lordship of Christ, 48, 50, 60, 120, 176
Lordship salvation, 50
Macedonius, 9
Marriage, 13
Martyr, Justin, 26, 34, 55, 69, 85, 89
Martyrdom, 52, 53, 55, 58, 144
Monotheism, 3, 13, 14, 87, 90, 93, 120, 185, 200
Montanism, 6
Mormonism, 51
New Covenant, 11, 16, 125, 200
Nicea-Constantinople Creed, 8
Nicene Creed, 1, 4, 5, 8, 9, 10, 11, 47, 60, 66, 79, 90, 91, 108, 122, 131, 145, 160, 169, 196, 206
Old Covenant, 11
Pan (god of forests, flocks, and fields), 124
Penal Substitution, 141, 142, 144
Pentecost, 63, 158, 172, 200
Persecution, 46, 51, 54, 56, 57, 58, 60, 141, 202

Philo of Alexandria, 12, 91, 102, 164, 168, 177, 192
Pindar, 49
Pliny the Younger, 51, 52, 53, 99, 100, 107, 166, 201
Pneumatachoi, 9
Pneumatology, 5, 7
Polycarp, 52, 53, 54, 58
Polytheism, 3
Pontius Pilate, 5, 6, 8, 15, 33, 142, 145, 160, 195
Prayer, 20, 22, 26, 92, 97, 100, 106, 107, 118
Pseudepigrapha, 21, 22, 23, 77, 209
Qumran community, 21, 22, 54, 98, 99
Rabbi Abba Bar-Kahana, 51, 76
Rabbi Akiva, 88
Reformers, 102, 141, 206
Resurrection, 4, 5, 6, 7, 8, 10, 17, 28, 30, 31, 32, 34, 35, 36, 37, 38, 39, 40, 41, 43, 46, 48, 50, 53, 61, 68, 80, 81, 82, 92, 116, 127, 128, 129, 130, 134, 140, 142, 145, 155, 159, 176, 182, 183, 184, 187, 188, 190, 198, 200, 202, 205
Roman Catholicism, 158
Rufinus, 7
Sabbath, 15, 16, 78, 147
Sanctification, 143
Second London Baptist Confession, 3
Second Temple, 13, 18, 20, 21, 25, 49, 75, 199, 209, 211, 214
Septuagint, 13, 12, 198
Shema, 12, 13, 14, 23, 87, 88, 90, 91, 92, 185, 197, 199, 200, 206
Sinlessness of Christ, 139, 143, 144
Socrates, 1, 55
Soteriology, 5
Spiritual gifts, 101, 200
Spurgeon, Charles, 209
Symmachus, 45
Targums, 77, 209, 210, 211
Tertullian, 6, 7, 8, 34, 53, 85, 104
Thanksgiving, 21, 22, 106
Theodotion, 45
Theophany, 18, 19, 21

Subject Index

Traitors, 54
Trajan, 52, 99, 107, 166, 201
Trinity, 7, 9, 11, 74, 91, 151, 200
Union with Christ, 143
Unitarianism, 13

Universalism, 189, 191
Virgin Mary, 5, 7
War of 1812, 97
Westminster Confession, 3
Zeus, 49, 154

Scripture Index

Old Testament

Genesis
- 1:1 ...... 151, 163, 176, 181, 189, 203
- 1:2 75
- 1:3 154
- 1:3-4 75
- 1:5 13
- 1:26 72
- 1:26-27 .... 64, 172, 181, 204
- 1:28 .... 72, 173, 204
- 2:7 72
- 2:24 13
- 3:8 187
- 6:2 72
- 6:4 72
- 8:20 142
- 9:6 164
- 14:18-20 116
- 14:22 116
- 17:5 37
- 19:24 214
- 31:13 165
- 35:10 37
- 41:51-52 174
- 48:8-20 174
- 48:20 174

Exodus
- 4:22 ....73, 174
- 4:22-23 .... 77, 210
- 4:23 210
- 13:3 15
- 15:3 ....18, 21, 76
- 15:8 18
- 15:10 18
- 15:12 18
- 15:18 ....18, 121
- 15:1-18 .... 17, 98
- 19:1-20 187
- 20:8 15
- 20:9-11 15
- 25:8 187
- 33:11 164
- 33:23 168
- 40:34-35 187

Leviticus
- 4:3 63
- 4:5 63
- 4:16 63
- 14:20 142
- 17:5 142
- 24:16 ....118, 213

Numbers
- 12:8 164
- 15:39-40 15
- 21:1-15 57

Deuteronomy
- 4:12 168
- 5:12 16
- 5:15 16
- 6:4 ....
  .12, 13, 87, 88, 90, 91, 108, 195, 199
- 6:5 200
- 6:20-24 15
- 6:4-5 ....12, 197
- 7:18 15
- 8:2 15
- 13:6-11 57
- 14:1 .... 73, 77
- 15:15 15
- 16:3 15
- 21:22-23 .... 54, 143
- 24:18 15
- 26:5 .... 14, 15, 17, 197
- 31:19 98
- 31:22 98
- 32:8 ....73, 116
- 33:2 158
- 33:26 214
- 34:10 164

Joshua
- 1:13 16
- 24:2 15

24:1-27 17	22:27 129
Judges	24:7-10 129
5:5 18	28:7 106
5:31 18	30:4 106
2 Samuel	33:2 106
1:14 63	33:6 166
7:1 211	35:23 47
7:14 211	44:8 106
7:18 156	46:10 116
22:1 98	47:9 116
24:1-17 74	57:5 116
1 Kings	57:9 106
3:24 142	68:33 214
8:10-11 187	72:8 64
1 Chronicles	77:17 18
6:31 98	82:6 72
17:13 ....74, 211	89:26-27 74
21:1-17 74	89:27 .... 116, 173
22:10 74	95:3 121
28:6 74	102:25-27 151
2 Chronicles	104:3 214
6:16 156	105:15 63
29:27 98	110:1 .... 129, 156
Ezra	115:4-8 123
7:12 64	118:1 106
Job	118:28 116
1:6-12 72	138:2 118
2:1-6 72	144:6 18
38:7 72	148:13 118
Psalms	**Proverbs**
2:2 63	23:7 1
2:7 74	30:4 75
2:6-12 64	**Isaiah**
2:6-7 .... 68, 81	6:1 117
2:7-12 64	7:14 75
2:8 129	8:13 .... 104, 199
5:11 76	9:6 .... 74, 75, 77
7:1 76	11:2 75
9:1 106	19:1 214
11:1 76	26:19 134
16:10 68	41:4 181
18:1 118	44:6 181
18:14 18	44:24 .... 91, 176
18:46 116	45:1 63
18:50 63	45:22 120
19:7 197	45:23 ...... 59, 60, 119, 120, 195, 196, 199
21:13 116	

48:12	181
52:13	149
53:4	55, 142
53:5	143
53:6	145
53:7	140
53:8	142
53:9	139
53:11	141, 143
53:12	114
53:11–12	142
57:15	117
57:20	19
60:1	134, 135
60:1–3	135
60:2	135
60:3	135
63:16	73
64:6	141
64:8	73
66:1–2	91, 176

Jeremiah
1:2	21
1:5	42
2:1	21
10:1–15	123
23:6	51, 76
23:23–24	158, 184
23:5–6	76, 187
31:9	73, 174
33:16	187
33:17	156

Ezekiel
1:3	21
1:24	18
2:1	213
26:7	64
43:2	18
48:35	187

Daniel
2:4	214
2:37	64
2:37–38	64
3:12	215
3:14	215
6:17	215
6:21	215
7:14	214, 215
7:27	214, 215
7:13–14	22, 213, 214
8:17	213

Hosea
1:1	21
11:1	73

Joel
2:32	49, 58, 60, 195, 199

Jonah
1:6	134

Micah
5:2	75

Habakkuk
3:11	18

Zephaniah
3:17	98

Zechariah
2:5	152
6:9–13	156
14:9	121

Malachi
1:6	118
2:2	118
2:10	73
4:4	17

New Testament

Matthew
1:1-17	63
1:18-25	127
1:21	194
1:23	75
2:2	65
2:4	65
2:13	127
2:15	73
2:19-20	127
4:3	78
4:11	127
4:23	26
5:9	192
5:14	136
5:15-16	124
5:43-48	141
6:7	207
9:35	26
10:17-20	51
11:25	106
11:27	32, 78
11:28-30	16
13:55	37, 38, 39
14:33	81
16:13	124
16:13-15	213
16:16-18	207
16:16	67, 68, 69, 81, 85, 123, 195, 199
16:17	67
16:18	67
16:21	36
16:22	68, 69
16:23	69
16:28	37
17:2	187
17:23	36
20:19	36
21:9	116
22:32	123
22:44	60
22:34-40	13, 87
22:41-46	157
23:12	115
25:31	187
25:40	142
26:30	99
26:39	128
26:51	33
26:57	33
26:63	69, 157
27:37	65
27:42	65
27:54	80
28:16-17	37
28:18	180
28:2-7	128

Mark
1:1	80
1:11	78
1:13	127
1:34	78
3:11	78
3:17	34
4:11	126
5:22-23	183
5:35-43	183
5:39	136
8:29	66, 67, 195
8:31	36
8:32	68
8:33	69
9:1	37
9:7	78
9:31	36
10:34	36
10:45	140
11:10	116
12:27	123
12:28-30	87
12:28-31	206
12:28-34	87
12:35-37	157
12:36	60
14:26	99

14:47	33
14:61	69, 118, 140, 157
14:62	118, 157
14:61–64	56, 158, 213
14:63–64	79
14:67	26
14:61–62	79
15:21	33, 34
15:26	65
15:39	80
15:44–45	36
16:5–7	128
16:7	37
16:9–20	37, 116

Luke

1:1–4	28
1:32	157
1:35	80
1:68	99
1:26–38	127
1:32–35	77
1:46–55	99
1:67–79	99
2:1	83
2:8–15	127
2:9	187
2:10–11	46, 47
2:11	47
2:13–14	99
2:14	46, 116
3:2	21, 33
3:23–38	63
3:38	72, 173
4:3	78
6:27–36	141
7:11–17	183
8:41–42	183
8:49–56	183
8:52	136
9:20	66, 67, 195
9:22	36
9:27	37
10:16	142
10:21	106
10:22	32, 78
10:25–28	13, 87
12:32	167

14:11	115
15:18	117
15:21	117
18:14	115
22:31–32	37
18:33	36
20:38	123
20:42	60
20:41–44	157
22:43–44	128
22:50	33
22:62	54
22:69	157
22:66–67	69
23:38	65
23:47	80, 81
24:4	187
24:27	140
24:34	37
24:44	140, 149
24:51	116
24:30–31	38
24:36–53	37
24:4–7	128

John

1:1	79, 122, 154, 160, 162, 163, 165, 169, 193, 203, 204, 211
1:1b	164
1:1–2	179
1:1–3	71, 78, 91, 150, 166
1:1–18	161, 162, 166, 169, 200, 203
1:3	160, 169, 203, 204
1:4–5	169
1:6–8	168
1:9	136, 169
1:10	91, 166, 167, 169, 196, 203
1:11	167
1:12	79, 167
1:12–13	80
1:13	168
1:14	79, 122, 126, 152, 166, 167, 169, 186, 187, 188, 193, 196, 205, 211
1:15	168
1:17	168
1:18	168, 169, 172, 204

Reference	Pages
1:42	37
1:49	69, 81
2:11	187
2:18–22	188
2:19	36
3:7	168
3:13	75
3:16	71, 74, 165, 169
3:16–17	83, 129
3:18	165, 169
4:9	55, 79
4:22	55
4:23–24	105
5:1	195
5:17	78
5:18	78, 80
5:19–27	188
5:21	78
5:23	78
5:25	136
5:37	168
6:38	75, 83
6:41–42	75, 83
6:44	67
6:51	75, 83
6:58	75, 83
6:69	68
7:5	38
8:12	75, 136
8:32	16
8:36	16
8:39	79
8:41	55, 77
8:48	55
8:58–59	56
9:1–11	136
9:22	26, 68
9:39	136
9:40–41	136
10:11–18	145
10:26–30	145
10:28–30	78
10:22	209
10:28–29	145
10:30	78
10:33	78
10:36	78
10:30–33	56
11:11	136
11:14	136
11:25–26	68
11:27	68, 69
11:38–44	183
11:41	106
11:43	136
11:52	79
12:41	117
13:33	79
14:6	124
14:9	153
14:26	51
15:26	50, 79
16:2	57
16:7	79
16:14	50
17:5	78, 79, 159, 179
18:10	33
19:7	79
19:12	65
19:15	65
19:19–22	65
19:30	31, 156
19:33–35	36
20:12	128
20:17	56, 80, 116
20:19–29	37
20:28	47, 165, 166, 204
20:31	66, 67, 69, 81, 85, 195, 199
21:1–25	37
21:5	79
21:15–17	145
21:15–19	54, 105
21:18–19	144

Acts

Reference	Pages
1:3	116
1:8	63, 128, 129
1:9–11	56
1:9–10	187
1:9–11	129
1:10–11	128
2:10	172
2:27	68
2:32	116
2:33	81

2:34	60
2:36	49, 127
2:46	25
3:1	25
3:14	68
3:21	192
5:31	116
5:34	88
5:41	118
5:42	25
5:34–40	88
7:53	158
7:56	213
7:58–60	57
8:36	84
8:37	84
8:26–35	139
9:4	142
9:20	81
9:22	65, 81
10:36	49
12:1–2	37
12:2–3	57
12:17	39
13:35	68
15:12–21	39
16:7	75
16:25	100
16:30	48
16:31	48
17:28	88
18:2	172
21:18	39
21:39	57
22:3	57, 88
22:17	25
23:6	36
23:8	36
24:5	26
26:5	36
26:18	136

Romans
1:3–4	48, 81, 82, 84, 127, 195
1:10	172
1:20	153
1:21	106
1:30	106
4:24–25	35
5:14	72, 173
6:4	36, 50
6:9	182
8:3	83
8:9	75, 77
8:14	80
8:15	77
8:20–23	190
8:23	190
8:29	183
8:34	156
9:1–5	73
9:3	64
9:5	82, 89, 205
10:1	46
10:9	46, 48, 49, 50, 51, 82, 182
10:9–10	60
10:9–13	58, 60, 184
10:10	48
10:12	49
10:13	49, 51, 195, 199
11:13	128
11:36	178
12:14	141
13:1	64
13:1–7	64
14:11	120
15:4	17
15:20	172
15:22	172
16:13	34

1 Corinthians
1:2	50
1:18	35, 192
1:23	54, 144
2:6	176
2:8	127, 176
3:11	124
8:3	88
8:4	14, 87, 89
8:4–6	90
8:5	45, 89
8:6	87, 89, 90, 91, 92, 93, 107, 150, 151, 160, 166, 169, 175, 177, 178, 189, 195, 199, 203

Early Christian Creeds and Hymns

Reference	Pages
10:6	17
10:24	113
10:19–20	88
11:17–18	101
11:20	101
11:23	39
11:23–26	17
11:33–34	101
12:3	48, 50, 51, 60
12:4–6	92
14:26	101, 102, 103, 106, 200
14:33	123
14:40	123
15:1	35
15:1–4	29
15:1–7	41
15:3	31, 39, 66, 112, 122, 196
15:3–4	28, 29, 31, 32, 34, 35, 37, 39, 40, 41, 42, 43, 50, 68, 81, 111, 112, 122, 184, 198
15:3b–6a	33
15:3ff	34
15:4	196
15:5	35, 37, 38, 40
15:5–8	34, 39
15:6	30, 46
15:7	33, 34, 38, 40
15:8	40
15:11	42
15:14	43
15:28	121, 189, 206
15:33	88
15:45	173
15:49	183
16:22	41, 51

2 Corinthians

Reference	Pages
1:5	142
2:15–16	192
3:14	11
4:4	172
4:5	46, 121, 195
4:6	152
5:17	177, 181, 193
5:18–19	193
8:9	179
11:13–15	51
13:14	51

Galatians

Reference	Pages
1:6–9	43, 51
1:14	88
1:17	39
1:18	40
1:19	37, 38, 40
1:11–12	42
1:15–17	42
1:18–19	40, 42
2:1	41, 42
2:2	42
2:7–8	144
2:7–9	42
2:9	37, 41
3:13	54, 143, 202
3:19	158
3:20	14, 87, 90
3:26	80, 85
4:4	179
4:4–6	77, 83
4:6	75, 80
5:1	16
5:22	74
6:14	35

Ephesians

Reference	Pages
1:1	103
1:3	80
1:3–9	137
1:4	181
1:7	192
1:10	189
1:13	190
1:20–22	176
1:22	180, 184
2:1	136
2:1–6	134, 137
2:11–22	135
2:19	124
2:20	124
3:14	119
3:17	104
3:21	207
3:1–11	135
4:4–6	92

Scripture Index

4:6 .... 14, 87
4:8 188
4:8–10 .... 5, 127
4:10...............................158, 178
4:11 145
4:13–14 133
4:15 180
4:15–16.................................182
4:24 173
4:30.......................................190
5:1–2 133
5:8 135
5:11 135
5:14 ..... 112, 133, 134, 135, 136, 137, 139, 169, 196, 202
5:18 133
5:19 ....103, 105, 106, 107, 108, 114, 134, 196, 200, 201
5:23..................................... 180
5:19–20 133
6:12 .... 135, 176, 192

Philippians
1:19 75
2:1 139
2:4–5..................................... 113
2:6 ..75, 83, 113, 122, 126, 139, 157, 160, 164, 166, 179, 186, 195
2:6–11..
....75, 82, 83, 111, 112, 113, 136, 139, 151, 162, 193, 200, 201
2:6–8................. 113, 115, 126, 166

2:7 ....114, 122
2:8 122
2:9 ....58, 118, 122, 129, 156, 159
2:9–11....60, 113, 160, 193, 195, 196
2:10................................ 118, 119
2:10–11. 59, 119, 120, 122, 129, 199
2:11 .... 46, 48, 58, 119, 120, 155
3:5 36
3:10.......................................141
3:20...................................... 117
3:20–21 .... 183, 205

Colossians
1:2 188
1:7 172
1:12–14 172

1:13 ....136, 172
1:14 192
1:15 ..... 113, 126, 150, 153, 171, 172, 173, 174, 176, 181, 182
1:15–16 178
1:15–20...
83, 155, 162, 166, 171, 193, 200, 203, 204
1:16 ..... 175, 177, 178, 189, 195, 196
1:16–17 172
1:16–18 175
1:17 ....178, 182, 196
1:18 .... 180, 182, 183, 184, 196
1:19 ....172, 184, 185, 188
1:20..... 189, 190, 191, 192, 193, 196
1:20–23 180
1:21–22..................................189
1:22–23.................................194
1:24 141
1:26–27 125
2:1 172
2:2 126
2:9 ....
89, 107, 153, 173, 185, 186, 205
2:10..................................... 180
2:12...................................... 36
2:15 .... 127, 176, 191
2:18 108
2:19 180
3:10.......................................173
3:11 194
3:15 ....74, 104
3:16 ... 103, 104, 106, 107, 108, 134, 196, 200, 201
4:3 171
4:10...................................... 171
4:16 103
4:18 171

1 Thessalonians
1:2 106
1:9 123
2:14–16.................................. 57
3:13 104
5:15 144
5:18 106

2 Thessalonians
1:7 128

1:8-9 192	160, 164, 169, 173, 179, 188, 193, 195, 196
2:15 2	1:3-4 .... 151, 159, 196
2:17 104	1:4 158

1 Timothy
1:10 131	1:5-7 158
2:5 .... 14, 87, 90	1:6 ....128, 150, 155
3:1-7 ....123, 145	1:8-9 151
3:14 123	1:8-12 151
3:15 .... 37, 123, 124, 125	1:10 151
3:16 ....112, 123, 125, 126, 129, 130, 131, 136, 144, 151, 156, 160, 166, 169, 173, 186, 193, 195, 196, 202	1:10-12 151
	1:13-14 158
	2:2 158
3:16. 127	2:6 213
4:1 131	2:9 159
4:14 145	2:10 178
5:17-19 145	3:1-6 159
6:3 131	3:7-4 16
6:15 199	5:9 91

2 Timothy
	5:7-8 159
1:9 126	6:4 135
2:15 .... 105, 124, 131	7:27 ....31, 156
2:22 105	8:1 156
3:8 124	8:13 11
3:15-17 131	9:12 156
4:3 131	9:14 79
4:4 124	9:26 31

Titus
	10:10 ....31, 144, 156
1:5 145	10:25 101
1:7 145	10:32 135
1:9 131	10:11-14 156
1:12 88	10:5-10 144
1:14 124	11:17 79
2:1 131	12:1 207
2:13 .... 89, 107, 126	12:22-24 207
	13:15 206

Hebrews

James
1:2 .... 91, 147, 149, 150, 151, 154, 157, 159, 160, 162, 166, 169, 173, 175, 177, 189, 193, 195, 200, 203, 204	2:1 152
	2:7 118
	2:19 87
	2:21 143
	5:13 100
1:1-2 14	1 Peter
1:1-3 149	1:11 75
1:1-4 ....147, 150	1:12 127
1:3 .... 151, 152, 153, 154, 155, 157, 158,	1:17 144
	1:10-11 140
	2:21 141

2:22	139, 143, 196
2:23	139
2:24	143, 144, 196
2:25	145
2:22–24	139, 143, 144, 160, 202
3:9	144
3:10	140
3:15	104, 105, 199
3:17	141
3:18	127, 141
3:18–20	5, 127
3:22	158, 189
4:4–6	5, 127
4:16	66
5:1	145
5:6	116

1 John

1:1	150, 211
1:1–2	126
1:2	163
1:5	135
2:1	163
2:8–10	135
2:22	65
3:2	183
3:8	193
4:1–3	122, 127
4:9	79, 165
4:14	82
4:15	82
5:1	66, 67, 82, 195, 207
5:5	82, 195, 207
5:4–5	2

Revelation

1:8	181
1:13	213
1:17	181
2:9	58
3:9	58
5:5	157
5:11–14	119
7:13–17	207
9:20	123
14:10–11	192
14:14	213
15:3	98
17:14	64, 199
19:13	150, 211
19:16	64, 199
21:3	187
21:4	190
21:5	190
21:6	181
22:1	157
22:3	157
22:4	187
22:13	181
22:15	191
22:16	157

Apocrypha

Judith
- 16:1-17 21
- 16:2 21
- 16:3 21
- 16:15 21

1 Maccabees
- 2:19-28 57
- 4:54 98

2 Maccabees
- 1:30 98
- 7:34 212
- 14:35 49

Sirach
- 4:10 212
- 7:11 118
- 43:26b 156, 181
- 50:18 98
- 51:1-2 21
- 51:10 212

Wisdom
- 2:10 80
- 2:12-13 80
- 2:13 ..... 80, 212
- 2:16 ..... 80, 212
- 2:17-20 80
- 2:18 81
- 2:18-20 80
- 5:5 212
- 7:25-26 154
- 9:1 168
- 9:7 212
- 18:13 212

Pseudepigrapha

1 Enoch
- 13:8 212
- 37-71 75
- 48:2-5 212
- 48:2-10 ..... 75, 212-213
- 48:4 23
- 48:7 212
- 106:5 212

4 Ezra
- 13:32 212
- 13:37 212
- 13:52 212
- 14:9 212
- 17:28-29 212

Joseph and Asenath
- 6:2-6 212
- 13:10 212
- 21:3 212

Psalms of Solomon
- 13:8 212
- 17:30 212

Testament of Abraham
- 12 212

Testament of Levi
- 4:2 212

Jubilees
- 1:22 212